NATIVE HEART

AN AMERICAN INDIAN ODYSSEY

▼▼▼▼▼▼▼▼▼▼▼▼▼▼▼▼

■■■■■■■■■■■■■■■■■■■■■■■■■■■■■■

GABRIEL HORN

WHITE DEER OF AUTUMN

■■■■■■■■■■■■■■■■■■■■■■■■■■■■■■

NEW WORLD LIBRARY

SAN RAFAEL, CALIFORNIA

© 1993 Gabriel Horn

Published by New World Library
58 Paul Drive
San Rafael, CA 94903

Cover design: Kathy Warinner
Typography: TBH/Typecast, Inc.

Library of Congress Cataloging-in-Publication Data

Horn, Gabriel, 1947–
    Native heart : an American Indian odyssey / Gabriel Horn.
    p. cm.
    ISBN 1-880032-07-4
    1. Horn, Gabriel, 1947– . 2. Indians of North America — Biography. 3. Indians of North America — Religion and mythology. 4. Indians of North America — Politics and government. 5. Human ecology — United States — Philosophy. I. Title.
E90.H67A3 1993
970.004'9702 — dc20   92-46448
                                                    CIP

First printing, May 1993
Printed in the U.S.A. on acid-free paper
ISBN 1-880032-07-4
10 9 8 7 6 5 4 3 2 1

I dedicate this book to the power of Orenda, that power of the past that is the sum total of the People's goodness manifested in the present to help guide us into the future.

I acknowledge the love and support of my family, my agent, my friends, editors, colleagues, elders, and ancestors, whose own power of goodness helped make this book a reality that records some of the struggles I faced living in this Wheel of Life.

Who we are at this moment in time is continuously defined by memories. We are the sum total of our past.

Contents

CONTENTS

▲▲▲▲▲▲▲▲▲▲▲▲▲▲▲▲▲▲▲▲▲▲▲▲▲▲

NATIVE HEART

THE DOOR

I STOOD MOMENTARILY on the steps of Mrs. Basic's old, wood-framed house and watched the morning star pulsating in the dawn sky. It seemed so big to me. It swelled as it approached and shrank as it faded back. It twinkled and twirled and danced in the deep blue. In my young boy's mind, the very idea of stars stirred a sense of yearning and wonder in me that has never waned. Stars are like islands in the void. Islands of light in the endless dark ocean of space.

Like the vitality of stars in the dusk of twilight, the grove-dappled shoreline where I once lived came alive each dawn. On the trail to the beach, palms swayed and pines whistled above the colorful citrus groves in the cool morning wind, and birds of many kinds helped bring a new day to life again. They winged and darted among the trees, whistling, singing, chirping, cawing, crying, and filled me with a sense of balance and beauty. Their sounds proclaimed the morning's birth, and made me aware of the struggles there are to live in this great Circle of Life, in this great Wheel of life. Among the dunes, sea oats, bent heavy with summer sun, glowed golden yellow in the first rays of early light.

2 I didn't know what to call all this that I loved then. I didn't know the name, Mother Earth, and I didn't know that the forces that kept the balance within her and the universe were all a part of something whole. In my young boy's mind, I didn't know that it was Mother Earth I was admiring. Nurturing, loving, teaching, and beautiful, she was the mother who would always be there for me. Whether I would one day find her in another foster parent's backyard or in a city park as an older man, in my heart she was always there, and it was from being close to her that my ideas about life would shape and form. And it was Mother Earth that would provide me the sustenances for living — love and strength in times of need. She was my real mother even then when I was a boy and didn't know enough with my head to call her so.

Living in a childhood paradise with Mrs. Basic, I got to see every day how everything around my world rim was somehow connected. I got to lay out with my older sister Angela and watch the stars at night. What connected me to the stars, and to the spirits who dwell among them, was another feeling I did not have words for then. I didn't know the words to call this sense of oneness I felt with the stars, with nature, and the land, this connection I had to all things, The Great Holy Mystery. For the young will often have the old sacred feelings that are passed on in the blood; it's only later in life when they meet the teachers and the wisdomkeepers that they are given the words to give meaning to the feelings.

At the end of the trail winding away from Mrs. Basic's house, just beyond the beach, small waves broke in the offshore breeze, and long lines of pelicans glided out over the water. That's how Mrs. Basic taught me to count, watching pelicans. "One time," I would tell my children many years later with a great sense of accomplishment still sounding in my voice, "I remember counting up to thirty-seven in one long swooping curve."

On this particular morning, though, I didn't have time to count.

I was nine years old that July, and could make fast tracks in the fine white sand when I had a mind to, and on that day, that's exactly what I did . . . until I reached the water's edge. Then I paused, still and taut like a fawn, and contemplated the island.

I'm gonna be there . . . soon, I thought.

The island. It was a jewel gleaming in the Gulf, a serpentine stone set in a turquoise sea. It seemed suspended there. Like the earth in the ebony ocean of space, the island's beauty beckoned the spirit in me as the earth must beckon the spirits who dwell among the stars. Mysterious and beautiful, always it pulled me, tugging at my child's sense of curiosity. The island. On this day I would finally be able to touch its green and wild world.

Growing up on the beach, I learned early that the Gulf is a giver of gifts, and the day before I was to be taken away from this boyhood paradise, I discovered that the Gulf had left behind a big door. It lay in a tide pool, wide and long and smooth, and reddish brown, like the summer color of my skin.

Such a door could have come from a big boat, perhaps a yacht, maybe a fishing vessel, or even a sunken Spanish ship. There were many of them out there. Sudden storms could descend upon a rich man's day of cruising the sea or a fisherman taking home his big catch. Just like that, it could blow them away like they never mattered at all.

The Spaniards and the ships of their great armada were not exempt from the indiscriminate forces of nature either, nor from the forces of Calusa Indians who used to live here. In one battle with the Spaniards, not far from the mouth of Tampa Bay, there's evidence that the Calusa sank eighty fiery vessels, the sea swallowing them whole. Nearly an entire Spanish fleet of battle ships heavy with cannons, and merchant haulers filled with Indian gold, were burned and sunk with their stolen booty by the Calusa. And though these brave natives could defend their country fiercely, they could not defend themselves against disease. The remnants of the Calusa people, and the other tribes who flourished in Florida, would live on, but only in the blood of other nations, like the Seminole, the Creek, and the Cherokee. They would live on in the hearts of others as well. And perhaps that's why I've always felt especially connected here, to the oaks and the palms, to the sea, and to the sun.

For days that spring, I had watched curiously as divers struggled against seasonal storms and fought off attacks by sharks in order to scavenge the area for lost fortunes. Their struggles against the elements seemed to be my first awareness of the "man against nature" mentality. And though it was common knowledge that most things of value were already taken from the old ships, these divers still searched, day after day after day.

My treasures, however, I took in the Indian way, from what the earth and the sea had provided. One of my greatest finds had washed up on the shore on the day the disappointed divers returned to the mainland. What I found wasn't Indian gold or a priceless gem or a shark's tooth or painted dolphins on a pottery shard taken from a burial mound; it was an old, cracked oar that was slowly turning to driftwood. Even though I had nothing to row with it, I listened to my inner voice and buried that oar just the same.

The hiding place I picked was where the anoles lived among the morning glory leaves that wound between the dunes and stretched out towards the beach. Anoles are lizards native to Florida that can change shades of green to camouflage themselves on leaves to hide from hungry birds and snakes. They're in danger of extinction now, but back then a whole long vine of various shades of green could move with a twitch of motion. It was only when I squatted real low that I could see the little creatures.

While I dug around the oar, they leapt and scurried about for shelter. One inadvertently landed on my arm and froze there. I watched as the creature's chartreuse, scaly skin quickly turned deep, dark emerald green, blending with the smooth brown of me. But while I was being awed by him, a sea gull suddenly swept down and snatched another smaller one right in front of me. The tiny creature was just too slow to change, or couldn't. I felt bad thinking I caused the death, but I also knew that the sea gull had to live too. I learned early that there must be death for things to live. It's part of the balance and the beauty in the Wheel. And it's The Way when it's done like this.

When I placed the anole on my arm down on a wide, round leaf, I didn't have to wait long at all before I saw the tiny lizard change colors again. Though other gulls scoured above, they could not see him. Nature was teaching me something about when to be visible and when not to be. I resumed the work of digging up the rest of the oar, careful not to tear the leafy green vine that provided refuge for the rest of the anoles.

When I finally pulled the oar out, I noticed that though half of the paddle part was broken off, it wasn't as badly damaged as I had imagined, and I figured it could still work.

I dragged the door into the water carrying the oar. It floated real nice, and I hopped on and started paddling. With the mainland behind me and the island ahead, I was a young boy riding away on the womb of Mother Earth, in the ocean of the Mystery, on a door. I was riding on a door towards the island I had contemplated since I could remember, contemplated in the same manner I had the stars. I even imagined that I was a star-traveler sailing to another world. I imagined that I was like a dolphin in the wild, free in the waters of life, free from the dangers of the white man's school . . . free, I imagined, like an Indian should be.

THE SHADOW PEOPLE

A S I PASSED over the sandbars and flats into deeper waters, the crystal clear morning slowly changed into a tropical September afternoon, and I could feel the heat of the Florida sun on my back, baking my skin deeper brown. It also painted sun-streaks through my dark hair that Mrs. Basic let me grow long that summer, maybe because she knew it would be awhile before I would ever have long hair again. Hanging past my shoulders, sun-streaked red and raven, my long hair gave me a spirit sense of untamed identity. And though I appeared alone as I paddled out to the island, I didn't have the feeling of loneliness. That feeling would come later in a dismal classroom among the shadow people, but now as a free and natural boy riding on a door in the Gulf of Mexico, loneliness was not a feeling at all.

The wind swept across the surface of the sea and made it shimmer in the sunlight like a galaxy of a million sparkling suns. It rippled the water around the door.

And they came, the dolphins, lots of them, with the wind, arching and diving and blowing. Their fins were shaped like crescent moons, silvery-gray and shiny, as they surfaced and circled and dove.

My smile must have been so wide it touched my ears. "Come on," I urged, pulling my paddle through the water faster and faster, "come to the island with me."

And they did come. Watching them play and listening to their sounds and splashes made me happy. Dolphins have a way of doing that to humans. Maybe it's because they're so free. Maybe it's because that freedom is the way they accept and love who and what they are and the balance they find living that way. That day that we traveled together, I also accepted who and what I was.

When I finally hopped into the warm, turquoise water of the island's shore, the dolphins were already making their way out to open sea. With white foam swirling around me, I turned and waved and called out to them; my child's voice raised above the swish of small waves and carried in the wind.

Though I was standing in water that reached to my waist, I could see clearly all the way to my feet. With my hand anchoring the door to my side, I watched blue crabs scurry away and schools of needlenose fish flicker by. As I headed toward the beach, two sting-rays stirred when I shuffled the sand and quickly fluttered away in their liquid sky. I remembered Mrs. Basic smiling when I stood as a toddler pointing at the water and shouting excitedly, "Butterflies! Butterflies!"

What words can describe how I felt now standing silently before the island I had contemplated ever since I could remember standing and watching the sea?

Wide-eyed with wonder, I explored the tree-lined shore. On one side, tangled mangroves stretched into the Gulf. On the other, a white beach curved around the island's tip. Before me, palm fronds of giant sabals waved like Indian hair in the steady breeze, and

8 pelicans skimmed over them, their wing tips brushing by. Behind the trees, the land rose high above the water towards a hill. It was the same hill my sister and I would watch the evening star dance above in the spring. As sea gulls squawked in the distance, I just breathed in deep and sighed.

The beckoning was finally over, and I dragged the door from the water and placed it up on the shore.

The paddle became my staff and would go with me. Planting it firmly in the sand, I took my first steps inland on a vaguely defined trail that twisted through clusters of palmettos, pines, and sabals. The shell-laden ground was cool under my bare feet. The pine needles were soft; the roots they covered were hard and veined across an ancient path.

As I climbed, the sounds of the sea faded, and the forest came alive with a myriad of chirps and songs. Crows cawed in the distance, and mockers and jays fussed at me passing under them. A diamondback curled in the shade and rattled.

When I finally reached the top of the hill, I was really tired. Leaning on the oar, I sank to my knees and rested. It had been a long journey for a young boy, but I'd made it. Looking up, I could see the beach where I'd left the world behind. It seemed far away with a lot of turquoise in-between. I wondered if I couldn't stay there on the island. The pale faces in black robes would never find me. . . . Shadow people wouldn't come here. . . . And soon they'd forget about taking me away to school, like they had taken away my sister.

If only I could stay. . . .

I would learn later in life that powerful dreams and even visions don't necessarily come when we want them to. But if we follow the path of heart, they come when we're ready. My first experience with vision was about to occur on this island. It was to become like a sacred haunting that would direct my destiny. Years later I would seek a vision in the old way. But now, as a tired boy, I laid upon the earth on my belly and rested my head on tired arms, staring out the corners of my eyes at the sunlight flickering through the fronds. The movement of the light momentarily transcended my reality.

It was in this vision-state of inner silence, of being not asleep nor awake, that I first heard the distant shrill sounds. They made me shiver. As they grew more distinct, they became the heartrending cries of women and children. Then suddenly, the horror of the noise was all around me. I propped myself up on my hands, and saw ghostly men in suits of armor striking and stabbing and tearing at everything. I tried to get up, but I was paralyzed. Terror had trapped my spirit in a body that couldn't move. Booms and blasts echoed in my head and shattered against the sky, and I saw the smoke from their long guns rising, thick and black and sinister. I watched the hazy forms of armored men setting fires to the lodges, and I winced as they smashed pretty pots upon the ground, shattering them to pieces.

I saw these ghostly forms emerge laughing from a burning lodge. Above their faceless heads they flaunted two long and feathered pipes. And to my horror these they smashed upon the earth in violent, angry actions. And I, a spirit in the body, an old gene, perhaps, remembering in the blood, felt the spirit of my own people dying. Other hazy forms shimmered all around. They wielded knives and swords and dragged a large drum from another lodge and tore it open. The metal of their weapons flashed silver and crimson beneath the shrouded sun. And I felt the heart of my people breaking. And all the while the silhouettes of the shadow people in shadow robes moved amid the swirling smoke.

The horror of the sounds stopped, and the silence was once again broken; this time by the loud cawing of a crow. It drew my mind back and snapped the grasp of fear that had paralyzed my body. The cawing of the crow brought back the day, and reality transcended time once again. I was crying as I ran, stumbling along the blurry trail ahead and falling back down the hill. Stumbling and

10   falling, until I couldn't run anymore. It was then that my gaze fell
upon something sharp and protruding from the ground.

At first I thought it was some kind of old bone that had rotted
and withered. I wiped my eyes and crawled closer to examine it
more carefully. The object appeared to be a long piece of rusted
metal. When I lifted one end, it broke abruptly, like caked sand. I
dug out as much as I could, but mostly it just crumbled. Though I
only held one piece of the rusty metal, I recognized what it was
from one of Mrs. Basic's books. I had stumbled upon a sword that
had somehow over time synthesized with its scabbard, and probably once hung on the side of a Spaniard.

Then I discovered another piece of metal. I had to dig deep
around it before I could finally pull it out. It was a gold cross.
Though badly tarnished where it was exposed, the part that was
buried shined dull and heavy. It was as big as my small hand. I knew
it must have belonged to the shadow people who watched under
their dark robes the day my people died and their sacred things were
destroyed.

My inner voice spoke to me again. It told me to leave. I had
seen what beckoned me there, and I knew why I had always contemplated the island. Now I understood as much as a young boy
could: I had to face the white man's world; there was no escape
from it. My heart wanted me to stay there on the island, but I also
knew now that they would come for me. They had discovered the
beauty of this place once before; they would find it again when they
came looking for me.

The tide had receded by the time I returned to the shore, and
the warm waters lapped soothingly around the door as I paddled out
to sea. The sun was slanting towards the west now, making its light
and heat less intense, and the trip back to the mainland would be
shorter at low tide. I kept searching the surface for dolphins, but
they were gone.

When Mrs. Basic saw me coming up the beach trail, she came rushing down the front steps. I recall her, nearly frantic, talking about my welfare and then pausing, as if a switch clicked her off. She bent close to study the piece of rusty metal and gold cross I held in my hands. While she examined the artifacts, my gaze fell on the ominous black sedan parked at the house. The black-robed people who once took my sister away were coming down the front steps.

▲▲▲

The next day I tried to be brave like they told me I should and to leave without any trouble as my sister had, but I couldn't count on that, and neither could they. Just as we approached the car I made my move to escape. With a nun on each side of me, I made a gallant effort to get away just as they were getting me into the car. I tried leaping through one door and out the other side, but one of the three nuns blocked my exit. Another grabbed my feet; I grabbed the steering wheel as if it were the Wheel of Life itself. But two nuns were pulling my legs. And I could feel my grip weakening and my fingers slipping from the wheel despite how hard I tried to hang on.

Then it was over. "Any more of that," the older nun shrieked, "and we'll send for the sheriff."

Mrs. Basic knelt at the car door and placed her hands on my shoulders. The younger nuns who held my legs during the brief battle stepped back. "You've got to go," she said. "We've got no choice. It's the law."

I looked out the rear window at Mrs. Basic clutching her dress and staring at us driving away; it was the last time I ever saw her. I kept watching her blurry form until they turned onto the main road. I pressed my back against the seat, and glanced into the rear-view mirror. The nun who was driving was looking at me as I looked at her. The older one I saw in the mirror that hung on the visor. She was cleaning and polishing the big gold cross. Next to me, leaning towards the window, the third nun was staring at the cypress and palm-laden world outside. Above the tree line she could see vultures circling. Perhaps she was questioning her own purpose in it all.

I remember telling myself that this had to be a bad dream and that I would wake up and run down to the beach and get back on the door. But it was like wanting to believe that what happened to me on the island had not really happened, that it too was only a bad dream created through my own imagination. I wanted to close my eyes and see dolphins, not the haunting images of black robes . . . of shadow people!

▲ ▲ ▲

My journey to the island on the door would become a dream by the time I would become a young man, and the ghostly Spaniards I saw there would become the ugly truth of the way things really were, and still are. . . .

As the cold northwest winds howl through the Indian housing projects outside the dark window in South Minneapolis, warm gusts across the gleaming Gulf blow across my mind. Yet I fall through my dream of the boy on the door, and the shadow people come. They are no longer the hazy forms of friars and Spaniards who haunt the lives and the dreams of me and my people. For over the centuries they have transformed into missionaries and zealots, pioneers and immigrants, soldiers and cops and FBI agents, gold rushers and oil barons, strip miners and developers, fat-cat politicians and prison wardens. They have become rapists and murderers. They are among those who often rove the dead of night and stalk as thieves and killers.

And so, as different winds of a cold northern night rap at a different door, I jolt from my sleep, but it's too late; they're already here. . . .

CHAPTER 3

WITH A GUN
AT MY HEAD

A MAN WITH COLD, violent eyes raised a badge in one hand and pointed a gun at my head with the other. He said something, but I didn't hear what he said; I only stared at the gun while my fists formed like frozen stones. An icy Minnesota wind whipped wildly out of the dark. My bones didn't feel the chill from the wind, only the cold in the stranger's eyes. And I wondered if this was how I was going to die.

Behind me, seven young boys gathered in the doorway, clutching sticks and clubs. They were between twelve and fifteen years old. They were prepared in their boyhood to fight like men.

We were the Heart of the Earth, an American Indian Movement survival school for native children. The school was, however, closely tied with AIM, and AIM and the government of the United States were at war.

Earlier that morning, before first light, intruders had entered and ripped files from cabinets and left them strewn about like trash. They broke furniture, tore apart the books, and ripped the phones from the walls. Some of the people said it was the Minneapolis cops; others thought the F.B.I.

14   Two other men appeared out of the dark and stood on either side of the man who stood before me. Each aimed their guns at my head. Yet two others, also with guns, bashed through the back door. It burst open easily, as did most doors in the Indian housing projects when the unwanted wanted in. The warrior boys and I stood sanely still. This, I thought, was the way of ancestral dog soldiers, and we were dog soldiers at that moment. It was as if we had staked our sashes in the ground and said, "This is a good day to die!"

There must have been strong medicine with us that night. Perhaps the most potent of it was in my words of reason. "I'm a teacher," I implored. "These are my students. . . . They're children! I'm a teacher. . . . These are children!"

In the cold air, my incantation became visible breath, and wrapped a cloud about the face of the closest man. It was a scene vaguely reminiscent of the time when the Aztec king Cauhtemoc stood before the overwhelming forces of the conquistadors after his great city Tenichtitlan was laid to ruins. Cauhtemoc spoke piercingly before the aimed muskets and cannons of the Spaniards. His words must have had the magic; they penetrated even the black heart of Cortés long enough to save the king's life and the life of his surviving warriors. Though I was no king, the rhythm of my words worked their magic, and created a cloud that seemed to momentarily obscure the killer's intent. Even the trees evoked their own kind of haunting magic. For shadows of leafless elms cast from the halogen street lamps stretched across the bare walls of the Catholic church across the street. They were like fingers of ghosts, reaching out to stop him.

Suddenly, like a distant wailing in the night, the scream of an approaching siren startled the gunmen. It caused their eyes to flick nervously, and stirred a sleepy ghetto awake. An ambulance passed, and apartment lights clicked on. Blinds were parted, window shades drawn up, and dark eyes peered from the silhouettes now gathered in the windows and doorways. Sensing the balance of power shifting, the two strangers who slammed in the back door slipped away. The ones who stood before me slowly lowered their guns, and cowered back hurriedly into the dank, cold night while a bitter wind howled after them.

DOLPHINS
AND SPANIARDS

I STEP THROUGH the door of memory where the strangers
stood and release my clenched fingers from stone fists. The bitterness flows from my opened palms into streams of spent emotions. The remembered cold of that Minnesota night fifteen years
ago is warmed in the Florida heat.

The laughter of my wife and children floats to me on balmy
Gulf breezes. Their brown bodies, diving like dolphins, glisten wet
in the white light of the sun.

We are safe here, I tell myself. On this distant beach, we
are safe.

"Oh, Little One," I laugh, embracing the wet brown roundness of my youngest son Carises as he bounds into my arms. I
hold him tightly, kiss his dark wet shoulder, and watch the shimmering water.

Shiny copper cheeks press against mine.

"Daddy."

"Yes, Carises?"

Small hands turn my face away from the Gulf and towards

the black almond eyes that melt into mine. "Come and play dolphins with us!"

The water. Ahh, the water!

We leap and laugh and hold our breath and dive. Down into emerald water, up to turquoise sky. I feel so free and wild.

My wife Simone emerges smiling, her long black hair gleaming over brown shoulders. We embrace, and she allows herself to float free in my arms. Her head rests near my heart. Eyes close, and we too are, like dolphins, in perfect harmony with all things.

But the irresistible laughter of the splashing children draws our attention. Their long hair hangs dark and wet like horse manes over their sparkling skin. This is what life is all about, I say to myself. This was the way it was before guns and disease, bigotry and hate. Just families loving life. Just families with no intellectual need to impose themselves on anyone else. Just families living close with nature, close to the land and the Mystery.

"Play Spaniard, Dad," pleads my daughter Calusa, pausing still between her two brothers. Her golden ten-year-old frame on long legs reflects generations of racial beauty.

"Yeah," shout the boys. "Play Spaniard!"

I squint my eyes and snarl and seize the role. "I've come fer yer gold and yer souls, you heathen savages!" My arm raises in challenge; my face contorts. My insanity is evident. Simone's feet quickly find the sandy bottom where she can support herself, and she swims away. She wants no part of a crazed conquistador.

Calusa giggles excitedly. Ihasha's eyes grow wide. His sinewy adolescent muscles anticipate the test of newly acquired strengths. Carises charges!

The ensuing struggle is intense, but brief. The Spaniard is promptly subdued. The children debate what to do with me. Calusa wants torture and dismemberment. A small price to pay, she declares, after all I've done to her people and her land. Carises enjoys the idea. Ihasha states that a slow death will give me power. Maybe I should die quickly. The children know their history.

I make one last break for open waters, but my imaginary stolen booty weighs me down. I am tortured and dismembered. The children pick me apart, careful not to let this conquistador die too easily. It reminds me how the Shawnee repaid some white men for what they did to Chief Logan's family. The ones who raped and butchered his wife and daughters. How they left Logan with no one in the world to love. How war evokes some strange force in humans. Logan got his revenge. Now, with pretend stabs and thrusts by invisible knives, the children get theirs. I let out painful roars and cries that gradually weaken to short bellows and water-logged grunts. Somehow, I manage to gather power at death even for a conquistador. Finally silence.

My hair matted and plastered with wet sand, my body limp, I hold my breath and fake death. Shoved away, I am left to the waves; the children shout stern warnings of worse things to come should I ever return.

DON'T MAKE WAVES
IN STILLWATER

WINTER FOG formed out in the Gulf and lingered there for most of the day. But as the sun began to set, the fog began to move in. Soon, a cool wet mist swept across the water towards the same shore where the children had once played dolphins in the summer sun and sent a Spaniard back to where he came from.

Now the fog arrived, ghostlike on the deserted beach. It brought other games for the children to play and other dimensions for me, their father, to fall through.

I sat alone. Simone was off in the distance collecting shells, while the children ran back and forth carrying jars and scooping at the wet air. They were trying to catch the fog. Above them crows flew from palm to palm. Sometimes they would land on the very tips of the dangling fronds, and they would sway there in the trees, watching.

Ihasha spotted one of their feathers, lying like an abandoned shadow in the sand, and picked it up. It was a long tail feather, so black its sheen was almost blue. "Dad!" he called, holding the feather in front of him while he ran towards me.

When he reached my side, he held the feather out. "Here,
Dad, you have it."

Twirling it between my fingers, I studied it. "Me-gwich . . ."
I said. "Ghost Dance feather." Ihasha's eyebrows raised. I twirled the
black feather again and studied it some more. "Are you catching the
mist?" I asked.

He smiled and squatted while his eyes stayed fixed on the
feather. He hesitated to answer, probably because he didn't want to
sound silly. After all, he was eleven, and that may be too old to be
catching fog in jars. "It was Calusa's idea."

"Hmmm . . . I used to do that. I'd like to now, but I just feel
like sittin' for a while." A small circle formed in my mind, connecting things and ideas and places.

"Why'd ya call it a ghost dance feather, Dad?"

"Because the ghost dancers used them on their shirts and
dresses. It helped them to travel to the other side . . . you know
. . . the ghost world. Somethin' about the power of the crow." I
paused, twirling the feather again, not really certain what the power
was, or is, in such an object. I twirled it and studied it some more.
"There are lots of dimensions to life," I added. "An elder once told
me that the crows are also the first in battle too. I suppose it all
makes sense . . . a ghost dance feather . . . the mist . . . kinda goes
together."

Ihasha watched me examine the feather. There was so much
he couldn't see. Who was I besides his father? I suppose it didn't
matter, not really. What mattered was that I loved him and he knew
it. And it satisfied him to know he gave me something special, a
feather to think about, to dwell upon. Like most boys, though, he
was anxious to get back to the things that kids do. He stood, still
holding his jar of captured fog. "You wanna catch some with us?"

"No . . . not now, Son. Thanks. I think I'll just sit here with
this fine feather and . . . sorta let the fog capture me."

The image of my son running back to join the others was a haunting one. For he seemed like a ghost racing back to the other side. Holding the crow's feather and sitting in the mist, I figured it no small wonder why I thought about ghosts and the other side. The last time I had worn a crow's feather was in my hair outside Stillwater State Prison in Minnesota. The last time I saw the mist and the crows together was there, too. The last time I held one in my hands was in the bundle where I carried the pipe stem. Circles. Everything's a circle.

Feathers are evocations of memory, and the one I held at that moment helped me recall. . . .

▲▲▲

The cold mist rose from the earth and settled around the bare elms in front of the prison entrance, creating that strange awareness of altered reality that could make a place of contained violence appear almost peaceful. . . .

But for me, when was anything what it appeared to be? And when is reality anything but a state of mind?

As I approached the concrete steps, a gust of cold air rushed past me. It felt as though it went right through me. I wondered if it might not be the spirit of one of the Indian men who had died in this place. I wondered if such a gust out of still air wasn't a sign for me to stay away . . . that this is a bad place . . . a dead place . . . a place where I didn't have the right nor the power to be doing this. Or maybe it was an agreement, that the path I took to get here was the right one. How could I know? My heart urged me forward, up the prison steps, and as I reached the door, I felt a growing connection between myself and the pipe that I cradled in my arms, and I became aware of another connection: that one was to my own death.

The notion that Indians die for what they believe, especially in prison, was not a paranoid idea that I had formed from a bad dream as a child, though that's what the nuns who tried to take my spirit away wanted me to think. "It was just a bad dream," they'd tell me. "You were a frightened little boy on that island. You just imagined that we were conquistadors." They'd laugh and smile and shake their heads and tell me that they were just out for my own good . . . to educate me . . . to save me from the devil and bring me closer to God . . . to make me a good boy in the eyes of Jesus. They told me not to think of myself as Indian, since I was lucky to have any white blood at all in me. "In some ways," they'd muse, "you're right. . . . We are like the conquistadors, but not nearly so adventurous." When I cried, they'd tell me that the old woman, Mrs. Basic, had the wrong kind of influence on me. As they cut my hair away, they'd say, "She let you run wild, you know."

Indians do die for what they believe. My vision or my bad dream or whatever they wanted to call what I saw on the island as a boy showed me that much. The recent killing of Anna Mae Aquash and other Indian activists in South Dakota and other places only reinforced it now as my gaze dropped from the prison door to the rabbit fur bundle in my arms and the beaded bag I held in my hand. The bundle wrapped around the decorated pipe stem, and the beaded bag contained the red stone bowl.

As I stood facing the prison door, the recollections began. I recalled what I saw and felt on the island as a boy — watching the hazy forms of Spaniards through the smoke — paralyzed by my own fear. I can shut my eyes now or at any time, and see them smashing the pipes, tearing at the drums, ripping the beauty out of this world. In the darkness of my own mind I can still see the shadow people who stood among them concealed in shadow robes, watching. No, I tell myself, it was no bad dream. And I am no small boy paralyzed by his own fear now.

22

Standing at the top of the steps, I turned away from the prison door. Shapes and forms seemed to shift and flicker in the mist that embraced the gnarled and dark trunks of the huge elms. I was not alone.

My eyes followed the crow sentinel as it flew from the iron gate at the prison entrance to a bare branch inside the compound. There, other crows gathered among the long, twisting boughs of the elms. They appeared like warriors. I knew what I was up against. I welcomed their company.

To understand what the Indian prisoners and I were dealing with is to try and understand the attitude Warden Wills had about Indians he couldn't control. His kind of attitude could cause the kind of bitterness to fester that could result in an inmate's suicide. Rumor was that what happened to Wills a few years back drove him over the psychological edge. While falling into a more bitter and sinister dimension, whatever sense of compassion or humanity Wills may have had for Indians must have frozen in a kind of free-fall from reason.

It seems that the warden had been under pressure a couple of years before from the Indian prisoners at Stillwater and activists from the Twin Cities Indian community. They wanted some kind of cultural event to take place inside the prison that could possibly lift the spirit of the men and also let them know that the community still cared about them. So, the warden agreed to a pow wow. The small event consisted of a drum, some singing, dancing, and some family members of the inmates. And it appeared like Wills had the pow wow and the Indian "agitators" all under control when something happened that would intensify his bitterness later on for "guys like me" and for the others who were involved in getting the pipe inside those steel doors.

At some point during the pow wow in the dismal auditorium, while the drum was beating and the men were singing,

24 someone had apparently slipped the warden a hit of LSD in a cup of coffee. No one knows who did it, and no one ever claimed to have done it. Some even believed that Wills had medicine used against him. Nevertheless, even though there were other people there, including other inmates and prison officials, Wills blamed the Indians.

As the story goes, Wills yelled some while being escorted through the general population that day. It doesn't take much of an imagination to hear him hollering about Indians being "nothing but a bunch of liars and thieves . . . dopers and dealers!"

By the time I had to deal with him, Warden Wills was not likely to show any sign of compassion or sensitivity for the Indians whose struggle it was to get the pipe inside the prison, especially Tuffy and the chief who were there at the pow wow when the warden freaked. Besides, we were the Indians that the system couldn't control. In the old days, we would have been called the "wild ones" in Florida — or the "hostiles" in other places — for that same reason. So I just considered the warden another manifestation of two thousand seasons of spiritual negligence, going back to Columbus and his kidnapping of peaceful Tainos, to Cortés and Coronado when the blazing conquistadors laid a bloody trail of Native people from Florida to New Mexico. I figured Wills was the kind of manifestation General Sheridan no doubt recruited during his "nits make lice" campaign against the women and children of the plains tribes, or that maybe he shared the same mentality as the cops who beat Indians like Simone's brother and sister in the back alleys and streets of Minneapolis.

At that time death for any of us was, indeed, a reality that I was facing as I stepped through the door of Stillwater State Prison that late afternoon nearly half a lifetime ago.

Inside, steel doors clanged shut behind me, and I stood cradling the Pipe. Its stem of sumac, wrapped in a layer of red flannel and covered with white rabbit furs, felt as soft as air. The bowl remained protected in its bag of white buckskin. The strength of loving hands lingered around the colorful and seasonal berries the women beaded in circular patterns upon it. Those berries could look so deliciously real that you'd think you could eat them. Within the stark prison, they were among the few things that showed signs of life. Even the two armed guards, who were my escort down the grim corridors of pale, yellow tile, had a sense of spirit-death about them.

Black men in blue prison uniforms paused with their mop sticks and watched as we walked by; white men with short sleeves curled up their hairy and tattooed arms stopped what they were doing and stared. Indians peered between the bars.

When we entered a small, windowless room, one of the guards, a tall, pale-looking man with close-shaven reddish hair closed the door. Against the wall was a table.

"Put it there," he pointed.

"I was told there would be an Indian guard here."

Both guards glanced at each other. The shorter one, who wore a dark mustache under a sharp thin nose, turned his head and said something to the taller one behind him and then left the room. I don't believe the warden anticipated having the director of human rights for the state of Minnesota waiting outside, but the director had signed in at the front desk shortly after I had passed through the first gate. I was no fool, and that was a part of the plan that I had made to help ensure my own safety as well as that of the men inside. Like the prisoners who mopped the floors in blue uniforms, the director of human rights was black too. His presence would help force Wills to cooperate if he had to, and having an Indian guard present at inspection was one of the demands Wills had agreed to. A little while later the shorter guard, who had left the room, returned, this time with the only Indian guard at Stillwater. This was something the warden boasted about to me and to others, as if having an Indian guard at the prison was some sort of grand

26   achievement.

"When was the last time you inspected a Bible?" I asked them, removing one of the furs from the stem. "How often have you inspected the communion a priest brings in? I suppose you check the holy water too."

I taunted them with these rhetorical questions, not because I expected them to answer, but because I wanted them to be aware of the racism that existed in this place. Ignorance could never again be used as an excuse.

There was no reply. There couldn't be. I'd stood at the steel-barred door before and watched the priests and ministers and rabbis go in. Never once did I see them or their holy objects subjected to this. Maybe it was the teacher in me, but I used the moment to try to educate these men; and maybe it was the AIM in me who wanted to make them aware and maybe even ashamed of how much a part of this bigoted penal system they were. Besides, this was the warden's condition. The pipe could not enter the prison without inspection. The compromise was my insistence on the Indian guard.

I lifted the layer of red flannel. "You know that looking at something so sacred and not understanding what it means can hurt you," I explained. I didn't say that to frighten them. As the keeper of such a pipe I was responsible for telling them this. In a way, looking at a sacred pipe is like looking at a Navajo sand painting. When a sand painting ceremony is finished, the sand painting used to attract the immortals is destroyed so the unprepared will not come into contact with it and be harmed. Though I had the bowl and stem of the pipe separated, the objects still contained power. The two white men stepped away.

The Indian guard remained near the table. I sensed his discomfort at being there, but I also understood his own sense of responsibility, not only to his job, but to the pipe. No matter how far government schools and churches had removed him from what he was, I could feel there was something in his blood that called him back to his ancestors, something that made him at least act respectful. After all, I thought, he should. He was seeing something that past generations had died believing in. I glanced at his eyes as he tried to avoid any extended contact with what he saw while I unwrapped the stem. He tensed and his lips pressed together when I removed the bowl from its beaded bag.

"I didn't want this done," I said to him. His uneasiness told me that he didn't either, but we had no choice if the ceremony of the pipe would ever be. I justified having gone this far because of the men inside and because I had not put the bowl and stem together. That I would not do. That would bring the pipe to life, and I would not do that, not for the system to degrade. No way. Not with such a bigoted sense of justice would I ever have exposed a living pipe to them.

Despite my warning, one of the white guards, the shorter one, briefly gazed at the two objects, bowl and stem lying on their wrappings. I felt he did this not out of some distorted sense of duty, but out of his own arrogance. And though he turned quickly away, it was too late. I saw this in his eyes. He had seen something his own religious and cultural background had allowed him no means to understand. The pipe I had carried into the prison that day was presented to me by an AIM warrior and an elder of the People about a year into my teaching at the Heart of the Earth school. It was not blessed by a mortal's ego, but by the very stone and wood which created it. In other words, Mother Earth blessed such a pipe. That's why I cringe when I see the Indian pipes with price tags stuck on their bowls. They're too precious. The one I carried into Stillwater that day had witnessed the births of native babies. Their names were called out to the Mystery on this pipe. It has listened to the

28

People's cries for peace in the world and within themselves. It has helped heal the wounds of the Native heart. This pipe was the last thing held by those of the People who were about to die and make their Great Change. This pipe had known the love of the People. All this is what gave it power. Even separated, the bowl and stem made one aware of such power. And this one white guard had now cast his eyes upon these two holy objects and had seen something so private and primal that it touched his own distant center and would never let him go.

The other guard, the close-shaven redhead, avoided any eye contact with the objects. I imagined that he would remain safe in his shallow, shadow world. I imagined that in his chosen ignorance, his life would stagnate there at Stillwater, never knowing that maybe the prison he was really guarding was the one in his own mind. I wondered if the memory of this time might not linger with him, though he would never let it tear away the barriers that kept him from seeing the beauty in diversity. But I imagined that the other man would never be the same. He would be haunted.

"This is a Great Mystery pipe," I told the Indian guard, who looked at the objects more as an Indian man than a prison guard.

It was as if the glassy, smooth and ageless red bowl, and the feathered stem, inlaid with ocean shells and wampum, had spoken to him, for he nodded and motioned to me to wrap them up once again. There was no indignity for the pipe, for me, or for him at this time, and I was glad he was the Indian that he was. I felt I had done right in this aspect of the negotiations with the warden.

Down the long, bleak hallway was the dingy and dimly lit auditorium where the Indian prisoners gathered on the stage as they had before around their drum, hoping that the time for them to pray together with a pipe had finally come. The first to greet me as my eyes adjusted to the lack of light was the chief. He was fair-skinned and blue-eyed. A bright red headband decorated his head. Behind

him was Tuffy. His long, curly black hair seemed free and wild in
this place of prison and denial. Though months of numerous phone
conversations created this moment for us, this was the first time in
this life that we had ever met. We embraced like brothers whose
paths of life had finally merged. We were brothers living The Way
among the shadow people.

Tuffy and I were the primary planners of this event — "agitators" the warden would call us. We had long engaged him and state
prison officials in verbal combat for this moment, and both Tuffy
and I had suffered through the wounds inflicted by bureaucratic
word wars and the threats, insults, and degradations that result from
such a battle. We were often reminded that "officially recognized
Indians" were working on religious expression for Native American
prisoners.

"You're no medicine man," the warden had sneered at me
months earlier from behind his desk in his plush office when Stillwater first rippled with anticipation. "You're a con artist." The tactic
was humiliation. Some historians and Indians who know such
things say it's what killed Wamsutta, the young Wampanoag
prince, in his dealings with the Pilgrims. Humiliation turns your
intentions into self-doubt. It twists your feelings about yourself and
your actions, and it rips at your heart's self-worth and your sense of
purpose. What good you try to do humiliation tears asunder. But it
wasn't going to destroy me. I couldn't let it destroy me. That's what
I had learned from the past.

"I never claimed to be a medicine man. I only keep a sacred
pipe that the Indian men wish to pray with."

"They're not men!" Wills shrieked. "They're liars and
thieves. They're dopers and dealers. And you're a con man."

I opened a folder in my lap and removed a letter of support
for the pipe to be brought into the prison. The letter was from the
office of a state senator who was then vice president elect of the

30

United States. I dropped it on the warden's desk. While he read it, I dropped another one from the director of human rights and another from a state congressman. "You're gonna let these men pray like Indians with the pipe they requested," I told him, "or I'll have the AIM schools outside with their drums along with all the media that a contingent of Indians attracts these days."

He pressed forward in his leather chair and glared at me with the cold, beady eyes of a killer, while his hands pressed down on the letters on his desk. "I'll get you for this, you troublemaking bastard," he snarled. "I'll get you for this." And I wondered how he would "get me."

▲ ▲ ▲

My young wife Simone may have wondered too when I left Minneapolis late that afternoon to carry the pipe to Stillwater for the first time. She was pregnant. And as I was driven away in a tanklike old Ford by two AIM warriors, I turned and saw her standing on the icy steps waving with one hand while she held her womb with the other. Her raven hair, draped over her pretty black and red poncho, was speckled white, and her rosy cheeks ran wet with falling snow. She was nineteen years old then.

As I watched her standing in the snowy doorway of our little rented house in south Minneapolis, I was seeing the manifestation of everything I ever loved in my twenty-eight years of life waving goodbye to me, and I wanted to stay. I wanted her and that soon-to-be-born son of ours to be the only ones in the world that mattered to me, but I was a pipe keeper who had been asked to carry the pipe to the men so they could pray. I wanted to give this back to our people.

A pipe keeper must love, I thought. But as the old Ford turned onto the interstate and wisps of snow swept across our path, I wondered too if what the warden said about me wasn't true. Perhaps humiliation was working against me as it had Wamsutta, prince that he was. Maybe I really am a "troublemaking bastard." Maybe I am an "agitator." Maybe I am a "con artist" just causing more problems for the guys in the prison, making life rougher on them. Maybe state approved and "government certified" pipe keepers should be doing this. But then, why weren't they? I even considered that maybe this whole affair was some attempt on my part to bolster my ego and prove something to myself. But every action up until that point told me, no: this was something the men wanted. It was a need they requested that I could help fill, and they deserved the right to request the pipe that I kept, or any other pipe. This was a basic human right that belonged to the People of this land and would not be denied!

As we approached the Stillwater exit, the soft snow changed into pebble-like pellets and then into hail the size of large stones. The hail battered the dented hood and the rusty roof and assaulted any doubts that were manifesting inside the old car. The noise it made shattering against the metal was deafening. I thought that any minute the windshield would blast away! What was shattered instead were any doubts that I or the two AIM warrior escorts may have conjured about what we were doing. Other cars pulled off to the side. Not us. We kept heading up the exit ramp, more determined than ever, and I knew then that we were men whose spirits were rooted deeply in the past and to our nation in a way that most people would never know.

The hail stopped as suddenly as it began, and we snaked our way up the winding road toward the prison. I saw the iron gate entrance ahead in the cold mist and the crows perched black against the grey air and watching, and all seemed right.

That was as far as the AIM warriors were allowed to take me. They parked the car in the lot designated for visitors and waited with the director of human rights at the front desk.

The white prison guards who had escorted me into the room where the pipe had been inspected led me down another cold corridor and through another entrance where we entered the prison auditorium.

32

Inside, the light was weak, but the spirit of Orenda, that collective spirit of the ancestors, was strong. It was too strong for the Indian men to be intimidated by the armed guards clustered at the doors. And though the warden remained absent from the shadows of the room, I could feel the bitterness of his presence. For in the empty aisles stood the men in grey suits. They were other prison officials, the warden's cronies, and probably some Feds. And as I scanned the dimly lit room, their presence became a haunting sight that seemed to have an eerie and historical setting. When I saw the Indian men gathered on the stage, their black hair reminded me of the crows that I saw gathered in the elms outside, and this gave me courage. When the Indian prisoners saw me walking down the aisle holding the pipe, accompanied by the chief and Tuffy, they turned or stood and looked up in silent recognition that the pipe and I had really made it. Some walked toward me and greeted me with handshakes or touched my arms, leading me onto the stage.

Relatives of some of the prisoners soon followed me in. They trickled down the aisles of the auditorium past the armed guards. One or two mothers and fathers, a grandmother and a grandfather, an aunt and an uncle, a brother, a sister, a former lover, a wife, a teenage son and a daughter, a cousin, a friend, and others all stepped onto the stage.

And that stage in the prison auditorium became very crowded, but not just with people. Among the Indian prisoners and their relatives and friends, something mingled and moved through the stagnant air, and the threatening presence of the armed prison guards and the warden dissipated into some vague or obscure reality that suddenly didn't matter any more. Orenda was everywhere.

And we began forming a great circle on the wooden floor.

At first, some of the people joked with me and the others who stood trying to locate the Four Directions in a place without windows, and when an elderly man remarked that this was a place where the sun never shines, the people in the circle laughed. And it was true.

We were in a room where no natural light had ever been. I imagined it before . . . perhaps in a dream. . . . It could have been a cave or a lodge. . . . Now I was here . . . in the dank and dark auditorium of a prison. . . .

After a good laugh and after deliberating and recounting exits and entrances, we finally found it . . . the East. And I sat with the pipe in that spot. I always sat in the East. It is the place of birth and rebirth. The sun shows me this. It is the place of origin and beginning. This the creation accounts tell me. That is its power. Like the sun at dawn, like the first light of day, like the dancing light of the morning star, and like the light that has glowed in the center of the pipe that I held, that power is the East and the light it brings.

Each of the hundred Indians there picked a particular place to sit, or they sat wherever they felt comfortable or happened to be until the circle on the wood floor encompassed the stage.

Everyone in the wheel watched with anticipation as I removed the sacred objects from their coverings.

"This is a Great Mystery pipe," I explained, as I put the bowl and stem together and held it up to them. "Now it is alive."

What we believe as a people is in this pipe. The pipe is our sacred bond with the Great Mystery. Holding it, we are connected to the Earth and Sky, and our words become the smoke. It strengthens our bond to this Creation and reminds us that we are forever a part of it. This is what I said.

As I rubbed my hand over the bowl and stem, I could feel the eyes of the people. And I could feel the weight of my responsibility

34

to them and to the pipe, to the past and to the present. The words I spoke expressed belief, and the belief belonged to the pipe and the people, living and dead, not just to me or to any one person. This was my intent: to give the people back the belief that once was theirs. What the Spaniards and the churches had tried to destroy and what the missions and schools and prisons and governments have all denied, the People and I would try to get back.

And I could feel something else at that moment, something pulling me along this path. Later, I would learn about something called destiny. But, at that moment, I only sensed it; for I knew I was on a particular path and that for one reason or another, it had brought me here, to this place, to this circle.

I looked at the pipe stem I held in my hands, running my fingers over it, loving and respecting what it was. I did this every time I took it out. And I contemplated my connection to the man who had shaped and smoothed the wood of sumac, who had carved this stem and created this pipe. I believed that he must have sensed its purpose, its destiny too. Perhaps the pipe itself was the vision of the maker. The bowl appeared ageless, and looking at it I could see a glimpse of the universe around its center. Its stem was nearly the length of my arm. It was long and oiled and smoothly carved, and it was inlaid with the kind of wampum shells usually found on lake bottoms and ocean floors. No one knew how these shells had been collected. They were shaped like hearts and carefully inlaid the length of the stem. And in between each shell heart was another, smaller shell shaped in a circle. They reminded me of the hearts of different people from the circles of different tribes and nations who come together as one and put their lips upon it and draw in its spirit-breath.

Sitting to my right was Tuffy. I helped him light a thick braid of sweetgrass and watched as he passed it to his left, sunwise, around the circle. It was the first time in the prison that such a ritual had been performed. The sweet scent of Mother Earth's burning braid rose into the usually stagnant and dank prison air. The people in the circle each drew the sacred smoke towards their bodies with their hands. They were bathing in the smoke, cleansing themselves of civilized trivialities, opening their minds and their hearts to what is beautiful inside them and what must continue to live.

It was at this time that I noticed my mother-in-law Elaine. I hadn't seen her come in, and I smiled at her, thinking about the work and the magic she too had made to help create this event, this assertion of Native American identity that was taking place in this prison designed to further fragment the identities of Indian men. Elaine was highly respected, not only among most of her people, but by the local politicians who learned from her almost daily about Native American people and how the Indian views the world that the white man created. Elaine had a way of making the white man aware of things without alienating those of them who had not totally succumbed to the system. I thought about her power as a woman of the People and the beauty and strength she brought to the circle of mostly men that day. She could never know then that a year later her own name, Woman-Who-Sweeps-Away-With-The-Crane's-Wing, would be bestowed on her and first spoken on the same pipe that she helped to bring to the men in Stillwater.

And while the purification ritual was taking place, I began working a pinch of tobacco into the pipe bowl. When I was done and the sweetgrass braid had completed the circle, I raised the pipe to the East and as I did this, I sang. The song had come to me in a dream from the Thunderbeings shortly after I received the pipe. It was a frightening dream where a Thunderbeing had taught me how to release my anger and anxiety, my tension and my fear, in a non-physical way. I was held immobile by their power. Only when I centered myself, when I reached a sense of inner peace and was able to let go of my anger and fear, was I free. The song came as I floated as a free spirit among the great cloud-like beings. The song has no words but evokes feelings like an approaching storm. It is sung in the pipe's presence to help penetrate and free the pain of the humans in the circle who hold it.

Creating a channel to the powers of each direction that I faced with the pipe, I sang the song that day at Stillwater that had been given to me by the Thunderbeings. Each time it would begin far away and travel towards us like the thunder: faint at first, and then suddenly bursting in our hearts and centers and then drifting away.

When I completed this aspect of the ritual, Tuffy struck a match, lit a stick of cedar, and held it to the bowl. Whether these rituals of presentation were properly performed or not, the fact is that all our actions were based on traditions we had learned with our minds and felt with our hearts. We weren't putting on a show for cameras. We were participating in our spiritual expression, and the powers that the pipe had attracted were all there.

Everything to get the pipe inside the prison had been done with the heart and the courage that such action requires. Everything in that circle was done with the heart too and with love for our people and our country and for what we believed. I inhaled strong; the smoke rose, thick and white. Releasing my breath, I then passed the pipe to my left, the way the sun travels across the sky, the way the sweetgrass braid had traveled, the way we had learned to pass such things to mirror the harmony in the great Wheel of Life.

As each person prayed and smoked and passed the pipe, I would glance up, trying to see the fire glowing in the bowl, trying to keep it strong. There were so many people that I feared that maybe the pipe would go out. Then what? Should I empty it and fill it again and continue the ceremony? If the pipe goes out, would that be a bad sign? Would that be the sign that I was afraid would happen? Would that be the pipe's way of telling me that what I did by bringing it to such a place was wrong? That I had no right to do this? "He's no medicine man," the warden and the certified Indians would say again. "He had no tribal authority to do such a thing."

I concentrated on that glowing orange light emanating from the pipe bowl. The men had asked me to come; this I told myself. I brought the pipe to them that they may pray as Indians. . . . I watched the fire in the bowl glow and dim as the people smoked. I watched its light glowing and fading, pulsating the way the morning star had when I stood watching it on the steps of Mrs. Basic's house. But what is far beyond the ego of men cannot be controlled by men, and I realized that whether the pipe would go out or not would be something that now only the pipe and its relationship to the people would decide. And though each person in that circle of a hundred strong smoked and prayed with the pipe, it never went out.

Throughout the ceremony I felt the People working with it. For I'm sure that each of us in the circle that day had something to deal with, something of our own self-worth to prove, and no one wanted the pipe to go out in his or her hands. And the pipe had to have felt the love of the People, so that when it returned to me, I took a deep breath, inhaled, and released.

Smoke rose as it had in the beginning, only this time it formed a large swirling ring that floated into the air.

At that moment I believe the circle was filled with all that is a part of the Native American soul. In the dark and dismal auditorium of a state prison, the spirit of the Indian inside the People was freed, and the invisible bridge that connects earth and sky and all things was made through the ceremony of the pipe.

When I had once again separated the stem and bowl and placed them back into the bundle and the beaded bag, other circles formed. One was around the drum and the Indian prisoners who sang and beat upon it while the rest of us danced in another circle around them.

38

"My name's Otto," said one silvery-haired man as he danced up to me. I wondered how someone like him could be guilty of any crime, let alone one that would wind him up in here. I imagined that the lines on his face were formed by the years he spent in this place, by the torture of confinement, though his dark eyes still held the spark that told others he was not spirit-dead. It was a spark men like Warden Wills did not have. "I'm in for forty years," he said, as he shook my hand softly. "Thanks, brother."

Another man danced alongside me. He introduced himself as Silas. "I've been in here for fifteen years. I hope you come again," he said, and he danced away into another world, another time.

"I'm J.B.," smiled another. His long braids swayed as he too danced to the steady, strong beat of the drum and the drummers' singing. "Maybe you know my niece, Holly Red Crow. She goes to the AIM school. Tell her J.B. says hi. It's been seven years since I've seen her."

"I will."

"Come again," they called.

And I would. Only there'd be no more inspections. From that night on, the pipe I carried would enter and exit that prison like the priest's communion, the minister's Bibles, or the rabbi's Old Testament. AIM warriors and I would defy prison authority on inspecting the pipe on several occasions, despite the warden's threats of locking us in there. Never again would we allow that to happen to the pipe that I kept. Even the Indian prisoners would create their own protests to forbid the pipe's inspection.

And soon, another event would take place in the state prison that had never happened before.

It would seem for some as though a pebble was tossed into a pond, with hardly a noticeable splash and a few small circles rippling out. But, in the reality of events, this particular stone was red and made of the ancestors' blood, and it would enter into Stillwater

with quiet force, and waves would form from its impact, flowing in
endless circles from their source. This was the night I would carry
the pipe into the "hole."

▲▲▲

When I left Simone that late wintry afternoon, she was holding Ihasha in her arms. He was three weeks old. As always, I did not
want to leave them, but I could not, of course, bring them with me.
For Stillwater State Prison was a battlefield, and I couldn't see how
a woman and an infant should be near such a place. I was also aware
that perhaps my primary purpose in life now was as a husband to
Simone and a father to Ihasha. I was to protect them. But how could
I protect them from this war? Even from this one battle? For wasn't
this just one of thousands in a war that began five hundred years ago?

Remember Uncle Nip's words. She was probably thinking
this as she stood cradling the baby in the doorway. My uncle made
me aware that my foremost responsibility now was to my wife and
our son. It was something that did not have to be stated again. It
was understood. Nippawanock made certain of this. He told me
about the needs of a woman like Simone, and the needs of a child.
But I had been engaged in this struggle before I'd met Simone. I had
to see it through.

I had to and she knew it.

She also knew that losing me now was an unimaginable idea
for her. Maybe she considered that even thinking such a thought
could possibly empower it to happen; maybe this was the reason
why she chose not to imagine it at all. Simone became my mate as
the patterns of our lives intertwined. She allowed herself to become
pregnant and have our child. How could she allow men of hate to
take me away from her? How could she allow them to deny Ihasha
his father? But what could she do? She couldn't allow me to be held
hostage to her and our son, or Wills and those who followed him

would continue to deny her people the most basic human rights.
No, these things against her people should be stopped, and Simone
knew this. Had I not taken up this struggle, I would not have that
which is old, that which she chose to pass on to Ihasha. No, Simone
would not allow the thought of her husband not returning to form
in her mind.

"Don't worry," I told her. "This is the last time." I held the
beaded pipe bag up to her. . . . "Look," I said, "you and your mom
put those strawberries on. Your sisters and aunts all helped. I have
this." The berries looked so real Ihasha reached his tiny hand out to
touch one while he drooled from the side of his cherry lips.
"Besides," I said, "I'm taking the human rights director with me.
It'll be alright." I kissed her lips and then her hair. "I love you,
Simone." I kissed Ihasha. "I love you too, son." And then I turned
as I had before and walked away.

She remained standing in the doorway with the baby in her
arms. I could feel her dark eyes follow me to the awaiting car.

Simone and I tried to reassure ourselves that it would be
alright, that we'd have a lifetime together, but we were never really
sure that we would. We were never even sure how long a lifetime
for an Indian was anymore.

At the moment when that strange and unwelcome sense of
loss would rise to overcome her, she recalled the dream she had
about us when we flew together as crows; "We loved each other
even as crows," she said.

And then there was another dream, the one she hung onto
most of all. In this dream she and I were old people. She described
us as being very happy, and she watched us in her dream as we
laughed together and rolled down a grassy knoll like playful little
children.

One dream gave her hope of another life together. The other
dream helped her to cling to this one.

I watched the cold Minnesota landscape moving past me as I headed for the prison for the last time, and I thought about the boy on the door, alone yet not alone in the great expanse of The Mystery. I thought about the metaphors: the door, the island, the dolphins, and about the wheel my small hands were torn away from and how I had somehow made my way back into it. I thought about the Spaniards that I saw on the island, and it filled my senses with the burning desire to set things right again. And I thought of Simone. Feelings for her fueled the fire as well. Now we had a son and the fire raged.

That night Stillwater was as black as the crow's feather that Ihasha had found on the beach and given to me: no stars, no moonlight, just the artificial light of the street lamps as we approached the prison entrance. Beyond the halogen glow I could feel the immense blackness. That is where I would draw the power. The darkness of The Mystery was my ally. In my mind I became one with it and the natural things of the night, for twirling in the slight wind were crow and owl feathers tied to one of my braids, and to the stem of the pipe.

Only one guard stood waiting to escort me at the first gate. Already I sensed the unusual, for there had never been less than two guards at other times. I pointed this out to the human rights director who had accompanied me there once again, and who had to stay behind the first gate.

Conspiracy coiled in the still silence.

At each check point a buzzer would sound, and another iron barrier opened and shut, clanging behind me while my lone escort hurried ahead.

Until now I had never realized how few Indians there really were in this prison. In our ceremony in the auditorium, there had always seemed to be so many more. Maybe it's because a hundred Indians in one room seemed like so many. But there certainly

42

weren't many out here in the general population of the prison, though. Tuffy and the chief greeted me but were quickly absorbed by the clusters and streams of white men and black men and men whispering in Spanish who moved about like walking dead people as we moved ahead, deeper into the prison.

As I walked farther on, I saw no Indians, only black and white and Spanish-speaking men who stood against the bars or leaned from the railings over the second level, all watching from their cages, as if something was going to happen. Some felt to me like the night-walkers and killers who stalked our country now. Others seemed like assassins. Maybe it was my own paranoia, but they all appeared to stare with anticipation. Cradling these beautiful articles of the pipe in my arms, I wondered if the pipe had somehow altered their own sense of reality, forcing some of them to reflect on their own torn roots, their own fragmented identities. And I wondered if they thought about what they believed in, and I wondered whether these thoughts could have any power to deter any plot to stop me.

I felt more vulnerable now and more afraid than ever before in that prison. But I kept following my escort. Then, as if I had sud-denly dropped some invisible weight from my mind, the fear I had been sensing fell away, and once again I was like a dog soldier on the night I stood on the steps of the AIM school with the children behind me and the men who held guns to my head in front of me. And while I moved past the cells of inmates and on to the next gate, I realized what had happened to me. I had finally learned a truth: I had become consciously aware that it was not me taking the pipe into this prison at all; it was the pipe that was taking me. It was as if I suddenly understood that this was how the pipe and I had been connected all along and how we were connected to the People.

Farther and farther and finally into the bowels of the prison I walked. This time I followed a different escort, past naked men showering before armed guards. The scene brought back the degradation that I had experienced once in such a place. How horrible, I thought, that humans were denied even their basic privacy. Through one more gate we entered; it was the last. It was the gate that opened into "the hole."

    It was one of the worst places on earth, something out of the "dark ages" mentality of the white man. Something out of the Spanish Inquisition. English dungeons. The KGB. It was filled with a cold kind of quiet that dwells in dead places made of concrete and steel. It was not like the area of the general population where I could still feel the spirit alive in the People. There was no movement or sound here, no feeling, except the sound of the iron gate closing behind me and the cold sensation it gave me when it slammed shut and locked.

    Two guards took me to a cell. At first, neither of them spoke. While I strained to see through the bars, I heard one of them tell me something about "time." He didn't realize that we were on Indian time now, natural time, not measured by the artificial means of a clock. The pipe would work its magic through the artificial time of civilized men, but he wouldn't know that and could never understand. It didn't matter whether he said I had twenty minutes or an hour in that cell, what needed to be done would be done on Indian time. But I nodded reassuringly for the guard's sake that I understood I only had thirty minutes.

    It was like another dream for me to remember those moments because, as they say about such things, they are of The Mystery. It is only through holding the crow's feather that my memory is stirred. It's like another falling through. . . .

    I have no recollection of walking into that cell. It was more like crawling. For it was one of those moments when time and place transcend, and I entered the lodge or the kiva, not the cell.

    At first glance, I saw my Indian brother. It's painful for me to remember what I saw. He was sitting cross-legged on the hard floor.

44

I noticed that his ankles were in chains. As my eyes adjusted to the eerie light, I saw that his hair was so long that it nearly shielded his chained wrists. It was so black that it boldly contrasted with the red prison suit that his kind had to wear in the hole. He reminded me of old pictures I'd seen of Satanta and Geronimo and other Indians considered dangerous and violent.

"Anin, Neeg." I greeted him in Ojibway.

"Anin, Neeg," he responded in a whisper.

We talked a little as I sat near him and unwrapped the pipe. I put the bowl and the stem together. His eyes were transfixed. Having been completely cut off from nature, he seemed especially drawn to its natural symbols: the wampum, the shells, the feathers of birds from different nations, the deer skin bundle of sacred foods, the snake skin binding stem and bowl together.

I handed it to him. "Hold it, Neeg."

He took it with both of his large hands and held it like a man would an infant. The silver of the handcuffs gleamed in the darkness, and he was careful not to let them touch the pipe as he embraced it and moved his fingers all over it. "It's beautiful," is all he said. Then his head dropped and his eyes closed, and I sensed he was feeling the power of the pipe moving through him.

And as we smoked and spoke our words into the Great Mystery that the Ojibways call Gitchie Manido, he and I watched the dark crimson of the pipe bowl glowing with the fire of life and connecting us to each other, to the earth, to the stars, and to all things. In the stillness and silence of that hollow cell, words of the heart were whispered to the Great Mystery and echoed free from "the hole" of Stillwater that night. They were freed in the sound of the words and in the smoke of the pipe.

There were many waves felt from that one ceremony there on the cold floor in the hole. It accomplished what Wills and others had probably feared all along and what they tried to prevent.

Soon, other pipes would be carried into Stillwater, and some of the men would begin making their own. They would demand the right to keep medicine bundles. Even talk of a sweat lodge floated in with the ripples made from the dream waves back in the hole, and visits from the students from the AIM schools where I taught would become more frequent. They would come with drums and singers who would help nurture the spirit of these men who were once again reminded by the pipe and their people that they were indeed men, not "liars and thieves, dopers and dealers." They were men. Whether imprisoned for wrongdoing or political reasons, they had struggled for the right to pray with the pipe, and they had won.

And whether Warden Wills was dealing with a power trip or a bad trip on acid, it's doubtful that he's ever come down. And though he allied himself with "officially recognized and certified Indians," he must have hated those of us that the white man's prison system couldn't totally control. But his attempts at denying people a basic human need no doubt still echo down the prison corridor till this day: "You don't make waves in Stillwater." And though that particular battle is over I can't help but think that the Indian people are like the dolphins I remember seeing on my door that day many years ago: they can die without their freedom. It's something called terminal captivity. They know that in such a place without a connection to that which is the Great Mystery in themselves, the great spirit of a nation dies.

▲▲▲

The laughter of the children down the beach is carried in the chilly wind and lifts my gaze away from the feather. Ihasha and Calusa leap over a dune's crest, hair whipping like wet palm fronds as they run. Carises, in the middle, is pursued with sticks. They descend on me quickly, panting, smiling, and wild with youth.

Calusa pokes her little brother. "You're our prisoner," she
declares.

46

"I made it," Carises growls, shoving the stick away.

I laugh and draw his brown body towards me. "What are
you guys up to?"

"We got fog, Dad," he says, showing me his jar.

Ihasha sits next to me. Calusa notices the feather in my hand,
and draws close.

"Are you okay, Dad?" she asks. She perceives things sometimes in me that I don't even see in myself.

"Yeah. I'm okay, Ca. I was just admiring this crow feather
. . . and I guess I was thinking." Each pair of dark eyes examines the
feather more closely.

Ihasha tells them that he found it. "It's a ghost dance feather,"
he says.

"And I remember a ghost dance song that I heard once," I tell
them as I stand in the heavy mist and stretch, taking deep breaths
of the wet, salty air.

Sensing the excitement about to happen, the children stand
too, taut and still. Their eyes fix on Dad; their energy primed and
prepared for the inevitable race that will follow.

I call to them.

Stand ready,
Stand ready,
So when the crow calls you,
So when the crow calls you,
You will see him,
You will see him!

And the four of us take off running in the mist along the
water towards Simone, while crows caw from the trees.

A SACRED PATH

"UNDER THE ORDERS *of the Catholic friar, Diego de Landa, thousands of Mayan books were brought by the soldiers to the town of Mani.*"

"Mani," I motioned with the book I was reading from, "is just across the water." The children peered out into the Gulf at the setting summer sun. "Over there is the Yucatan."

Their eyes followed a gold, shimmering trail of sunlight. It reached from the shore where they were to as far as they could see. I told them Mrs. Basic used to say that if you traveled on that path, you would come to a beautiful land where great temples and colorful pyramids once decorated the earth and celebrated the creation.

A dolphin surfaced and blew as he crossed the trail of light. Another one. And another. There were three. Four. Five. "That's as many people as we got in our family," said Calusa.

We watched the family of dolphins arc across the sun trail, heading south that late summer afternoon. We watched until they became tiny specks and disappeared.

I rested the book on my knee and wondered what the kids were thinking, what they were feeling. The doubts and challenges

48

of fatherhood tumbled in my mind: What would they think when I finished reading this story? Should children know such things? Would it be too upsetting for them to learn about the books and what the Spaniards did? Maybe there were better ways to help get them to appreciate books. Certainly there were. There wasn't a night that Simone didn't read to them. They knew their father was a teacher, and that I used books. They knew I wrote books. But maybe there were safer stories. . . .

Safer stories? I amused myself. Is there really such a thing as a safe story? I'd heard my own kids talk about dolphins in ways even adults couldn't handle. Carises could tell you how the Japanese fishermen shot and beat the dolphins to death with guns and clubs, how their nets stretched out for miles in the Pacific, and how scores of dolphins and whales and turtles and countless other forms of sea life were killed to catch tuna. Carises said that the same thing was done by other countries in the Sea of Cortés in order to catch shrimp.

Calusa informed us that to eat a can of tuna that wasn't labeled "dolphin safe" was supporting the killing of dolphins. Sometimes they would dramatize the point, the two youngest leaping and swimming in the water playing dolphins while Ihasha pursued on his raft. He was the tuna boat. They were convincing. They knew the names of every type of dolphin, and they could also tell you about the many who died for the one captured and placed in a tank for experimentation or trained in an aquarium for people's amusement. I understood what it was like to be torn from the Wheel as dolphins and whales are, and separated from those I loved, to be re-educated, or trained.

I used the moment to remind the children that a good deal of their information about dolphins came from books, just like the one I held. As I began to read from it again, Calusa gazed down at the sand. "Is that why you write books, Dad?" Her eyes never left the bird she was sketching with her finger.

"Sure," I said. "I want people to know the truth too. Besides, writing books goes along with my vision."

Carises started sculpting a dolphin in the sand; Ihasha worked on a pyramid.

And they listened as I continued to read. . . .

"*The Mayan books were brought into Mani and built into a great pyre.*" I explained that a pyre was a big heap of things that burned. In this case, the heap was made of Indian books. "They torched it," I explained, holding up the book I was reading from as an example. "You see, kids, friar de Landa felt that the Mayan writings were of the devil.

"*He also ordered the soldiers to hang many Indians by their feet and some by their arms. While being whipped by the friars, the Indians were forced to watch the destruction of their cherished books.*"

I turned the page. There was a picture on that page of the atrocity that had been sketched by a Spaniard back in 1562. I showed it to the kids. They glanced at it; then they studied it. They would never forget it.

I resumed reading.

"*We can't begin to realize what was lost in those fires. Much of the native knowledge of medicine and astronomy is gone; their poetry is gone.*

"*'Our priests wept,' the people said, their faces wearing masks of pain. 'How do we mourn for such a loss? Nothing could have been as cruel as the burning of our books . . . except the enslavement of our children. And the children, we would hide them or carry them into the forest.' Mothers who couldn't escape would choose to smother or poison their infants rather than have them stolen for slavery.*

"*'But the books! We could not stop the fires. We could only cling desperately to our memories and weep. They took generations of our hearts and minds, the books, and they threw them into the fires. And we could not stop them.'*

"*. . . And so it was. The wisdom of the ages disappeared in the black smoke of burning books.*"

50   The children and I sat still and quiet. The setting sun was
turning red. For a moment it was as if there were no sounds, no
movement. It was as if our world had paused to hear and to remember and to mourn.

Then, like a loon's call across a wind-swept lake, I heard my
name. Simone was coming from the house and heading toward the
beach. She emerged from the path that wound over the dunes, and
stood searching among sea oats that stood taller than she. "The
news is coming on. . . . You asked me to get you. . . . Dinner's
almost ready," she said.

I waved acknowledgment, and she turned and headed back
to the house.

"Dad?" Calusa asked, erasing her bird.

I placed the book at my side. "Yeah, Ca?"

"Can we go for a swim before dinner?"

I knew why they needed to swim. They not only needed to
renew themselves in the water, they needed to experience the path
of light that leads to the land of huge temples, pyramids, and
libraries once filled with colorful books, the sacred path you can follow to a land whose people loved their books. "A golden path of
light that leads to such a place," I tell the children, "is a sacred connection to our past." And as I watched them heading toward the
shore, I couldn't help but remember when I was a boy and liked to
swim in the sun trail. Anyone who's ever swam in one knows or
feels its magical connection to time and the Mystery. The dolphins
must know.

I nodded and smiled. "But come in pretty soon and help
Mom out, okay?"

I stood and stretched and took a deep breath, then headed back
to the house. Behind me, the children dove into the path of sunlight
on the water where the dolphins had just crossed, the path that leads
to the Yucatan. Behind them in the sand the book I had been reading from remained, the pages flipping in the early evening wind.

When the kids returned to the house, Simone got them busy.
There was much to do, she told them. There were dishes that needed   51
washing, corn that needed shucking, trash that needed to go out. . . .

Carises grabbed the trash.

Ihasha leaned on the kitchen sink and placed his hands in the
warm dishwater. "Mom, did Indians really have books?"

She stood at the stove, dropping fresh corn into a pot of boil-
ing water. "The Mayans and Aztecs did," she said; then she paused
and considered the question some more. "But they weren't books
like ours. Their books opened the way an accordion does. Like
when you opened one, it was the unfolding of a story. But they
were books. And they had very colorful pictures and symbols in
them called glyphs. A book like that is called a codex. We know
from those few that survived the burnings that they were very
beautiful."

"Then it's true that the Spaniards burned them," Calusa said,
stripping the husk from the last ear to be placed in the pot.

"Yes. It's very true."

Ihasha smirked, "I wish somebody would burn some of the
books they give kids at school."

"Remember what your Uncle Nip told you, Ihasha . . . you
too, Calusa . . . that you can find some value in any book."

Carises, who had been quietly listening, lifted the trash bag
and headed out. Before he came into the living room, he stopped at
the back door and picked up the book he'd left there when he came
in from the beach.

Like Carises, I too had been quietly listening to the conversation in the kitchen; and, even though my eyes remained fixed, more
or less, on the TV, I could also see what was going on in the other
room.

"Watchin' the news, Dad?" Carises asked, holding the Hefty
trash bag with one hand over his shoulder, while handing me the
book with the other.

"Yeah, Carises. I'm watchin' the news." I glanced at the book.

"Oh," I said, acting surprised. "Did I leave this on the beach?" Carises nodded, and I thanked him in Ojibway, the language of his mother. "Me-gwich, then." I kissed his soft brown cheeks, then looked at the book again. "Sure glad nothing happened to it and that you thought enough of books to take care of this one."

His little pearl teeth gleamed behind the smile on his lips, and slowly he started on his way out with the trash. Then he paused.

"Dad, did they really have colored pictures in their books?"

"Oh my, son, they sure did. Beautiful ones. Bright colors too. All kinds of colors. They probably had a color for every flower there was in their world."

His moist black eyes glistened like quiet pools. He stood staring at the floor as if momentarily he was staring at something in his memory. The trash sank to his feet and rested there. His gaze lifted slowly then, almost reluctantly, to the television news, and we watched men dressed as conquistadors and black-robed friars march up the beach and through the horde who lined the shore for the annual celebration of the landing of De Soto and the Spaniards.

A SENSE OF HISTORY

T HE PARK SIGN entering Dade City, Florida, reads "Sight of the Dade Massacre." Many tourists and their kids stop here. They say it gives them a sense of history. I say nonsense. I say it serves to reinforce their myths and stereotypes. The fact is, it's called a massacre because the natives won. Indian warriors, American soldiers. Both with weapons. Major Dade and his invading American army was annihilated in the palmetto-laden forest.

"A matter of semantics." That's the standard response from those who defend and perpetuate the myths of history: "It's a matter of semantics."

History is not a matter of semantics. It's a matter of acquiring wisdom; that comes from learning from the past.

Yet United States history is based upon word-play. This is how the history writers become the bastion of Western propaganda. They disguise truth through ambiguity and semantics. Major Dade and his troops weren't massacred like the park sign advertises, for no dictionary defines a massacre as "an armed conflict between hostile armies." That's a battle! And that's how Dade died — in a battle.

54   And when they are challenged about such things, these schol-
arly men and women of the past usually resort to a few standard
arguments. The response is quite typical. They accuse the chal-
lenger of being "mad" because the Indians lost the war. But if this
was true, how can a surrendering nation that has lost a war negotiate a treaty? What World War II negotiations did Japan take part in
after two atomic bombs were dropped on that country? Their surrender in the Pacific was unconditional. Even their national religion,
Shintoism, was banned by the United States. The fact remains that
in order to sign a treaty, which is a negotiated settlement, a compromise must be made and agreed upon by one nation to another, both
of equal stature, and not just for one generation either, but to be honored by future generations as well. This often evokes a standard
response from U.S. history scholars: They claim that they shouldn't
be obligated to those treaties because they were agreed upon and
signed long ago. "We must go forward," they admonish.

I say we can't go forward until we know where we've been.
Unless we know the past, how can we have a future?

This idea, "to know the past," threatens to rock the founda-
tions upon which U.S. history is based. So the past is not known.
"It's the only possible history," says Earl Shorris in his book, *Death
of the Great Spirit*, ". . . for [Indian] history lies so close to the foundation of the state that it could endanger the entire structure. So the
history of the Indian is not (necessarily) suppressed, but it is not
known. The Indian is of little use to the nation. . . . Tyrants may be
evil, but if a democracy practices genocide, who will be called the
villain? If there can be no history of goodness, there must be no history, for ignorance is better than a history of evil."

And you know what D.H. Lawrence said is true: "The
American landscape has never been at one with the white man.
Never. And the white men have probably never felt so bitter anywhere, as here in America, where the very landscape in its very
beauty seems a bit devilish and grinning, opposed to us.

"The desire to extirpate the Indian, and the contradictory desire to glorify him, both are rampant still, today. . . .

"But you have there the myth of the essential white America. All the other stuff, the love, the democracy . . . is a sort of by-play. The essential American soul is hard, isolated, stoic, and a killer. It has never melted."

And so it goes.

History as we've been taught in school is more propaganda than knowledge of past events, but many buy into it. For them, it's the only way to buy into the system and have the chance to chase that illusive "American dream." The cost is their identity. A Mexican of Nahuatl ancestry will claim that Spanish is his native language. A Mayan woman will say that she is half white. Uncle Nip explained how to regard this racial degradation once. He said, "Indians do not come in parts. You either are an Indian or you're not. You couldn't be half this, half that. You are all Indian or not Indian at all. Blood runs the heart."

One time he explained this concept of racial identity to a college student who asked him if he was a full blood. It seemed the student insisted that Uncle Nip couldn't possibly be full Indian, since he was so fairly complected and even had blue eyes! Uncle Nip told this person that he [Uncle Nip] couldn't help it if he'd been bastardized by an inferior race, but that he was Cherokee. And he wasn't part Cherokee either. He said one drop of Indian blood could overpower anything that Europe ever produced! Then he turned to me and said that a person who was insensitive enough to say such a thing to him deserved such an answer.

What's the use? I bet that's what Red Jacket must have thought when he was chosen by his people to respond to the Reverend Cram two hundred years ago, when the first missionaries came among the Iroquois. I'm sure Red Jacket must have figured that anybody who could actually come among a people other than his own and tell them what to believe was, perhaps, a bit beyond reproach.

56

The whole idea of proselytizing is a little bizarre; people who are comfortable in what they believe don't have the need to impose themselves on others. Nevertheless, Red Jacket's response kept the missionary at bay, at least intellectually speaking. "Brother," Red Jacket said, "we understand that your religion is written in a book. . . . You say there is but one way to worship and serve the Great Spirit; if there is but one religion, why do you white people differ so much about it? Why do not all agree, as you can all read the book?"

A matter of semantics?

We've been trying to teach our children both sides of history. Not that I don't mind slanting things a little for the Native Americans, but I think we do a pretty good job. It's not all that hard, you know. All we do is try to be honest about history and tell them that what they read in books or magazines or see on TV or in the movies is true or not as best we can know it. And this we try always to support with the literature and documentation that's available. And whenever I'm thinking that maybe our children get too much truth, Simone straightens me right out. "When are they too young to know the truth?" she asks.

So, with the help of Simone and a man named Ray Fadden, I feel at peace in seeing history and the world from an Indian perspective. And I'm certain that I'm not alone.

Simone, the kids, and I had been riding home from our first and final visit to the Major Dade "massacre" sight when I first told the kids about Ray Fadden. They were little then. I think Ihasha may have been six or seven, Carises three or four, Calusa somewhere in the middle. It was getting dark, and it had been a long ride back home. The children were drowsy and looking forward to a good night's sleep in their own beds. . . .

"I was about twenty-one, maybe twenty-two," I began, "when I went to visit Ray Fadden up in the mountains of New

York. He was one of the last of his kind. He lived in a cabin in the
mountains with his wife. The two of them sort of took care of the
mountains. They loved animals, and Ray was a fierce protector of
their right to live. But he also was a teacher and a history keeper. So,
next to the cabin that he lived in, he built another one, only this one
was shaped like a long house. He made it into a museum.

"On the trail toward the museum you went past these little
areas that exhibited Indian contributions to the world. He had one
exhibit, though, that I'll never forget. It was about the size of a large
room and was encompassed by a barbed-wire fence. It was a horrible lookin' thing. Inside the fence were oil cans, refrigerators, TV
sets, old tires, air conditioners, lots of junk from the civilized world.
Outside the area was a plaque that read:

"CONTRIBUTIONS OF THE WHITE MAN SINCE HIS ARRIVAL
IN THE WESTERN HEMISPHERE 500 YEARS AGO"

As Simone, the kids, and I cruised along to the hum of the
engine into the Florida night, I recalled more of my visit with Ray
Fadden. "One day he sat me down on a wooden bench in the long
house and read to me from wampum belts about the origin of the
People. He read the belts like he was reading from a book. He helped
me understand things about myself and my feelings. He made history come alive because you felt like you were a part of it, not something removed from it. Sitting on that bench while Ray Fadden read
to me was one of the greatest influences of my life.

"That's why," I'd tell my kids, "you're so lucky being Indians. Anyway, Ray Fadden also told me something about American history and the way it's told in the white man's books. He said
that an American history text was nothin' but a book of lies written
by a thief."

I guess I put the notion of history into the kids that night on
our drive home from the battle scene where Dade and his American

58

troops were killed. Carises said he wanted to play history in bed with his "men" when he got home, which he was hoping was soon. I imagined that Ihasha fell asleep thinking about Ray Fadden. Calusa just gazed out the window at the blackness of the Florida forests and was probably thinking about the safety of all the animals she loved.

Another Mohawk man who challenges these thieves who write history is David Goyette. David just returned from a protest at the Museum of Science and Industry in Tampa. The museum featured the controversial exhibit, "First Encounters," a state and federally funded project commemorating, in 1992, the landing of Columbus 500 years ago. The exhibit cost $600,000. One curator for the state museum in Tallahassee called it a "gloss-over of history." A St. Petersburg, Florida, archaeologist referred to it as a "shameful omission." A specialist for the Florida parks, who knows Florida history as well as any living person, also commented on the exhibit. He said that the exhibition was a "blown opportunity to truly educate people."

Others proclaimed their displeasure over the exhibit's Indian protesters. One woman was seen on TV saying that the demonstrators were spoiling the children's enjoyment.

Goyette explained to the media that far more statistical and historical information was given to scenes of the Jewish holocaust at the hands of the Moors in 1492 than to any torment and genocide that Native Americans suffered upon the arrival of Columbus and the Spanish conquistadors who quickly followed.

The parallel with the Jewish holocaust scenes may have even been acceptable to Goyette if the exhibitors had made the obvious connection. No way. There was virtually no mention of the 1700 Native American nations and tribes that have been wiped off the face of the earth since Columbus landed. There was little or no reference to the agony inflicted upon these people by Columbus and his Spanish followers. "Accidental" and "unfortunate" were the words used to describe the European diseases that killed our Native people by the millions. How's that for semantics? There's no implication that these diseases were regarded by the white man as acts of "Divine Providence," or that they were intentionally distributed among the People in order to kill them.

What about the choice of conversion or the sword? What about the scene that de las Casas describes in his journal, where the Spaniards waged bets to see if they could split Indian people in half with one swipe of their swords? What about how this future Catholic priest also described Indian infants, still nursing, being wrenched from their grasping desperate mothers and flung to the Spanish dogs for food? What about their overpowering guns? Even Indian slavery was "glossed over." When Goyette asked why the curator in archaeology at the Florida Museum of Natural History in Gainesville, who was mainly responsible for the exhibit, described Indian slaves in one scene as "laborers," the curator responded by saying it was a matter of "semantics."

When a friend and editor at *The Tampa Tribune* phoned and asked me why the exhibit was offensive, I told him: "Because the white man spent $600,000 on an exhibit that romanticizes genocide."

"But how could Goyette say that Columbus was a lot like Hitler?"

"Because, my friend, each regarded his own kind as superior, and the exhibit, by not pointing this out, perpetuates that mentality of superiority, not only over other humans, but over the entire earth. Maybe he should have said that the Spaniards were more like Nazis to make his point clearer to you. But the message is the same. History that is not 'glossed over' has proven this mentality to be very dangerous. It has wrought incredible hardship on indigenous peoples all over the world. It has exterminated nations of people, plants, birds, and animals, and it has devastated the environment of the entire world."

60

"But Columbus was an explorer," the editor argued. "Hitler was a dictator." There was an extended pause when I chose not to respond. "I guess," he continued, "there should have been more of the exhibit dedicated to the Native American perspective."

"There was little or no mention of the great civilizations and societies that were native to this hemisphere and flourishing when Columbus landed."

I suggested that it was not mere coincidence the United States is naming its new space probes after early "New World" explorations and explorers. "In all these years," I said, "what have we learned? Don't you think one of those ancient philosophers was onto something when he said that a People who do not learn their history are forever doomed to repeat it?

"We can't change the past, but we've a moral responsibility and obligation to learn from that past. How else do we dare venture off into the future, perhaps into other new worlds? And what if, like Chief Seattle said, our destinies are intertwined, and you're going to experience the decay of everything you hold sacred some day too? Maybe it is the order of nature, like wave follows wave and season follows season. Or maybe, the way I see it, we are, indeed, all part of the great Circle of Life and that the circle cannot exist as we know it if any one part is gone. And the Native American, the Indian, call us what you will, is that part which may be disappearing."

I don't know what else could have been gained by this dialogue with my editor friend, except that we are still friends and that he still asks me to review books for his paper because he respects that native perspective. But I also wonder about what he must feel as a father, knowing that he must look at the world differently than most white people. I wonder where, or even if, he draws the line between the truth and what he believes his own kids should know.

Indians have the same choice as the editor from *The Tampa Tribune* does, at least as far as assuming responsibility for what sense

of history our kids have. And we see it everywhere. It doesn't have
to be pointed out to us. Along with the distortion of history, there's
the giant hypocrisy. They hear that minority people deserve to have
rights. They learn that in this country "minority" usually means
black, or now even Asian, hispanic, and gay. Jesse Jackson talked
about positive self-image, racism, and brotherhood while running
for president back in the Eighties. He even formed the Rainbow
Coalition — rainbow, that's what the Ojibway call "the return of
the blessing." And there he was, a black man, speaking about racial
dignity during a rally in Cleveland, home of the big-nosed, bucktoothed mascot of the Cleveland Indians baseball team, "Chief
Wahoo." I wrote him about it, twice. In my letters I implored him
to help eliminate such racism and degradation in professional sports.
He wouldn't touch "Chief Wahoo" with a twenty-foot political
pole. Blacks in baseball was his pitch. "Minority managers." What
if the image of a thick-lipped, wide-nosed stereotype of a negro
called "Willie Watusi" had greeted him in Cleveland?

As Earl Shorris said, Indians don't exist, except in those places
where they are useful to the state. And Jesse Jackson was of the state,
and his Rainbow Coalition was no "return of the blessing."

Perhaps the closest any transplant Americans have ever come
to understanding the Native American situation in this country
were the Transcendentalists of the mid-nineteenth century. They
included Emily Dickinson, Thoreau, and Ralph Waldo Emerson, to
name a few of the most prominent. Like the Indian, their religion
was simply the oneness of things. They were students of nature.
They were obstacles to the white man's progress. They were
observers of hypocrisy. Dissenters.

Emerson once wrote in his essay on non-conformity, "Thy
love afar, is spite at home."

Indeed! How many times have Native Americans read and
heard how wonderful that the President of South Africa has freed

Nelson Mandela! Yet I could hardly find a person in this country who's known about Leonard Peltier in the sixteen plus years he's been in prison. In Russia, they know about Leonard Peltier. In Jamaica, they know about Leonard Peltier. But not in the United States. "Thy love afar, is spite at home." It's not hard to imagine what inspired those words by Emerson over a hundred years ago, or what caused him to make such an observation. In those days, he was referring to American condemnation of slavery, not in the United States, but in Barbados.

For many Native Americans, Peltier was one of the true leaders of AIM, the American Indian Movement. In many ways, he was a chief in the old tradition. He led by example. Peltier is a man of heart. The deaths of two F.B.I. agents in a shoot-out during the Pine Ridge invasion in the Seventies took place at a time of war. Though Peltier's trial for their alleged "murders" was a fiasco of justice, he still languishes as a Native American political prisoner of the United States. Good for Nelson Mandela! But what about Leonard Peltier?

Leavenworth Penitentiary, where Peltier is expected to die, is not far from Kansas City, home of the N.F.L. team, the Kansas City Chiefs. Their novelty is having an Indian on a horse gallop along the sidelines wearing a headdress and waving a lance to celebrate a touchdown.

Several years ago, back in '74 or '75, while I was briefly employed with the Indian education office in Minneapolis, I took to the road. One day I was asked to go out to a suburb called Burns-ville, and speak about Indians at one of the elementary schools. I'd been doing this type of lecturing and interacting with audiences for years, even while in college. I held little back when speaking to university students or adults. No doubt, I may have at times sounded like an angry militant who was ready to take the country back by force, if necessary. Of course, the reality of that happening was not likely, although I'm sure there were some listeners who truly wondered. But this was the early to mid-Seventies, and Native Americans were, literally, fighting for the survival of their identity. I tried to educate whites to this fact as well. Sometimes my presentations brought home that message.

When it came to kids, however, that was a different story. Kids hadn't really hurt anyone yet. They were kids. Born into a world they had little or nothing to do with. They were kids. And there is always hope for kids.

We formed a circle there in the Burnsville elementary school and began discussing the philosophy of the traditional Indian. I explained how the Indian believed everything was related. That he regarded himself as no better than anything else. That, to him, trees were alive. Animals and plants too. Even rocks were alive. And rivers and streams. I explained how the Indian regarded the Earth as Mother. That to sell her and pollute her body was as unthinkable as selling or giving poison to one's own mother. As the kids scooched closer to me, our circle grew stronger, and I read to them the words of the People themselves, for I always traveled with the books.

This time I read from one of my favorite books, *Lame Deer — Seeker of Visions*, by Richard Erdoes and John Fire:

"You know, it always makes me laugh when I hear young white kids speak of some people as 'squares' or 'straights' — old people, hardened in their ways, in their minds, in their hearts. They don't even have to be old. You can be an 'old square' at eighteen. . . . To our way of thinking the Indians' symbol is the circle, the hoop. Nature wants things to be round. . . ."

Then "the squares" entered the room. Three men. By the way they were dressed, I figured that one or two of them were probably administrators, the other seemed like plainclothes police. They seemed to cast long shadows over the children as the kids turned and gazed up, fearfully. I looked up from the book. "The squares"

64   casting shadows stood with their backs to the door behind them. With arms folded, "the squares" and their shadows stood over us and stared at me.

Despite the interruption, I continued reading. *"Is not the moon round? And the sun? And the Earth? Are not the planets and stars round? Do not the planets move in circles around the sun? Do not the stars move in circles in a galaxy that's round? Even the trunks of trees are round and the antlers of a deer. The horizon. The rainbow. That's why the circle is a fitting symbol for the Indian. His lodge was circular, or he sat in circles in his longhouse. His village was a circle within the tribe which was a circle within the nation which was a circle. Circles within circles. With no beginning and no end. This was a beautiful and fitting symbol!"*

I glanced at the wide-eyed children as I spoke. "In a circle, we are all equal. There is no part more important than another. In a circle we see each other's faces, not the backs of each other's heads. In a circle, there is a sense of unity. Of oneness."

The three "squares" began closing in. I resumed reading from Lame Deer. *"Square is the white man's symbol. Square is the dollar bill, the jail. Square are the white man's gadgets — boxes, boxes, boxes and more boxes — TV sets, radios, computers, washing machines, cars. These all have corners and sharp edges, points in time. White man's time. With appointments, time clocks and rush hours. . . .*

"Square are the white man's houses, his offices, his factories. His schools. You become a prisoner inside all these boxes."

They forced the children aside with their big legs and shoes and stepped over those kids who didn't quite move out of the way enough. They did this until they stood right before me, like shadows over me. One of them said that I would have to leave. The eyes of the children studied the eyes of the squares, and then they studied mine. There was no light emanating from the faces of the children as there once had been. They seemed sullen and disturbed, but I could sense they were beginning to understand. No lesson I could have taught them, no text I could have read would have better depicted how a sense of history is better not experienced in this country.

"No," cried one of the children. "Why?" asked another. The men in suits and ties did not reply. They took my books and escorted me out of the building, and it was at this point that something truly unusual happened to me.

One of the kids, about a fifth or sixth grader with shoulder-cropped blond hair, ran up to me as I approached my old Mustang in the school parking lot. "Please," he called. "Please, wait!"

"You could get in a lot of trouble leaving school and talking to me like this," I said, shielding him from the building. His breath was short and quick.

"Please, listen," he pleaded.

I squatted before him. "Sure," I said, "what is it?"

"Well, you know how some people tell you one of their relatives was an Indian?"

"Yeah."

"Well, you know how proud they are of that?"

"Yeah."

"Well, my great, great uncle was no Indian. He hated Indians. My great, great uncle was George Armstrong Custer! And I'm ashamed. I'm really ashamed!"

I was struck dumb. I looked into the boy's red swollen eyes. He wasn't making this up. "I can prove it," he cried. "We have all the proof at home. My dad showed it all to me. I never hated Indians. . . . I just wanted to say I'm sorry."

I brought him to my chest and hugged him, and I thought how these things can happen living in the Wheel.

"We both feel bad about what Custer did," I said, trying to console my little friend, "but you had nothin' to do with that. You and I are alive now. We can only learn from the past. . . . We can't

change it. You and I . . . we can be friends. . . . We can even be
66   brothers. We'll see."

I felt bad and strange as I drove away, leaving him standing
alone in the school parking lot. But as I headed out of suburbia,
I felt something truly special had happened between us. The boy
got to say he was sorry. By this selfless expression, I hoped he would
be free of this incredible burden — a burden he either chose to carry
or was born with. Saying he was sorry for what his ancestor did
was something he wanted to do, something he needed to do in
order to help set things right again. And I got to be the one he said
it to.

▲ ▲ ▲

One other striking moment that yielded a sense of history
occurred back in 1974, while I was teaching at Heart of the Earth
AIM Survival School in Minneapolis. The scene merits some
description.

The word school usually connotes a building, a hallway that
leads to classrooms, an office, a library of some sort, a gym or recre-
ation area, and heat. In Minnesota winters, you need heat! Heart of
the Earth was not such a school. At that time we were located in
the Little Earth Housing Projects, and our school consisted of a two-
story apartment that included a kitchen that was used for an office,
a living room where we socialized or sang around the drum with
Old Man Bill or Chester, and two bedrooms and a basement that
were used for classrooms. My classroom was the basement.

So, it was there we'd huddle beneath our winter jackets,
Dakota and Lakota teenagers, some Ojibways, a Cree, an Apache,
a Mandan, a Seneca, and me — all together — longhairs in a circle
of straight-back metal chairs, reading and studying the chapter
about Little Crow's War from Dee Brown's book, *Bury My Heart at
Wounded Knee*. What spurred the organization of a caravan to

Mankato was when one of the students, a very bright and hand-some Apache youth named Mark, asked if anyone had seen the historical marker which read: "This is where thirty-eight Sioux Indians were hanged." Most of us, having never been to Mankato, shook our heads that we hadn't.

Mark explained that it used to be there, in Mankato, just as you entered town, but that he didn't see it last time he went through. Since this history was so close and so recent, I thought we should go to Mankato, following the same path of the war, and the same road where Indian men, women, and children were paraded through the streets of the southern Minnesota town in cages while being spat upon, yelled at, mocked, and even stoned.

We first stopped at the marker alongside the road to Mankato where the Indian agent and trader, Mr. A.D. Myrick, was killed and where his body was discovered with grass and dirt stuffed into his mouth. The marker gave no mention of the starving Santee who he told to "eat grass and their own dung" if they were hungry. It gave no mention of how the annuities that were guaranteed the Santee never got to them, but made Myrick and his heroes, Ramsey and Sibley, wealthy. It just told how the Sioux killed him and stuffed grass in his mouth.

By the time our five-car caravan made it to the outskirts of Mankato, we had attracted an impressive following of local police and probably F.B.I. cars. As we snaked through the town searching for the marker and wishing to honor our slain Santee brothers, they followed. The caravan grew and grew until it seemed that there were more cars following us than there were in the origi-nal caravan.

We stopped here and there and everywhere, but we could not find the marker. Finally, we headed for the courthouse where we asked what happened to it. We were told it was something the mayor of the town thought it better not to show. "It wasn't good for the town's image." We asked what happened to the marker. We asked where they put it.

We were given directions how to get to the waterworks department at the edge of town, where the heavy equipment was kept. We were told it was placed there. When we arrived, our caravan had diminished considerably. Though Heart of the Earth had managed to stay together, the cops and feds had lost interest or gotten lost.

The waterworks department was enclosed by a big fence. One of the workers said he believed the marker was buried in the back under a mound of dirt and gravel. Most of the kids climbed the fence and held it up from the other side so the elders and the teachers could slip underneath. Quietly, we headed back behind the main building to the gravel mound.

It stood about twenty feet high. The boys and girls and the drivers of the other cars and I climbed and surrounded it. We started digging through the cold stones, and one of the Ojibway boys soon discovered the plaque of the slain Sioux. It was small and not too deeply buried. We all huddled over it and read the words silently that described what was once billed as "America's greatest mass execution." There was no problem with semantics here:

ON THIS SPOT WERE HANGED
THIRTY-EIGHT SIOUX INDIANS

Tobacco was passed around the quiet gathering; every kid and each adult whispered a private prayer as they placed the tobacco on the marker or somewhere near it. I just turned and faced the fading winter sun, and I don't recall saying anything as I sprinkled the tobacco I had been holding in my hand. I was just feeling bad that these men, who probably had families and others who loved them, had to die that way, and I was also feeling a sense of history, that sense of history that comes from livin' it.

CHAPTER 8

THE NAMES OF CHILDREN AND OTHER ENDANGERED LIFE FORMS

A NARROW LAND BRIDGE at low tide stretches out to an island where the warm waters of Tampa Bay meet the Gulf of Mexico. It was probably designed and created long ago by the Calusa people who used to live here. Over time, the bridge was worn by tides and storms, and now it only appears at low tide. It is more than a bridge connecting the ever-encroaching civilized world with a quietly defiant and primal land, it is a bridge linking past and present. It connects what was with what is. . . .

The island itself basks in the water that is always. It is one of our favorite spots. The children and Simone named it Joey-Gah. It was a name they learned reading Seneca tales together for a week of winter nights before going to bed. Joey-Gah means raccoon, and there are quite a few raccoons who live here.

We left the Mustang far back near the entrance to the county park. I once learned the hard way how fast the tide comes in here. Once I stranded the car on the island when the water rose to the bottom of the doors and appeared that it might go even higher. Fortunately, it was the time of the new moon and the tide receded a bit sooner than it would have had the moon been

waxing full. Now, we don't drive across the bridge; we walk the distance between the park entrance and Joey-Gah. The sky is grey and
low clouds move swiftly over us. I pause and tell the children to look
at the sky, to observe the movement of the clouds. I ask them to try
and feel the wind as it moves. Even though it sometimes whips in
gusts, the movement, the blowing, is constant.

"See how the lower clouds move more circular than in
straight lines from east to west or north to south, like when a storm
sweeps in off the bay or from the Gulf. It moves like a wave. You
can see the line of clouds drawing near."

Everyone looks up and watches. "That's when we start singing, huh, Dad."

"That's right," I said, smiling. I felt good when Carises made
that connection, like it was a kind of affirmation that children really
can carry on the beliefs we teach them. "Because the land needs the
rain. But these clouds are different. They're the bands of a great
storm that wants to be born . . . that's trying to draw the energy
towards its center so it may have life.

"Notice the clouds, kids, because you live here and because
you may not have the TV weatherman to count on all the time.
Besides, even with all the technology they have today, they still
can't predict where a hurricane will decide to hit until the first bands
are nearly there, and even then a hurricane can change and turn and
head in another direction, all the while gathering energy, gathering power."

"This land we live on . . . all of southern Florida," adds
Simone as we head up to the narrow land bridge that will take us
to Joey-Gah, "used to be called by the Indians who once lived here,
'The Land Where The Wind Is Born.'"

The wind blows steadily. It causes the fronds of the island's
sabals to whip about as the children walk barefoot ahead of us
toward the bridge. And the green leaves of the wild oaks twirl and
glisten like jewels above them.

Though the sky remains grey and wet clouds swirl above, there is no rain. There is no thunder or lightning. I explained to the kids that these are signs that a great storm is trying to be born. "The energy is heading towards the center," I tell them, "always towards the center."

And though the wind remains constant, it doesn't grow stronger, and Simone and I finally cross the bridge behind the children and land on Joey-Gah. The first sights are the sea gulls and crows, blue jays and mockers, darting down to the tide pools and rain pools for tadpoles, stranded minnows, or just a drink of water.

Life intertwines here on Joey-Gah. Life is real here. A pair of great horned owls will swoop down at dusk from a wild oak. Snowy egrets wade the island's white sandy beaches, and a rare Florida crane will sometimes reveal its red-crowned head from behind a dune. Blue crabs skitter in the water among the sea grasses, and brown pelicans drop from the sky like feathered spears into the green sea that surrounds this island gem.

And the island is the home of some of the most ancient species of plants found in the world. They grow from the sandy earth as their ancestors did when dinosaurs foraged. Their vitality for life is the sun; their sustenance is the rain. In these ways they are much like the Indians who once lived here and who walk upon the land now.

Cedars, centuries old, live here. Red-tail hawks perch in the cedars, and two or three raccoon families scurry through scattered palmettos below them. It's not unusual to glimpse a king snake winding through the mulching fronds and cool shade of clustered sabals. Even Grandfather Diamond-Back suns himself here in the hot sand among the tall sea oats. On one side of the island are red and black mangroves. Those that appear like "walking sticks" are the red ones. Those that have roots sticking out of the sand like fingers are the black mangroves. Their purpose is to trap sea-stuff like seaweed and leaf litter to form new land. Water moccasins protect the mangroves.

72   In the summer, giant cumulus clouds expand and contract and rise up like white mountains. We call these clouds the Thunderbeings.

Out in the clear waters, dolphins leap, and the children watch and listen, like other native children once had before De Soto and the Spaniards came. As they race down a shady, shell-white trail that snakes through the trees and palmettos, their natural senses are keened. On the back of an earth serpent trail, they race through what was, what is now, and what may soon cease to be. Somewhere in their minds, at whatever level they can understand, through whatever gene it is that allows them racial memory, they know that the shadows of the conquistadors have returned; only now they are known as real estate brokers, bankers, developers, and oil tycoons; now they're disguised as contractors, laborers, and politicians. Together, they will pave over old trails, level burial mounds, make new roads and parking lots of asphalt, and they will smother the land. They will build condominiums the colors of Easter eggs and stab the flesh with towers of concrete and steel. They will bring their human waste. The new conquistadors fill the ranks of their armies no longer with Spanish soldiers. They have changed too. Now they invade this fragile land as fishermen and shrimpers, spongers and boaters. They come as tourists. They come with the same old-world mentality; they come to get away from what they've created somewhere else. They come always to take more than they need.

"I hope they can remember all this," I say to Simone while we walk and watch the children ahead on the trail.

She squeezes my hand. "They will," she says. "And they'll thank you for giving it to them, just like I do."

They will know that more than the memories of extinct tribes live on in their names. If they can remember moments like these in places like this, they can tell about it at some future time: How beautiful the world used to be! It will be for the children like a vision that can never be taken away.

And that's why Simone and I named our children for tribes and nations no longer living. We hoped that the names of extinct 73 people would influence their abilities to protect what they can and to remember what they cannot protect. The awesome idea of extinction vibrates in the sound of the names of the children. The Ihasha, the Calusa, and the Carises are of the Mystery now. They are some of the oldest words, yet they sound new among the newest. They are names that are evocations of sound that, perhaps, in the great expanse of infinite chance, can help set the balance in this land right again.

The children race down the island trail to the shore. Their brown skin blends with the colors of the trees, their hair the shade of wild, twisting branches, waving like the windblown fronds. They race ahead and down the trail of time. Then, like ghosts, they fade and disappear.

It is like a dream I am living. How much longer do we have, I wonder, before we Indians disappear and become ghosts like our ancestors on the trail of time?

"Dolphins!" Carises cries, standing knee-deep in the water, pointing to the center of the channel where the bay meets the Gulf. "Dolphins!"

Ihasha and Calusa stand on the shore behind him and watch too.

Simone and I also pause and stand watching the children watching the dolphins.

"He calls them, doesn't he?" she says.

I know that this is not a question. It is an observation. "It seems that he does, Simone. It seems that he does."

"And they come. They really come. Look. . . ."

The children strain to hear and see the wonderful creatures as they leap and blow and play near the shore, the children's imaginations stretching, their hearts pounding.

At first, they didn't notice the two white men who waded nearby. They wore T-shirts and black rubber boots that reached to their hips and hung from their shoulders by thick suspenders. Calusa, with her fawn nature, spotted them first. She nudged Ihasha. Old instincts made Carises turn abruptly away from the dolphins towards his brother and sister, who were staring at the two men.

Each wader carried a net filled with blue crabs — so many blue crabs the children were appalled. One of the men paused. He said something to the other man. He picked up a crab. It dangled by its claws. The children identified it by size and claws to be a female. The other man, not holding the crab, pointed at it and laughed. They both laughed. Then, in one swift and violent motion, the helpless crab was yanked apart, her body splashing below, the man still holding her claws. The children were statues, frozen by the single act of horror. The man holding the claws by his fingers threw them away like garbage, and the two continued wading through the water, reaching down into the sea grass and tossing more crabs into the nets as they passed. It was low tide; the crabs were nesting. Easy prey this time of year, this time of day.

When the nets were filled, they were emptied into coolers left on the beach. Inside the coolers, the crabs struggled for life, buried beneath each other and the darkness of the heavy air.

This is not The Way.

"Take only what you need, kids," Uncle Nip would tell them. "The animals are your older brothers and sisters. And only take life when you have to, when you must. It's The Way of the People. When you do, don't take the biggest. Use discretion. Leave the females, of course, because without them there can be no more."

Cortés, De Soto, Columbus, and even George Armstrong Custer understood The Way. In their strange, vile, and twisted minds they must have understood. Their old-world mentality certainly knew about genocide. They just figured that they, through their birthright, were somehow exempt from The Way. That men made in the image and likeness of a God who created everything have the right to do anything. It's okay for them to kill the birds: Cortés and his Spanish soldiers burned the aviaries that were kept by the People of the Sun. In this single act of utter violence the old-world mentality exploded in an incinerator of flames and thousands of beautiful and once-cherished birds burned alive. To this day stories are told about how their screams and cries echo still through the concrete canyons of a civilized Mexico City in the quiet hours before dawn.

De Soto was a Spaniard in the old tradition too. How often does one hear about the savage brutality he inflicted upon the natives of Florida, how he had them torn apart by dogs, severed their arms if they didn't find him gold, cut off their noses for amusement. And the one who lead the way, Columbus, made Indian girls sexual slaves, and killed men who opposed him. The old-world mentality lived in them all, but it found new life in men like Custer, who killed women and babies, and who ordered the shooting of a hundred ponies, their life breath mingling with the mist that hovers over the South Dakota snow.

Genocide is real to me. Extinction is real. My children bear the names of it. To see these crabs treated as Cortés had treated the birds, like they were lifeless unfeeling things, evoked in each of us a strong sense of bitterness. Then we got angry, and we decided to help set things right again, to help bring the balance back.

We quickly located the men's jeep. It wasn't hard. Bright red and shiny new, it appeared as out of place as the men who drove it in. We approached it carefully and quietly. Ihasha noted the chrome letters on the side: CHEROKEE CHIEF.

I told him that it was a good lesson in irony.

At the rear of the vehicle, Calusa stood biting her lower lip, contemplating the license plate. She was stringing together other times, other places. "New Jersey," she muttered.

A large cooler rested on the back of the jeep's hatch. Carises climbed up and lifted the lid. "They're in here!" he cried. "Lots of them."

76

When are the events or actions the all? Like everything, they too are only an aspect of the whole. Ideas, ideals, and intentions, they are the master facts. They transform the event, transcend the act. Yet the act must be set in motion.

Ihasha and I lifted the heavy cooler. Carises, Calusa, and Simone kept their eyes fixed on the beach. It was time to liberate the crabs.

"Let's go," I said.

Through the trees and palmettos, we moved like the joey-gahs. The power of the place and us being so much a part of it made it almost impossible for anyone to see us. As we headed toward the beach, we felt the allegiance of everything around us. This is what it's like to have that feeling that this is your land, that you are a part of the land, and it is a part of you. I wondered if only Indians could feel this way.

We approached the shore cautiously. Men who torture and are cruel to animals are no doubt that way to people; at least, that's what went through each of our minds as we made it to the water.

Then, like intruders that they were, there they stood, the two white men, holding yet another cooler filled with crabs. Not a stone's throw away from Carises, they dropped the cooler and headed back in the direction they had just come, and away from Simone and the children and me. I wondered how the men could not have seen us.

"Carises was standing right out there," I said to Simone. "Why didn't they see him. . . . I mean how could they have missed any of us?"

She shrugged, relieved that they hadn't. "I don't know," she said. "I could've sworn one of 'em looked right at me."

"Maybe we're really ghosts, Simone. I mean maybe, in some strange way, we are the ghosts. . . ."

"Can we let the crabs go now, Dad?" Ihasha asked, interrupting the eerie feeling that had encompassed both Simone and me.

I nodded. "Let 'em go, Ihasha. Give 'em back their lives!"

One by one the crabs hit the sandy bottom and scurried away. One by one, each of the coolers left on the beach was emptied, and the crabs inside were freed. All the while, the excitement and energy of the crabs and the people fed the constant wind and nourished the storm trying to be born.

As we raced back across the narrow bridge connecting past and present, I wondered some more about what had happened back on Joey-Gah. I wondered if we had truly traveled on the trail of time, and that somehow, maybe, we were the future ghosts that day. In my mind I could hear the voice of Uncle Nip: "Ghosts are of the land they love, kid." Ghosts are of the land they love.

When we reached the mainland where our car was, we took refuge from the sudden downpour under a dilapidated pavilion. There we watched the interloping white men make their way off Joey-Gah. Their new jeep slipped and skidded along the disappearing bridge, tossing and slinging wet sand and salty water all over itself. And I thought about the connection of all things, including time. We watched together as the mechanical CHEROKEE CHIEF headed slowly down the shell-paved road into a wall of water that fell from the sky. I held Simone in my arms, and as she cuddled in, I kissed her silky black hair. The children spoke excitedly, recounting deeds of bravery. They stood and shook their small fists into the air and driving rain, and called out a familiar warning to those men who cast their shadows like Spaniards over this land, who came to take more than what they needed from the land.

"Never come back again!"

THERE IS ALWAYS
A BALANCE

T HE GREAT STORM that gathered energy passing Joey-Gah
Island that summer afternoon when we liberated the crabs
was never born. The clouds, however, did leave their blessing of
rain on the land, but they did not become that awful power that
merges with the wind and becomes the hurricane. That storm will
be born some day and will sweep away the Easter-egg houses and
air-conditioned malls that have taken the place of thatched homes
and shell mounds. Some day such a storm will come. But, for
now, the Gulf Coast beach where I live with my family is as tran-
quil as ever. The Florida summer has slowly and subtly transcended into autumn, and the season when the great storms are
born is ending. Autumn nights now cool the warm waters of the
Gulf, and the days have become drier and cooler. And that feeling
that comes to me every fall, that peculiar feeling of being back in
time, had returned once again.

Teaching classes at the college at night and writing in the
morning had given me the afternoons. Simone and I decided to
keep the children home this year and assume the major responsibility of educating them. It would not be easy. When it came to

the children, however, Simone was the most patient mother I had ever known. And, besides Uncle Nip, she was the most well-read person I'd ever known. Between the two of us and the close circle of friends and elders that we kept in contact with, the task looked promising.

Afternoon thoughts swayed with the motion of the hammock. I had tucked the published journal of Columbus between my side and the embroidered Mayan netting that supported me. The shadows and the sunlight flickered through the bushy fronds of the sabals. Even Columbus couldn't bring me down. Because I wasn't anywhere, not up, not down. I just was. And as I lay back suspended in that moment of indifference, I thought about my age. Forty-four. . . . I say this in my mind, swaying back and forth. Back and forth. There is magic in such a number. There is calmness in such a motion.

Thoughts of Uncle Nip reeled with the sway of the hammock. I missed my uncle. I still ached and longed for the physical body. Though it seemed like Nip lived in every other way, I missed the contact. I could listen and hear the ghost voice in my mind. I could close my eyes and see Uncle Nip, and I could dream and see him in my dreams. In our house were all Uncle Nip's books with all the notations in them, the brief memos scrawled along the borders of the pages or on pieces of paper tucked inside the covers. They told us what he was thinking about certain passages. Some of the books still carried Uncle Nip's fragrance or the scent of his house, and occasionally Simone or I or one of the children would pick one up and sniff it. Loving memories of Uncle Nip fill our hearts.

Yet, I needed to hear the ghost voice. I needed to understand about the thread that separates past from present, the vision from the dream. I wondered if maybe I hadn't already found the thread, and that maybe I just wasn't aware of it. Like when I was a little boy and felt such a strong love for the land but didn't know the words

Mother Earth until Uncle Nip told me. Or when I felt myself a part of everything around me then but didn't know about the Great Mystery until Uncle Nip taught me. These things that I had special feelings for . . . maybe I had discovered the feelings of the thread already, but Uncle Nip wasn't physically alive and able to tell me what to call it or what it was. I listened for the ghost voice, but it would not come. This was just something I had to figure out for myself. At forty-four, it appeared that I was the elder now.

I swayed in the hammock beneath the glitter of sunlight, and I wondered about a lot of things. I wondered why I turned out the way I did. I wondered why I think the way I do. I could have been a Christian. I could have been an American. I could have cropped my hair short, bought a suit, and got a job that would have better supported my family. An Indian friend of mine, who is an executive with a major defense contractor, once urged me to get a job there, as a supervisor. He said that such a job would enable me to get a new car for my wife, a big house with a pool for the kids. But how could I greet the morning sun with the pipe if I took such a job? How could I hold the pipe, address the Great Mystery, and pray for the welfare of the earth and the animals and the birds, yet be a part of the destructive aspect of my species by working as a supervisor for a corporation that profits from war and the exploitation of the natural world? My Indian friend, who often drinks too much these days, cared about me enough not to press me further when I declined the offer.

I had made other decisions. Choosing not to establish myself in the white man's world and in his school system, I went Indian. I didn't have to work at Indian schools all those years and feel compelled as a teacher and a father to retain an Indian identity within myself, my children, and my people. I could have been anything. But I was an Indian. It's always been this way. So I wondered if being an Indian was ever an intellectual choice with me. In the quiet flickering sunlight I acknowledged the influences of Mrs. Basic, who allowed me to experience the world the way an Indian boy should. I acknowledged all that I had learned from Uncle Nip. But then, I wondered what it was in Mrs. Basic that enabled her to do that for me. I wondered what it was in Uncle Nip that made him the way he was.

Indians are changing. I say this to myself. The center of the People is shaken, and though there are those native hearts who struggle to bring it together, there are yet others who work to tear it apart, and many more who don't care if they succeed or not. These are the ones who have lost their center. Many of them who live in the cities have cut themselves off from the land. Their children are denied the love for the earth and the connection to their traditions, such as seeking a vision. And there are those Indian "progressives" who live close to the land on reservations, but they call oil drilling and strip mining and clear-cut logging economic progress. One tribal chairman in Florida wanted to open his reservation up for white hunters to kill, for a price, exotic animals. Many Indian dancers don't dance for power anymore; they dance for money at pow wows. And some "activists" have even made a living off of causes. Even a few college intellectuals call themselves "breeds" because they have lost their identities and don't know anymore who they are. Others of the People have no concept of the Mystery, yet call themselves traditionals. They pray to an anthropomorphic God with the pipe, a god that is somewhere in the shadows between the Mystery and the god of the Spaniards.

Many more of the People have become Christians. A few of them are used as missionaries. I heard one story about a tribe who still lives in the rain forest along the Amazon. This tribe taught their children, since first contact with white people, to run away whenever they saw a white person. This even protected them from the spirit killers, the missionaries. Then, one of the more recent religious sects of whites that has sprung up in this country attracted an

Indian flute player to their flock. They sent him into the rain forest
with his flute, and the Indians who had been taught for generations
to run away from white people didn't run. The way I heard the
story was that more missionaries followed the Indian flute player,
only they were white, and they carried with them such things as
measles and mumps, the diseases that white people don't often die
from but Indians do.

And, of course, there are those of the People who regard
themselves as Americans now and salute the flag and sing the "Star
Spangled Banner."

Why not Nip? Or me? Why not the others who have clung
to the old ways of seeing things? What made Simone the way she
is? Why have we raised our children to hang on to their native ori-
gins and identities when they will probably suffer because of that
very thing. No wonder our lives are intertwined with the dolphins
and other endangered life forms. We represent what is in the way
of human greed. Where's the balance? Where's the thread that ties
it all together?

These are the things I wondered about. The hammock
swayed higher, and I rode the stream of consciousness further and
faster. Dreams and visions and decisions made and needed to be
made all flowed through my mind. Living in the white man's
world, using Indian medicine to survive in it, believing in Indian
thought. I'm forty-four and have done it so far, but how much
more? How long can I live in these diametrically opposed worlds
and go on as the natural world shrinks and becomes more of an
intangible reality than something I can hold or touch? The world
of the Indian is dying along with the world of the dolphin. I'm
afraid that the natural world I love will die like Uncle Nip, and I
won't be able to touch it anymore. To luxuriate in its beauty, to experience its power. My children won't be able to hold it. Simone will
be lost without it. What's the thread that holds worlds together but

keeps them separate? What's the thread that separates things like past from present, dreams from visions, reality from itself, yet holds it all together?

The sound of waves lapping at the shore before me and Simone reading to the children from the house behind me make everything seem right again. It is no illusion, I say to myself. We are still here. I reached for the book that I had tucked away, and examined the cover. "Columbus came and went," I mutter. "Ignorant bastard." The book fell to the ground. I didn't want it sharing my space.

The sunlight flickered through the palms, and an offshore breeze carried a hint of coolness in it. The sky was blue and clear. I felt the balance, and I whispered this to the wind. "There is a balance," I say aloud. And it's not something I always saw or felt. Not at all. There was a time when I had told Uncle Nip that there was no balance.

▲ ▲ ▲

I was nineteen then and going to college. The place that nurtured me as a child and consoled me as a young man was being bulldozed away. More and more people kept pouring onto the land, or what was left of it. At nineteen, I couldn't see any balance. Everywhere I looked, all I saw was devastation; therefore, the balance didn't exist anymore.

"Where's the balance, Uncle? You said that in the Mystery there's always a balance. I don't see any balance. All I see is the destruction."

"The earth is a speck of dust in the universe," Uncle Nip responded. "Just because you don't see a balance doesn't mean there isn't one.

"I assure you," he added, smiling, "that we are — whether your ego thinks so or not, whether you see that we are or not —

part of the balance that exists always in the Great Holy Mystery. Everything's a part of the balance, kid . . . everything."

▲ ▲ ▲

And, at the scary and sacred number of forty-four years, I had finally experienced the consciousness of that balance. For the first time in my life, I recognized the relationship between the beauty and the horror of life's experience. It was something so simple that it could be seen in the journal of a man who shifted the balance of the world, and it could be felt in the gentle autumn breezes that carried pelicans above the water. It could be heard in the sounds of love emanating from my home. Lying in a hammock one fall afternoon, I experienced the balance that existed at one time everywhere in America. And it was real to me that day because I felt it and was aware of what it was. Swaying in the hammock between two sabals while the sunlight flickered above me and the autumn breezes swept over me, while images of Simone and the children passed tenderly through my mind, I felt the balance, and it existed within me.

A crow swept down and perched himself on a dangling frond above the hammock. He arrived at the same time Carises did. I greeted them both.

The crow tilted his head, peered at me, and hopped onto another frond. He snatched a huge hopper in his black beak and flew away, probably back to his own nest and family.

Carises climbed into the hammock with his dad and scooched comfortably alongside me.

I kissed his head and felt the wild and thick sun-streaked darkness of his long hair. It was like kissing the boy who was me long ago. I squeezed him. His softness melted into me. "Everything okay, Carises?" I asked.

"Yeah, Dad. I just got a question."

"Oh?"

"How do you count coops?"

"You mean like counting coup? Like how an Indian counts a strike? That's pronounced *coo*. Like the sound a mourning dove makes sometimes."

"Yeah. That's it. Mom read to us that a warrior wins eagle feathers by counting coos. She said to ask you what it is."

"Well, to count coup and win an eagle feather, a person had to be a skillful and brave warrior. He could only count coup in battle."

"Did he have to kill someone?"

"That wasn't the idea, Carises. You see, when Indians of the Great Plains couldn't avoid war, that is, when all words had failed, they went to war. Now war, as they understood it, was fought without guns and lots of killin'. Instead, they went into battle with coup sticks. The idea was to get close enough to the enemy, who was more than likely wanting to count coup on you, and strike him first, or even touch him, with your coup stick, in front of everybody. That proved you were a more skillful warrior that day. It proved you were brave, and it humiliated your enemy. Because he was so humiliated, if not sportin' some wound from a hard strike, he left the battlefield. It was quite a sophisticated way of settling territorial disputes when the words had failed. But there was rarely someone killed in such a battle, Carises. There was a winner, of course, and a loser. The winner got to go home, talk about his brave deed, and dance his victory. And, because of his bravery, he was presented an eagle feather. The loser . . . he got to go home too."

"Did you ever count coos, Dad?"

There was a pause, and in it the caw of crows traveled back to us. "I guess that crow's family got excited about his catch," Carises observed.

The question he asked needed an answer.

Funny thing, I thought, how in the autumn it's so easy to get nostalgic. "Yeah . . . I guess I did, Carises. It's just that . . . it was so long ago I sorta had forgotten about it." I pushed myself up on the hammock, so that my head was elevated but my legs were still stretched out comfortably. Carises used my arm as a pillow. We looked up at the sky through the palms.

"You know that stick, Carises, the one I used to have hangin' on the bedroom wall . . . it looked sorta like a cane?"

"Yeah. . . . It had copper tacks on it, and it was shaped like a boomerang at the top. It was made of smooth wood and painted black where it curved." Carises made a curving gesture with his small hand.

I smiled at the child's memory. He must have been only three years old when I took the stick down and replaced it with a painting. An eight-year-old records a lot in his memory. "Well," I continued, "that was Uncle Nip's coup stick before he gave it to me."

"It had an eagle feather on it, Dad. Did you win it?"

I smiled again, this time out of wonder for my little son's curiosity. I hugged him some more and said, "You're so beautiful, Carises. I love you."

He smiled too. I guess because it felt so good to hear those words, to feel so loved, he snuggled closer, skin on skin with his dad. "I love you too, Pop," he said.

The love between a father and son made a balance in that part of the world, in that speck of dust in the Mystery, and Carises and I could each feel it. Such love had great power, and we could feel it in the gentleness and tenderness of thought and things.

Puffs of white clouds sailed across the blue like wisps of raw cotton. Palm fronds sounded like rattles in the soft wind. The hammock swayed between the sabals. The sense of peace and balance that existed at that moment, the autumn slant of the sun on that particular day, the feelings that could make a man feel like he was back in time, a son feel that he was loved, and the need to learn and the need to teach all played a part of the balance. All played a part of the story.

"Yes, Carises. I won that feather."

I KILLED
SAVVY SEMINOLE

A N ANIMAL, when snared in a trap, will gnaw his own foot
off to escape. After I directed the battle against The Seminole Bank of Tampa, I contemplated suicide.

Had any of my student peers known about suicidal signs,
they would've seen them in me. But this was 1970. These were
the days of LSD and mescaline, hash and marijuana. Of student
protests and arrests. Fear of the draft and anguish over war. These
were the days of mind expansion and soul disruption. So much
was going on then within the minds of the country's youth that
my internal struggles were not seen as suicidal by even my closest
friends. Alienated and disillusioned with the world themselves,
they didn't see the signs in me, for they were searching for ties to
the past and acceptance of their present. They couldn't know my
anguish. They couldn't see the signs.

A few days before I had given away all my record albums
and my stereo; I said that I didn't want anything of the white
man's world. I didn't possess very much that belonged to that
world either: some music, a few books, an old black-and-white
TV set. I told a couple of friends who had assisted me in ridding

the world of Savvy Seminole that I had had enough. But the feelings I had went deeper than the words. I felt that I could never and
would never be a part of this world.

The Tampa night was unusually quiet. College exams were
over. The Christmas holidays allowed many students who rented in
the area around the university campus to head back up North. It
was between semesters and the first time that I had to myself. Even
my work-study job at the university press didn't resume until January. Uncle Nip was visiting old friends in Oklahoma, and so I was
alone. . . . And there I was, inside my two-room house, on the
couch, with a bayonet clutched in my right hand, contemplating
suicide.

My dog E slept peacefully against the front door in his usual
spot. . . . He hadn't heard death come in.

Earlier that week, my neighbors, also college students, had
said E chased away two strangers from outside my place. The men
wore suits, they said. I figured that they had to be Feds or some other
kind of cops and that they were after me. Paranoia did strike deep
those early days of the Seventies, and for good reason. I had learned
as a small boy that shadow people of the church or the government
had ways of penetrating one's life and ruining it. And I assumed the
worst: that the men in suits were trying to plant something on the
remains of the dead '55 Bonneville I kept out back in the yard. It
was the home of Florida weeds, palmetto bugs, and a rare Indigo
snake, and it was the perfect place for a "plant." I was certain that
the cops would come back later and bust me for possessing whatever illegal substance they left behind. It was usually an easy task
to bust students on drug charges then, because something as small
as a marijuana seed embedded in a shag carpet or under a chair cushion was enough. That's all it would take. Once that evidence was
discovered, a bag of something illegal would somehow turn up in
an investigator's hands, and the arrest would be made.

But not every student activist had an uncle like Nippawa-
90   nock who made certain I stayed as clean or as conscious of my
responsibilities as I could be. "You watch yourself, Kid," Nip had
warned, knowing that I was no saint and that I hung around with
an anti-war, anti-establishment crowd who indulged in the times.
"You can't be out drinking and driving or smoking weed or dropping acid and be a leader," Nip would say. "You have a responsibility
to the People. If you get caught, you not only ruin your life, but you
hurt and embarrass your race." Uncle Nip always stressed the concept of the People with me. It usually worked.

And having a big black lab like E guarding my house and a
harmless but large and rare snake guarding the junk car outside also
helped keep the shadow people of government away.

But I knew that I couldn't keep them away all the time. I
learned that living in the white man's world made me vulnerable
one way or another, at one time or another. There were just too
many rules, too many laws. There were just too many ways they
could get you, I would say. And I was right.

Having protested the arrest of a Native American weeks
earlier, and having become the leader of the newly formed United
Native Americans at the University of South Florida, I was known
to the local authorities, and, considering the times, probably federal
ones too. Within a five-day period, I was stopped two times by
police and questioned, both those times at gunpoint. The second
time I wound up in jail. It was another routine traffic inspection, the
sheriff said. Forced, spread eagle, against the car and frisked, I was
charged for not paying a ticket and arrested. And that was the way
the shadow people of government got me.

I pointed to the pollution pouring out of the smoke stack of
a downtown chemical company and said to the cop who was driving me to jail that maybe he should be arresting the men responsible
for that pollution, and he looked over at the black smelly shit rising
up to the sky and said that I was probably right.

I was temporarily held in the center of a small room where there was a chair with scratched aluminum arms. They forced me to sit down. They called the chair I was sitting in "the barber's chair." A burly looking man, with bushy eyebrows, crew-cut hair and a clean-shaven face and neck, kept offering to shave my head. "Come on, sweety. I'll make you look like a man." He'd wave the hair clippers in front of me. "Savvy?" he'd say with a sinister smile.

I clenched my teeth and snarled, trying hard not to jump up and punch him in his fat stubby face. Instead, I focused my eyes straight ahead, like an angry dog, glancing only slightly to follow the movement of my tormentor. I'm sure he was studying the tension in my face and hands, and could see my veins and arteries showing in my arms. I look back at it now and know that he must've had a lot of experience badgering men in that chair. And when I couldn't be drawn into the scheme, the fat pink-faced guard raised the clippers closer to my face and sneered, "How 'bout I take a little off the sides. Savvy?"

He pushed himself right into my face, and I locked into his eerie gaze. It was mean and menacing. Then I asked him something. I guess I did it because I wasn't afraid of him anymore. "Why are you threatened by long hair?" That was my big question. I didn't say, "Fuck you, asshole!" That would've given him something to justify in his mind what he was intending to do. "Why are you threatened by long hair?" What kind of response could he have given?

He just stood straight up, and for a second he gave the slightest impression that he was actually considering a verbal response. But it seemed like the words I spoke and the bravado with which they were spoken had temporarily confused him. Without warning, like he'd rehearsed the movement many times before on others who sat in this chair, he punched me in the solar plexus with the force of a man who knew his power and where to deliver it. I shot forward. My hands, which were tightly clamped around the

92

chrome arms, contracted violently into clenched fists and could barely keep me from sliding onto the floor. With my breath blasted out, I gasped once, twice, three times, trying to suck in some air. Blackness nearly overcame me.

As I struggled for breath, I drew myself up. One of the other guards smiled insidiously and asked if I'd like a Mohawk instead. The burly one laughed as spit dribbled from the corner of his mouth. Still snickering, he wiped the dribble away with the back of his fat hand. His cold blue eyes had no flicker of light in them. They were as dead as he was.

With a guard on each arm, they dragged me out of that room and finger-printed me in another. I was reminded that I had forty-eight hours to keep my scalp — in other words, two days to get bailed out. Then I was photographed and hauled down a narrow concrete corridor of pale yellow and taken to a shower stall with no screen for privacy. They ordered me to strip and shower, and when they had decided that this phase of my induction into prison life was over, they tossed me a pale blue prison uniform and ordered me to put it on.

By the time Uncle Nip bailed me out, only five hours had elapsed, but they were some of the longest hours I'd ever spent. On the way home Uncle Nip told me that he was arrested once in Miami, and how humiliating an experience it had been for him too. Nip said that he'd been accused of murder. The police told him that an eye-witness had identified him as the killer. They stripped him, roughed him up, smashing his nose, and they cut his hair. It was the cutting of the hair that most affected him. It was something that hadn't been done to him since some righteous Christians first got to him when he was a boy just off the Quapaw reservation. Later that night, the police told Nip that they had made a mistake, and had captured the real killer. They let Nip go, but not without warning him to go away and to not let his red ass be seen again. "I was cut

off from the world, Kid . . . thought I'd die there. So I guess leaving
with short hair and a broken nose weren't the worst things that
could've happened." I glanced over at Nip, at his curly and silvery
hair. I figured it wouldn't get much longer now, since the older we
get, the slower our hair seems to grow. Leaning back against the
headrest, I observed Nip a moment more, and I wondered if there
wasn't a human experience that my dear uncle didn't know about.

As we drove along the interstate, I turned my gaze out the
window at the bulldozers and fallen trees, past the familiar signs
that read CONSTRUCTION AHEAD. Florida was exploding with people. "Come on down!" was the call, and they came. Endless waves
of them were washing over the land and devastating it. The destruction of the environment was more than apparent from the car window. The white man called this population explosion and stress on
the land "economic progress." He called the dead trees and developed wet lands "construction" and "job opportunities." As the en-
vironmental devastation passed by, I knew that the natural world I
loved was changing, that I felt no part of the civilized one that was
replacing it, and that I'd sooner die than ever be locked up like that
again. I'd sooner die with the trees and the animals we passed along
the interstate.

▲ ▲ ▲

That's why I wanted to die then, as I lay on the couch.
Indians and trees and animals were all the same to the shadow people. That's what I was calling them all then — shadow people. To
me, they cast a long darkness over this world, always looking for
profit and never seeing the beauty in things. Governments and politicians of every color play word games while our world loses something beautiful every day. Japanese fisherman, Greek spongers, Arab
oil sheiks, European bankers live for the money and the material
power that money can buy them. Korean herbalists will pay

thousands of dollars to have a Florida black bear killed for a gall bladder that's sold as an aphrodisiac for thousands more. Asian tuna boats roam and rape the oceans slaughtering thousands of dolphins and other cetaceans with nets that reach out for miles, and American logging companies see dollar signs growing up mountain sides and never trees that have lived for a thousand years. They all have one thing in common: They lust for money the way the Spaniards lusted for gold, and they cast a shadow of death over this world.

It all comes down to greed. Greed and power. They have psychologically and spiritually severed their ties with the earth. And, like the trees and animals, I knew that if the Indians couldn't be tamed or didn't serve the monetary purposes of the Shadow People, they were destroyed. I knew this. I knew that my people were being killed in the Brazilian rain forest and that it wasn't even a crime to do so. And I knew that the Shadow People would get me in the end too. It's history. It's part of the past, and the past and today are no different.

I thought this, and never considered that there was a thread that weaves them together, yet separates them subtly and finely. I only knew that the Shadow People destroyed everything of beauty in this world and that they would destroy me too. I even wondered if somehow I hadn't been a witness to my own death that day years ago when I rode a door out to an island in the sea. Maybe I really died there, in that massacre, and what the shadow people of the church got from me was only what was left of the memory and spirit that got born back somehow, and they even tried to kill that. The spirit that remained in me at that moment on the couch that night in Tampa wanted out of this white man's world of greed, this prison outside the prison, and that's all I really knew.

There was no escape. I couldn't stay alive and not fight to protect my land and the animals and the integrity of my people. I couldn't. It was just something in me that I didn't understand then and I would never really understand. And one way or another, the humiliation the white man planned for me was unavoidable, and it was one reason why I was laying on the couch, contemplating my own death that winter night when I was only nineteen years old. I wanted to kill myself and not allow the white man another chance to kill what was left of me, what was left of my spirit. And I was afraid and tired of always having to be brave at facing life. So, like the animal who gnaws his own foot off to escape when snarled in a trap, I contemplated suicide.

Because of my arrest and the battle to rid this world of Savvy Seminole, the idea of failing at school and the burden of leadership, the possibility of failure in my uncle's eyes, and the constant battle to retain identity, I just couldn't carry on anymore. I could find no escape from the shadow people or myself. I could only find reasons not to live. For I was blind to any balance in my life. I was afraid of the future.

At that moment on the couch, I felt that there was just me. I knew Uncle Nip was old, and I didn't want to burden him anymore with one identity crisis after another. I did have my dog E. But, even after all the times he had protected me, probably some I didn't even know about, I didn't suppose that E could protect me then. My dog had been my guardian against those who would bring harm to me, but how could he guard me when I was determined to kill myself? And as much as I loved E, I can't remember thinking about what would happen to him after I died. That's how self-centered humans can be, especially when it comes to suicide. That's how withdrawn into myself I must have been then. It's hard for me to recall what went through my mind at that moment.

I just remember laying on the old couch, pressing a bayonet against my chest and thinking that of all the ways to die, I chose this one.

It would, no doubt, be a gruesome and painful way, and I could only guess that my thoughts at the time had a lot to do with the choice. Even suicide was a political decision. A gun would have been using a weapon that the white man used to kill animals. And I'd always hated guns. I hated the idea that these artificial extensions of civilized men had somehow allowed people to believe that because they had such power to kill, this is what made them superior to other, far more intelligent life forms. For me, guns symbolized the white man. They symbolized his civilization.

Hanging myself wasn't even a consideration. I would not choose to die the way the thirty-eight Santee warriors were forced to in Mankato, Minnesota. Hanging was the white man's choice of how to kill my people. I would not hang.

Another option was for me to overdose on drugs. This was the easiest. Drugs were plentiful around the college campus. But an overdose on drugs would only allow the media and the government to exploit my death and embarrass my uncle and my people. After all, looking back, I realize I was by far not the most important person in the world, but at that time I was the chairman of the United Native Americans for South Florida. I had led one of the most widely publicized protests the area had seen. The media and the police would have their day if the cause of my death was a bad trip.

No, by dying this way, with a bayonet in my gut, they couldn't allege that I died of an overdose. To die this way was more like a sacrifice. I would die as a warrior sacrificed.

This is what my nineteen-year-old mind was thinking while holding the bayonet. Through the gruesome kind of death that the bayonet would provide, I hoped that I would, at least, pay the shadow people back a little for what they did to my people, for what they had done to me. In a warrior's sense, the slowness of such a death would enable the spirit power to grow. What was left of this spirit would be freed then from further humiliation. It would be sacrificed back to the Mystery. My body would stay behind as a grim reminder of the conquest and the horrible ways the People had died . . . how the white men took their European methods of terror and brutality from one continent to another, from one century into the next . . . how the early colonists and American soldiers used their bayonets to cut off the genitals of the People . . . how they made tobacco pouches out of the testicles of men, and how they stretched the female parts across their saddle bows and hats to wear as decorations and ornaments. The French corrupted the Iroquois word for the female sexual part, otiskwa, to squaw, and that's what the white man has been calling Indian women ever since. The civilized armies of the white man used bayonets to slice open the wombs of pregnant women, the unborn nation spilling onto the earth. They used them to sever women's breasts.

They don't teach this in American history classes, elementary or secondary. But that year I had read the newly published historical accounts of savagery in the conquest of this land. The truth that I and every other Native person felt was now published as fact, and it enraged me. The American holocaust was recorded by eyewitnesses who documented such things in their journals. Indians began reading the documents. More Americans should have. For if a people don't know the past and where their country has been, how will they know where they're going and how to act when they get there?

If American history doesn't teach the past, then how can the truth be recognized and how can the horrors of human behavior be kept from happening again? I would ask these things of the civilized world while it plans more journeys to the moon, more explorations of other worlds. The answer is always, of course, that they will happen again. When the people of the United States opened their eyes one day and saw the dead women and babies photographed in the ditch at My Lai, they wondered how good American soldiers could do such a thing. "It's the worst tragedy in the US Army's history," a TV anchorman said.

They can't imagine American soldiers taking part in the brutal killing of babies for entertainment while in the performance of their duty. What teenage recruit raised on an American history text and TV ever can? That behavior was always reserved for the enemy. It's impossible for most people to imagine how indoctrinated hatred and bigotry, fear, and lack of compassion for life can create a frenzied slaughter of humans, but it happens. Some Indian children, as old as my son Carises, could sometimes run away and at least try to save themselves from the soldiers; but infants were easily snatched into slavery or shot to death. When the soldiers made war on the Apaches and raided the village where Geronimo's family was living, they killed everyone who was unable to run away. The soldiers took Geronimo's baby and tossed him high into the air. And the baby gasped from the force and height he was thrown. He fell, and his soft brown body stiffened on the hard, dull-grey bayonet of a laughing soldier.

I thought about these things on the couch with the bayonet in my hand, and I wanted to pay the white man back with my own gruesome death. By using a bayonet, I would not allow them to violate me any further with their laws, their education, their degradation of my identity. For I would not allow them the satisfaction of killing me by humiliation. When they find my body, I thought, with this ugly thing stickin' out of it, maybe this'll be their grim reminder of the horror they've imposed on this world. Maybe this'll violate their strange sense of order in their civilized world. Maybe then they can sample my blood off the floor and find out just how much is Indian, just how much isn't. At least, this is what I reasoned as I slowly pressed the pointed pewter blade into my own flesh, pressed it harder against the center just beneath my ribs, pressed until it penetrated, and my muscles contracted.

Then, I paused. Not because of the pain. I was almost numb to that. But because something moved across my mind.

I sat up. I didn't feel the blood trickling down my side when I removed the bayonet. I could only feel my rage. The hideous face of Savvy Seminole was there, in my mind, for that instant. And I realized that Savvy was not really dead at all.

The bayonet was still in my hand, but it laid by my side now. I reclined once again, remembering that day I was with T.C. and his two little daughters. I remembered that moment when we sat in T.C.'s car at a busy Tampa intersection, and the image of Savvy Seminole intruded into the lives of these two beautiful Indian children. . . .

▲▲▲

We had just pulled up to the stop light and we waited while the girls played in the back seat. Above us loomed the billboard of Savvy Seminole. His bucktoothed smile, big nose, and red-skinned face mocked us. But, at first, we wouldn't see it. Perhaps each of us, two young men and two children, didn't want to really see it. An anvil crashed into Savvy's ugly feathered head by his own hand, creating his silly expression; the message was some kind of bad pun that was supposed to show us how the Seminole Bank "compounded" its interest rate.

The Savvy Seminole billboards were scattered throughout the Tampa Bay area. But not until what happened finally happened did I really see Savvy Seminole in all its degradation. A similar advertisement of a black or a Jew would not have been tolerated. After all, this was 1970! The Civil Rights Movement would have brought an immediate end to such debasement against the blacks, who were now starting to become consumers and making more deposits into the system, and subsequently, becoming more like the white man and a part of the system. To offend the consumer and the customer is not in a bank's best interest. And besides, the president of the Seminole Bank and the chairman of the board were both Jews. They would swear to the media the day of the confrontation that they were truly "sensitive" men whose own people had been persecuted.

T.C. was of Comanche and Kiowa and white blood. He joked about his initials, saying that they stood for "Tough Character." Though anyone who knew T.C. thought of him as more of a gentle man, T.C. regarded himself as Comanche, and these were proud people. Historians have referred to these Native Americans as the "Lords of the Plains." They were no savage, silly-looking, mindless caricatures like the Savvy Seminole perpetuated. The Comanche and Kiowa were handsome and honorable people. The Comanche would not surrender their country without a struggle. They would not surrender their spirit. When the great chief Satanta killed himself, he was a prisoner of war, and only Satanta could free his spirit and the spirit of the People. He did this by leaping to his death from the window of the prison hospital. He let the People know he would pay the price for his pride and dignity with the sacrifice of his life. He too would not be trapped in the white man's world of humiliation. Satanta knew such strong spirit was of more use to the People in the Mystery where it could be recycled than debased, taunted, and weakened by the white man's prison. That's the way some Indians like Satanta thought. That's what I was thinking too, on the night I held the bayonet to my chest.

So, when T.C.'s seven-year-old daughter leaned over the front seat, pointed to the creature staring at her from above, and asked, "Daddy, is that an Indian?," my whole being became enraged. T.C. turned to stone. It was as if all the humiliation that either of us had absorbed in our lives and managed to contain had finally been penetrated by the softly spoken and piercing words of an Indian child.

When the traffic light changed, T.C. just sat stony still, arms wrapped around the steering wheel, looking ahead. I hardly heard

the honking horns and swearing drivers passing by, only the echo
of his daughter's words. T.C.'s dark sunglasses reflected the hideous
image above.

Diana sat in the back seat, her black, almond eyes set in a round
and pretty porcelain-like face, her teeth glistening like pearls behind
full and ripe cherry lips. The expression she wore was bewilderment.

Her baby sister Tina sat beside her. Her short, chubby legs did
not quite reach the edge of the seat, so she pressed her cheek against
the door and gazed up to see what her sister had asked about. What
was she thinking? What would a child think of herself? It was probably the first time she became aware of racism without knowing
such a word existed. Tina was the picture on a postcard, an Indian
baby from Oklahoma, the kind tourists send home with short notes
and an American flag stamp. The tourists are not aware that these
Savvy Seminole moments ever occur in the lives of Indian children.
They are not aware how the images they portray of Indian people
affect children and how they, themselves, see the American Indian.
Whether it's the Indian maiden on the Land O' Lakes milk cartons
or the Chief Wahoo image on the Cleveland Indians' baseball uniforms, they fester and affect the People and how others see them.
The Savvy Seminole incidents smolder and can intensify as a child
grows older until he lies as still as I was on that couch contemplating suicide to escape the humiliation of those images and that
mentality.

My eyes must have flashed fire, because Diana put her hand
to her mouth like she was frightened of me, like she had seen a
monster in me that she didn't know was there. She could see my
reflection in the cracked mirror which hung from the sun visor in
front of me. Diana had only known me as the friend of her dad's
who gave her rides on his motorcycle, a friend who played hide-and-
seek with her and brought her candy whenever I would visit. Now
I was suddenly the reflection of a wrath she had probably never seen
in a man, especially in a man she thought she knew. She glanced

at my fists pressed against the dashboard and then back up at Savvy Seminole.

"No, kids," I said, still staring up at the billboard, "that's not an Indian. That's not an Indian at all. That's Savvy Seminole. He's how white people like to see us."

Diana made the connection. She wanted to understand how these "white people" regarded her people, how they regarded her. "Why do they do that?"

"I guess, because they really don't care, Diana. They think we're dead or somethin'. Because maybe he's how they want to see us. In a way it makes them feel good about themselves, knowing they took a country from a bunch of silly Savvy Seminoles." I paused and turned to look at the two little girls in the back seat. "But he's not an Indian, kids. And he's gonna come down."

▲▲▲

So, one Tampa night during winter break between semesters, there I was, just another Savvy Seminole sprawled out on some old couch, ready to kill myself. Just another "Savvy" to the white man. Then why not push the blade further? What stopped me? It wasn't fear of dying. Too many young Indians don't look at death that way. That's why so many kill themselves. It's a way out of this life, a way out of the humiliation. "Go on . . . shove it in," I said, my eyelids squeezed shut, my lips pressed hard against each other. "You'll never be anything but a Savvy Seminole. That's why he's in your mind now . . . because you're really him. You'll always be him."

▲▲▲

During the protest, I had been afraid. Though I regarded this as a sign of weakness, it probably wasn't. I had much to consider: I would not allow T.C. to jeopardize his life on a picket line in the deep South because of his two children, so the protest may appear like "this was just one Indian who got a hair up his butt." That's what I had heard someone in the bank saying to the press. And what 103 would happen if the protesters — mostly students, some clergy, and a couple of the radical university professors — decided to quit before an agreement with the bank could be reached on when Savvy Seminole would come down? If the protest fell apart, Savvy and the bank would win. What would happen if the bank paid some bureaucratic Seminole Indian puppet to make a statement that there was nothing the Seminole Tribe Inc. found offensive about the sign? I also thought about what would happen to me when the battle was over. I wasn't going to jail again. So where would I go to get away? And what would I say to the media in front of all the cameras? These were big things for me to face then, and I was indeed afraid, yet when I thought about all these things, they weren't really at the root of my greatest fear. That particular fear was something I couldn't identify just then. It wouldn't have mattered. I went ahead with the plan to organize and lead the protest of the bank in spite of this nagging, stomach-wrenching sense of a fear I couldn't identify.

I had not yet heard Uncle Nip's explanation of bravery; he told me at some point down the road of life that a warrior is fully afraid before a battle, but that he acts in spite of his fear. This is what makes him brave.

"A man who charges a machine gun nest, screaming insanely and without regard for his own life nor anyone else's is, at that moment, an insane man." That's what Uncle Nip would say. "His act is one of insanity. It is the brave man, who cherishes life and wants to keep it, that charges the hill out of love for his comrades and his land and his family. . . . He's the truly brave one who routs the enemy, the one who acts in spite of his fear."

Outside the bank building the picket line stretched a long way down the busy Bush Boulevard, and traffic moved slowly, and sometimes it came to a standstill. Occasionally, someone would shout from his car, "Right on, brother!" Other times, people taunted and made mock war-whoops, the kind they see and hear on TV. Beneath a militant and confident determination, though, something made me afraid in a way I had never been, not even in jail. It wasn't the taunts either.

It wasn't the TV cameras that followed me, nor the newspaper reporters who held microphones up to my face. It wasn't the local police who watched, nor the F.B.I. agent who told me that he was part Cherokee too, but moved away disgruntled when I suggested that he pick up a sign and march with the rest of us. As determined as I appeared that day, as splendid as I may have looked with my blood-red bandanna, my long dark hair, and my beaded choker, I was afraid of something I couldn't identify, and I trembled inside on account of it. I was dressed for victory, yet something in me was being defeated.

As the bank's chairman negotiated in the board room, I saw what I was to the white man. Mr. Klein did not talk to me. He directed his words to the ministers who joined the protest, to a professor of sociology at the university, and to the student leaders from the university who came to lend support. Even when the bank president finally returned with the bank's agreement to change the billboards and not use Savvy Seminole anymore to advertise the bank's services, he didn't address me. Mr. Klein gave his statement to the ministers and the students; he told them without even making any eye contact with me. The bank president was no different. He stood on the speaker's platform set up by the media inside the bank and gave his statement to the press and the TV camera people. But he would not address me. I was something less than a person. And that's what I feared. I felt like a Savvy Seminole. That's why the victory over the bank felt like a defeat for me.

Throughout that day of protest, I was like a dolphin in an aquarium. In a zoo the body of the dolphin is trapped and the spirit of the dolphin that dwells in the body and animates it and gives it

life is trapped too. It is trapped in the body, confined in a place where
its only freedom is defined by people. Though I could move more
freely than the captive dolphin, I too was trapped. The place of
confinement was not a twenty-by-thirty-meter concrete pool, but
rather the world around me. The shadow people see the dolphins
the way they choose to see them, as something less than human.
That's how they chose to see me. What could the dolphins do about
it? What could I do? If either of us strikes back, we are considered dangerous and removed. The dolphins will themselves to death
to allow the spirit a chance to escape and to join the Mystery in the
pool of goodness that belongs to the Mystery and to them by extension. They do this while the spirit is still there, while they still have
the power that the shadow people have not sucked out.

▲▲▲

And that's why I was ready to push the blade of the bayonet
further into my body.

In a trance-like state, I was shoved suddenly awake. "Damn
it, E," I snapped. "Do ya have to go out now?" What would you
know about killing yourself? I thought but didn't say. "Can't you
just lay there quietly for a while and leave me alone?" The idea
sounded silly — leave me alone while I kill myself. It didn't work.
My eyelids flicked opened and shut until I got my bearings. A wet
tongue licked me across the mouth. "Damn it, E."

The night was damp and cold as I stood watching E lift his
leg by the old Bonneville, marking territory. My life-breath formed
puffs of smoky mists and rose up through the old oak that I stood
beneath. Its branches were nearly bare; together, our naked arms
raised to a starry sky. I wanted to go into the stars. Then I noticed
the leaves that still remained clinging to the tree. I thought about
how they were clinging to life while I was wanting to throw it
away. In the sound of a breath, I said that I was sorry.

When E and I walked in the back door, there was Uncle Nip sitting on the couch. He startled me. But before I could comprehend the impossibility of that happening, Nip was gone. I moved slowly toward the couch, scanning the room, as if going through the motions of wondering where Nip had gone, when all the while I knew that what I saw was Uncle Nip's second self. It is something the Aztecs called the nagual. Nip had once described to me how he was training himself to leave his body at will. He said he had done it once before and that if you had walked in on him at that moment, you'd have seen two of him.

The bayonet was on the floor near the couch. Seeing Nip there somehow made me aware of the pain that I felt from the wound. I could also feel the blood on my side.

I fell into the couch and sat staring at the wall. E pulled up against my leg and stared too, only up at me. His blue-black eyes spoke love, his black hair felt soft and luxurious as it moved between my stroking fingers. I didn't want to feel loved, damn it, but I was. I didn't want to love, but I did.

I thought about Nip. I knew that my battle against the Seminole Bank and Savvy Seminole had been necessary, but I worried. I was aware of what the law enforcers were capable of doing to me. I was aware that I was born into a war against a people who seemed hopelessly lost and that such a people were capable of anything when it came to protecting their power. Though I would one day reflect on the battle to rid the world of Savvy Seminole as a "good fight," I knew it was just a test. There were going to be other battles more important to the People, like the one to get my college degree.

E lifted his head from my knee and leaned back, letting me know he wanted to be scratched and stroked on his chest, along the thin "permissible" strip of white allowed on black labradors when being judged at dog shows. This white strip was a way of telling if they were, indeed, full-blooded labs. I would tease E about that and remind him that Indians were regarded the same way. That's where

I always scratched, though, on that white permissible line, and where E loved it the most. I scratched and petted E until the dawn's first light when we wound up lying together on the floor. It was then, when the first pink-painted sky showed itself through the parted blinds, that I knew the feeling of wanting to die was no longer there. It was gone with the night.

That morning I rode my motorcycle over to Uncle Nip's. Even if Nip wasn't there, I just wanted to be around his house, take in the scent of the orange trees, and sit on the grassy earth where the old one shared his blood with me and first called me nephew. I just wanted to be there, but was surprised when I pulled into the driveway to see his car back in its stall. Nip was home.

"I cut my visit short, Kid, because the weather was too cold. I could feel too much of a strain on the heart. Besides, most of my friends had died back there. It just made me feel too old going back this time. . . . What about you?"

"I guess you know what happened, huh, Uncle?" It must have been the special breakfast Nip had made: bacon and eggs, toast and jam, fresh orange juice. Coffee. The dark and sorry expression on my face faded like the night to the day.

"You know, don't you, Uncle?"

"Know what? That you tried to kill yourself last night?" I gazed down at the table, partly ashamed, partly embarrassed.

"Kid," he said, his voice slightly raised, his blue eyes peering at me while he lifted the coffee pot from the stove, "who would've had to identify your body if you died? Who would have to bury you?"

He poured the coffee. I picked at the good food and slowly ate. "Did you ever think how selfish an act suicide is?" He didn't pummel his young nephew with words; he was too appreciative that the power for which he had trained himself had worked that night, that he was indeed able to separate his ghost from his body or whatever had happened, and that he had me near him now. He explained how the Cherokee believed that if a man committed

108

suicide, his soul, or spirit, would wander forever in a void of blue. He told me that once he loved a boy like me, and the boy had killed himself. "It was years ago," he said, his voice trailing away.

Nip explained how people are responsible to those closest to them. He was right, I thought. Who would take care of E? How betrayed my dog would have been if I had killed myself that night. I imagined how hard E would've fought the police. They probably would've shot him.

Damn! I thought. How selfish. And I'd hate the idea of Uncle Nip having to identify my body. He had to bury one kid before who he loved; another would be too much. He'd had two heart attacks.

"Great breakfast, Uncle." I said, hugging him at the door as I was getting ready to leave. His hug was strong. It squeezed some tears from my eyes. "I'll be okay," I whispered, soon realizing that his eyes had teared up like mine.

And I would be.

It had been two weeks since the battle with the bank, and the billboards had been taken down, for customers didn't appreciate having to pass through a picket line to do their banking. Though the chairman and his board removed Savvy Seminole from the land, it was me who killed that part of him that I believed was part of me on the night I didn't kill myself. After Savvy was gone, a pretty sun symbol decorated the once offensive billboards. It was a classy advertisement for a bank, and a meaningful one too. For the sun is the symbol of rebirth.

Savvy Seminole was dead. Diana and Tina and other children would never have to set eyes on him again. And no Indian parent, like my friend T.C., would ever have to see that hideous face staring at their children. They wouldn't have to answer the humiliating question, "Daddy, is that an Indian?" ever again.

That was my first coup.

CHAPTER 11

DREAMS AND VISIONS

WATER. In Manabozho adventures it is renewal. Perhaps that's why I always found the way to the shores of the earth at different times in my life. The stories of Manabozho, the Ojibway cultural hero and trickster, taught me why I come to the water.

Ahh, the water! The water, sparkling with life; it glistens in the white heat of the mighty tropical sun. Diamonds of light. Crystals of light. Seeds of light twinkling in turquoise and shimmering in the sea that embraces this fragile and shattered jewel of the land I love.

Uncle Nip hugged me close. He embraced me again like the sea embraces the land. He was the soothing constant that would help heal the damage done to my spirit in the way the sea must soothe and help heal the spirit of the land. I had just returned from Wyoming and my first teaching experience. You might say I'd just returned from the front lines. The trip to Florida had been an especially long and lonely one. I was a broken young man, and I wept in my old uncle's arms. My face pressed against the scars of the old chest. Even after two heart surgeries, the old one's embrace was still strong. I could not talk; I could only cry.

110

"For an Indian," Nip explained, "there's nothing as powerful as a vision. Not an experience of consciousness nor an extraordinary dream creates that sacred connection to the Great Mystery. Only the vision does this. But a vision occurs maybe once in our lives, Kid. And it's granted only at that moment, when the Mystery unfolds itself and reveals something of itself directly to us.

"But surely you know this."

"Why am I so lost then, Uncle? Why did I lose so much?"

"You've lost sight of the vision. You could've stayed and dreamed you kicked the BIA and school board asses to hell. But that would've been your dream, Kid, not your vision. You were granted something special when you were just a child. And though dreams are also special and also of the Mystery, they are not visions. They occur in our unconscious. They can guide us on the road of life, but they do not become the center of our lives."

Having cried myself out, I withdrew from my uncle's embrace. "I'm twenty-three, Nip. My wife's left me . . . I was fired from teaching. I was even banned from the grounds of any school on the reservation, maybe even the state. . . . I don't know. Is this why I went to college? What a way to help my people!

"I wanted to stay and fight them, Nip. I wanted to dream the fight and to know what it was like to stand up to them. But I only dreamed that they came for me with guns, and I woke up in a roadside rest to the smell of diesel fuel and trucks shifting gears. Instead of making a stand and defending myself, I just left."

"And well you did. They would've killed you, Gabriel. They would've tossed your body in a ditch and left it there. The People can be better served — I assure you."

Nippawanock stood. His glassy blue eyes revealed some of the pain he had once felt. Nip too was a young man once, filled with ideals and the passion to try and make them happen. He knew the rejection. The degradation. The sense of loss. But he knew his sense of duty as an uncle outweighed any sense of wanting to avoid helping me to understand what had just happened, what I needed.

"Such dreams can be powerful, Gabriel. But they can become what we want or what we fear. They can obscure a man's vision. Instead of the guidance he needs to walk the path of vision, he loses sight of the vision, and the dreams become the focus of his life. If he dreams of the past, he may walk in the past."

I knew what Nip was referring to. I had told him on the phone that I decided to stay and fight it out . . . with guns if necessary. "After all, Uncle," I argued, "am I not a man? Am I not a warrior?"

And my wise old uncle knew these thoughts and understood them because he had had them too. From the time they took a scissors to his hair back in Quapaw in 1928, to that moment at the University of Mississippi when he was suddenly dropped as a doctoral candidate because of anonymous letters that slandered him, he too wanted to kill them. But they were shadow people, faceless and spiritless beings, Spaniards in the old tradition. "They'll kill you in the end," he told me. "Is this how you live the vision of the boy to whom it was given?"

Nip walked across the room and stood before a painting. It was of an Indian man who was receiving insight from the Mystery. Of all the art my uncle collected, this was the painting that I liked the most. Nip pointed to it. "The vision and the dream are not the same, Gabriel. To distinguish the difference can be like finding the thread of the Mystery that separates the past from the present. What you need is to fast and pray. Seek a vision now."

And so, at the age of twenty-three, I found myself trying to distinguish between the vision I had when I was a boy and the dreams that came to me when I was a man. And I got lost somewhere in between.

When I was a boy and witnessed the Spaniards' destruction of what was beautiful among the People, I was set on a path that would lead me into manhood. It was the path the vision compelled me to walk, even though I wasn't always aware that I was on it. And it was along this way that I met my Cherokee uncle, because my uncle was living his vision too. The paths crossed. Named in Wampanoag by his adopted mother, Princess Red Wing, Nippawa-nock, or Star-That-Rises-To-Greet-The-Dawn, would encourage me to learn the arts, read the literature, and earn a college degree. He would help me fight against the indoctrination I received at the hands of the Christians who, in the fervor to save me, never considered my right to exist as an Indian. Nip instilled in me that the needs of the People were more important than my own wants and ego. As a teacher, I could help meet those needs. As a teacher I could help restore and nurture what the white man in his schools of ethnocentricity had denied me and my people. As a teacher, I could help bring something back to the People who had it nearly all stolen away. So, like an Aztec gardener whose vision it was to care for flowers and poems, Uncle Nip would care for me.

"Go on your fast now," Uncle Nip urged me. "Go for your vision. Go out alone and fast and pray and seek a vision in the old way. If you're to continue as a teacher of the People and remain on the path of heart, this you must do. And it is time."

This was the power of the vision that Uncle Nip had tried to instill in me. He would say that it integrates itself in the living man and becomes the force that is the Mystery of his life.

The vision I had when I was just a boy allowed me to identify the horrors of human dogma as I became a young man. It allowed me to understand the weaknesses of men and the dangers they can impose on other life forms. In child ways I understood these things even when I was a boy and didn't know that I did.

When I fall through my dream of the little boy who rode the door across a turquoise sea and laughed with the dolphins, when I fall through that time when I felt the wind whipping my sun-streaked hair behind my coppery shoulders and saw the water glistening like a million stars, when I can remember the life of the person I knew I really was, the shadow people come. And I awaken.

At twenty-three years old, I needed the power to face the shadows, for I felt my connection to the vision of a boy slipping away by forces I couldn't control. But still, I could feel the love of the great Mother Earth within me and all around me. Like the water that is constant and embraces the land, I felt as secure in my relationship to Mother Earth as I ever had. And still, as always, I could feel the spirit of the land fill me.

"Go on your fast now," Uncle Nip said. "Go for your vision."

So, after battling degradation and injustice and nearly taking my own life, after earning my college degree, after teaching among the People and being fired from my first teaching position, and after falling in love with a woman who left me for another man, I found myself again on an island. And again I fell exhausted upon my mother. Only this time I was not a frightened boy, but a young man who had lost sight of his boyhood vision and his adult intentions. I was a young Indian who began seeing my own people in the shadows, and I began to slip back into the past. I was losing the struggle to live. I had lost someone I loved and what I loved to do, and I lost sight of the thread that Uncle Nip had said somehow separated the vision from the dream, the past from the present.

CHAPTER 12

THE QUEST

THE TINY ISLAND where I chose to seek my vision stretched just off the Gulf Coast, not far from Madeira Beach. After Hurricane Elena swept across it a few years ago, the tiny island was transformed into not much more than a small sandbar. And not much lives there now. Before the hurricane, the island was a yearly nesting site for the great loggerhead turtles. Now, not only has the island nearly disappeared, but so has the great nation of loggerheads — gone by way of fishermen's nets, by way of power boats, by way of poachers and shrimpers. It must have been a sight to see these huge turtles amble purposefully from the sea each spring onto the shore during the dark of the new moon. And how it must have been to see their young hatch out. Only once a year would these tiny forms of new life head for the full moonlight that reflected off the foamy-white crests of waves that washed on shore. And the baby turtles would make their way, guided by the light, towards the water. They would skitter and scramble and zig-zag and beeline their way maybe thirty yards from where they emerged out from their eggs in the sand.

Long ago, the Indians would come out to watch them. Silently, adults and their children would gather behind the palmettos and pines and watch. From that distance they would see the wonderful sight, and they would whisper stories about the strong-hearted turtle and how the first land was placed on her back and how the land grew and became known as The-Island-Where-The-Turtles-Nest. They would tell these stories and they would make charms for their babies from turtle designs and use their shells ceremoniously to carry sacred herbs or as rattles to accompany sacred healing songs or as calendars to mark the thanksgivings and the passings of each of the thirteen moons.

And though they didn't live on the island, the Indians, like the great turtles, had certainly used it wisely. Instead of leaving behind pollution and waste, they left pottery shards and arrowheads and bone fish hooks. Items like these could be found most anywhere along the white sandy shore, which was once lined by native pines, palmettos, and sabals. Now just skeletal remains of decayed fish and sharks' teeth are all one would find here. Small clusters of sea oats and sea grass are all that are left. At high tide, during a full moon, the Gulf waters nearly cover it. Because of its smallness and distance from the mainland, developers didn't bother with it, even before Elena's fury. Because of the shifting sands and the erratic depth of its shore, boaters stayed clear of it. Because of the powerful currents that could easily sweep a raft out to sea or a strong swimmer under, tourists avoided it. Because of all this and my connection to the island of my past, at age twenty-three, I chose this island to seek my vision.

Without eating or drinking for four days, I sat on a turquoise towel within a circle that I drew in the sand, and I cried out in the ebb and flow of my emotions for some direction, some purpose, to my life — a life that had devoured my intentions. In my hand I held a small stone. The stone was created at the exact spot where lightning had once, in the blink of an eye, connected the earth and sky. It was created at that moment in a place far away from the tropical sun and the Florida shore where I had chosen to seek a vision. Such a stone was born of the Thunderbeings and believed to have strong medicine.

I was out dancing one day under a bright and cold Wyoming sun. In my inner torment and confusion, I would dance. For it was through the dance that I would call up the power that made me an Indian and attached me to the land and to the stars. And gazing at the hard, dry ground, I recognized the shape and sacredness of a stone, and I picked it up. I rolled it between my fingers because it was so round. I studied it as it set in the palm of my hand, turning it and wondering about its roundness. I took it to Vince Lonewolf, and he painted it with a sacred red ochre found in a secret place in the mountains of Wind River, a place known only to him and one other old Arapaho medicine man.

As small waves swept onto the tiny island's shore where I fasted, and night breezes wisped across the water and murmured through the pines, I clutched that stone.

And when my emotions were spent and my eyes drained of tears, I contemplated the stars and the Great Mystery that is all things. I concentrated on that part of myself that I shared with all things. I struggled to let go of the idea that there was an anthropomorphized God in heaven who would bestow on me certain favors if I asked. Instead, I cried to the Mystery in the old way, for pity and for ways that I could grow and help my people. I cried for understanding. And the small circular and painted stone lying on my turquoise mat was my intercessor. I spoke into it and wondered upon it, and I searched for the connections to the smaller mysteries of my own life that led me to this place surrounded by the water.

The water . . . it's where the dolphins are. It's where they chose to be. I tell myself this the first night of my fast.

But only the cricket sings softly near the circle drawn upon the sand.

In my thirst and hunger on the second day, I began to truly feel the power of the sun's heat. The great white orb moved so slowly across the sky that the day seemed a lifetime in itself. I'd watch the water. Sometimes it would dance in the sunlight; other times it would appear flat, like a mirror. It would reflect the sun's image as a great circle of white light set in glass. Occasionally a shark's fin would slice the flat surface of the sea and ripples would distort the image of the sun and remind me that I would still have to swim back when my ordeal was done.

As the mighty sun sank in the Gulf just beneath the place of sky where the evening star would appear, I saw its turquoise center. At first, I wondered if my eyes were simply straining too hard and that I was imagining this. But the image remained. It even became more prominent, taking the form of a turquoise nugget. And as night quickly came after the sun's departure, I laid myself across my mat and watched the other, more distant, stars appear.

Throughout my second night I tried not to fall asleep, keeping my focus on the stone and my purpose for being there. But the song of the cricket grew louder, until I began to fear it. The fear didn't take hold of me suddenly, but gradually, almost without me noticing. Then it was there. I held the small stone, but it didn't seem to comfort me the way it had. Nor did it any longer give me a sense of security. The second night was filled with fear, my fear. The third day was filled with my confusion.

By the third day, my lips were cracked and dry. My tongue was swollen. I imagined what it would be like just to touch the water to my lips, and I did this. Reaching beyond my circle but never leaving it, I cupped a bit of sea water at high tide and touched it to my lips. Only after I felt the wetness and coolness of the water did it burn. Now I wondered if I had not broken my fast. I tried rationalizing that not drinking the water had kept the quest alive.

As the sun sank that third day, I drifted away until I awoke
118 to the swish of waves on the florescent shore, under the last fainting
silver of a waning crescent moon.

That final night the singing of the cricket encompassed me.
I searched the perimeter of the circle, leaning as far out as I could,
and swept my hands as far as I could reach them, hoping to find the
cricket that had become the enemy, the menace of my time there,
and stop his incessant singing. I blamed the cricket for distracting
me, for not allowing me the chance to focus on my purpose. I
thought that the cricket was the cause of my having to be there so
long without a vision, for I'd heard and read about others who had
received a vision in much sooner a time than the four traditional
days assigned. I wanted to find that cricket and kill it if I could.

I left the circle in the deepest part of night, when even the
waning crescent moon had set in the sea. I searched frantically. I
hated that sound because it overwhelmed all other things that might
have been going on. Yet I was terrified of it too. What could make
such a sound? Had I offended the spirits of the place? Damn! I cried
again and again. I even smashed my fist into the sand. Still the
deafening sound of the cricket singing would not go away.

I did not sleep that night, but just before the still-silent dawn
of the fourth day the waves broke off shore like whispers, and I
heard the familiar cries of dolphins once more. Weakened from the
days I'd spent without food or water, I struggled to stand and I
swayed, gazing at the sea as they passed. And then, as though my
gaze was drawn down to the sand, I noticed the footprints all
around me. I saw the mess I had made during the night of my once
unbroken circle, and I fell defeated to my knees. Through my
anguish a slight sound came, like a lone chirp into the gentle dawn.
It was the cricket calling. This time it showed itself. Limping past
me, I could see that what had terrified me was a harmless creature
no bigger than my thumb.

Weakened and nearly broken I saw one more thing. Not in a vision. Not in a dream. . . .

Out from the sand rose a lonely loggerhead. She moved toward the shore a short distance away. I sat, like the stone on my turquoise mat in the broken circle, and watched her. And then she disappeared into the sea.

CHAPTER 13

CARRYING
MY MIND AROUND

"WAS THAT YOUR VISION, Dad?" I glanced up from the road at Calusa's pretty face looking at me through the rearview mirror. I especially loved her eyes. They grabbed me then. Wide with wonder, sparks glistening in their pools of blackness, flickers of light like spirits dancing, darkness as thick as the space between the stars.

Her father's recollection of his first vision quest had become the story of that particular drive. "No, Ca. I wasn't ready for a vision. . . . I hadn't dealt with my anger . . . nor my fear." Ihasha and Carises sat in the back seat of the Mustang, listening.

Simone let the hot wind blow through the open window against her face. There is an old Ojibway song that she likes to recite for me every now and again, and it was the one I was thinking about as we rode the 'stang across the John's Pass Bridge from Treasure Island to Madeira Beach. "My thoughts are so heavy," the song goes. . . . "It's as though I were carrying my mind around. . . . What's the matter with you?"

The words sing of simple aspects of the human condition, a condition that has sprung forth from the Great Holy Mystery since the first people. It's an expression shared by the ancients as well as the contemporaries. They are words that have, from time to time, adequately described the state of my own mind. It was such a state of mind that I carried on my first vision quest, and that I was carrying then, years later, as we headed up the John's Pass Bridge.

The bridge we were crossing did not link the past and the present. It was not a bridge in the old tradition, like so many of the old songs. It was probably because that fine thread that separates the past and the present that Uncle Nip used to talk about had once again disappeared. This bridge only links one tourist trap to the next. Conquistadors and developers, Spaniards and Americans. What's the difference?

The bridge is lined with scores of tourists who seem to live only for the here and now. They're part of that "me first" generation, that "me first" mentality that many Americans misconstrue to be "personal freedom." They have no concept of a future beyond what's in it for them. They have no concept of a Seventh Generation, of keeping in mind not only the present but the future generations — generations who may never see a dolphin breach or a pelican dive.

These tourists hang their fishing poles and casting nets over the iron railings in large numbers to take what they can from life now, for themselves. Swarms of sea gulls torment them, hovering above them and their lines and their nets. The gulls excrete in their excitement on the iron plates and pavement of the bridge and on the windows of the tourists' cars that pass over it.

A fisherman swats at one with his pole. Another curses them. They even curse the presence of brown pelicans. These great birds perch precariously on sagging power lines, waiting for a trout dropped from a hook, a castaway tossed over the side, a flounder snagged on the metal railing that the fishermen rest their rods upon. Occasionally, pelicans will risk navigating their huge wingspans between the power lines and suddenly dive. When they emerge, they float upon the surface of the emerald water, shaking their tail feathers, working with a catch. Or they will quickly rise again and dive again — each plunge between the lines as dangerous as the next. Too often, though, the fish they catch carry in their mouths a fisherman's hook and line. Beneath the bridge power boats, hauling more fishing tourists out to sea, speed out into the Gulf or into the bay. They occasionally smash into a hooked pelican or even slash into desperate manatees or dolphins that have strayed too close to humans, their sonar confused by the onslaught of engine vibrations.

We ride the Mustang down the John's Pass Bridge into the concrete canyon of Madeira Beach. On the black-topped road dividing condominiums and tourist shops, I search for a place to pull over. Everywhere there are parking meters. The heat from the asphalt is stifling. The sea breezes are cut off by the buildings. "It was never this hot in April," I tell the children. "That's why they built a nuclear reactor just north of here — for their air-conditioning. And radioactive waste leaks into the air and water. You can't see radiation, kids. So people tend to think that if they can't see it, then it's all right because they need the reactor to keep them cool."

"You should write a book about that some day, Dad," Ihasha suggests.

Maybe I will, I think to myself. Though I don't know much about the scientific aspect of nuclear reactors, I can write about how primitive people only take what they need from their environment. How they adapt to their surroundings rather than alter them to suit their own needs, or worse, their own wants and desires. How it would prove wrong to profit from that energy which belonged to the stars. "Maybe I will, Ihasha . . . maybe I will."

Ihasha says that he saw on TV how some scientists were trying to find ways to color the different kinds of toxic waste leaking from nuclear plants. "All that'll do," I say, "is show people the poison that's going to kill them. I suppose that way they'll know how they're likely to die from it . . . and how long and painful the death will be."

Calusa says that she read in a book how crabs have been found with three claws and that strange-looking fish have begun to appear: some with two heads, some with two tails, some with no tails, some with one eye, some with no eyes.

Carises says nothing. He only stares out the Mustang's open windows from between the bucket seats. The hot wind blows against his face too.

Though I try, I can't conceal the way I feel about things, and I wonder how this affects the children. I can't hide my disgust. The first Europeans who came to this land had no respect for it. This is no secret. They came to take what they could for themselves. Most of what I see screams or cries out this truth to me. Now they come as tourists who have traveled here for more contemporary reasons: to escape the lives they live in crowded northern cities, to break out of their citified office boxes, to escape the industrial air, to seek the picture-postcard scenes that developers have replaced with huge hotels and massive arrays of condominiums. They don't even know that the palms they see in the travel magazines are not the native sabals that once lined the beaches. Like most of the native people, the native plants of Florida have been replaced with other species from other parts of the world. The impact has been devastating. Exotic plants have done to the native ones what the transplant Americans have done to the native people of this land. Native plants and trees don't do so well in parking lots and De Bartollo malls. Parking lots are now usually decorated with exotics from Burma and India. Malls are usually done in plastic. They don't even realize the bright yellow sun in the pictures of the travel magazines is a hot, intense tropical sun, and it drives these human visitors from the cold

124

of the north into air-conditioned condos and malls. They cannot take the heat of the real thing.

Ihasha wonders why they don't use solar energy.

Carises wonders why they just don't leave.

I have to pause. . . . Again, a father must weigh his influence on his children. But they have their own minds. They can see for themselves. Besides, they know I love them. They know I love the land. Then let them know me!

"The oil barons who control the oil, Ihasha, and the business tycoons who control the power companies also control politics. And the money they make and the material things they accumulate usually controls them all. The oil barons discourage the development of alternative energy, like wind and sun, because of money. And as long as they've got the money, they can hire the votes and the guns to get the oil and keep their power. Until they can figure out how to make big bucks off the sun, they'll never change.

"Developers are the worst. . . . They don't care about the land. They don't care about the animals or the eagles or the dolphins or what impact their condos or malls will have on any of us. They care about making money.

"And the more developments, the more malls, the more condos, the greater need for electricity, because by now they've created an intolerable environment, too much like the one they wanted to escape from with too many people. It's almost as though a gene in our species somehow mutated and has made civilized humans like a cancer on the body of the earth. Wherever their civilization goes, it consumes what is good and beneficial on the body of the earth."

"The men who own the oil company we use," adds Simone, "also own the nuclear power plant just north of here. They can't support the development and research of solar energy because they haven't figured out a way to own the sun."

I glance into the rearview mirror once again. Calusa is no longer visible. Instead, I see only the face of Carises, his coal-black 125 eyes scanning the sidewalks and parking lots. His question about why they don't just leave is a haunting one. It's one I've asked myself. "They don't leave, Carises, because they think everything's been put here for them. They don't really consider how they affect other life forms. They consider only themselves. I don't know how to change how they think except by doing what each of us can do to teach them and to live as close to The Way as we can, taking only what we need. I don't believe our people knew how to change them, which is probably why we fought them so hard. But what we do know about cancer is that once it consumes all that is good and beneficial to the living body, it too will die. Radiation kills cancer. With a hole in the ozone over North America, maybe that's how they'll die."

I wonder what else my youngest son is thinking. I wonder too if I, as a father, had not just inflicted upon my children my own disgust for what civilization has done to this land. Maybe I'm too negative. Oh hell, I say to myself. They can read the orations of Red Jacket, Metacomet, Tecumtha, Geronimo, and the rest. They all saw the same thing, the destruction of what the Native American knew was beautiful. Maybe I should concentrate on what's still beautiful. This I remind myself. That's why I came here, to the water, to feel the beauty of this place again, to show the children where I fasted for my vision. It feels like I've been carryin' my mind around for so long. . . .

I drive slowly in the right lane while rental cars in the left whiz past with tinted windows closed tight. I don't want to stop. I can't stop. It's too hot to stop. But then I point out the window. "Over there . . . over there!"

I find a niche, turn off the engine, and open the door. "Pines used to line this shore," I say, standing in the blazing sun. Simone steps out with the children behind her. She already knows this. I brought her here before the kids were born, when the tiny barrier island could still be seen from Madeira Beach, and she could see the island Where-The-Great-Turtles-Nest, as I knew it then — before the last hurricane hit and the last wave of civilization was just washin' in. And I told her the whole Wind River story that drove me here and compelled me to seek the vision then.

I told her about the phone call from Uncle Nip urging me to leave and about the night a zealous group of red and white cowboy patriots from the Riverton VFW drove onto the reservation, the headlights of their pickup trucks bursting the darkness around the trailer I rented for fifty dollars a month. Indian and white legionnaires jumped out, wielding clubs, or hung out the windows of their cabs aiming guns. That's how my teacher-friend, John Parks, described it. He said he was heading back to Riverton where he lived when he decided to take the long way into town, down through the reservation. He said it was late, about midnight. He said that he saw a lot of lights down at my place. Knowing I wasn't home, he pulled over not far away. With a good view of my front door, he cut the engine of his pickup and switched off the lights. E's barking was the first thing he heard.

"Come on out you commie bastard!" one of the legionnaires yelled. He was pounding a baseball bat against the aluminum trailer door. John said the man's VFW cap had covered a flat top, Fifties crew cut that made his head appear square when the hat bounced off during one of his bashings. John said that you could hear the fury in E's bark.

A 306 semi-automatic protruded from one of the trucks.

"A hundred bucks for your braids!" they laughed.

"Come out you AIM fuck!"

WIND RIVER

W HAT SEEMS NOW like an assault against me at Wind
River started the warm September day when I arrived
there back in 1973. It was as if the oppressive spirit of the white
man that had controlled the People for so long was being threatened by the movement that was taking place within the spirit of
the People then. In a small way I was a catalyst in that movement
because I was a teacher of the People.

I was anxious to get settled in, and reported for work about
a week early. Lack of accommodations on the reservation for my
Cherokee wife Linda and me forced us to spend our first night in
a motel in Riverton, Wyoming, a small city located on the Wind
River Reservation border. Riverton was populated mostly by motel
owners, cowboys, ranchers, bankers, developers of one kind or
another, and oil men. Since Linda and I had only been married for
a few months, we thought that our stay in a motel could have
even felt like a honeymoon of sorts. But things aren't that simple
when you're an Indian sometimes, especially an Indian with
braids back in the early Seventies.

128

Our first night in Riverton was a night of terror, for a car crashed through the wall and window of our motel room when we were just drifting off to sleep. I heard a car racing down the main drag of town and then the screeching tires. Suddenly, I heard a loud thump when the car hit the high medium dividing the road. Then there was silence as the car left the ground. I opened my eyes as the window of our motel room exploded with light. The impact was terrifying. The car stopped halfway through the room, sending chunks of cinder block and shattered glass everywhere before bursting into flames. I could barely see the head of the driver through the smoke. I could see he still had his cowboy hat on. I remember not caring if he burned in the wreckage.

My dog E was nearly killed, and my butt was severely lacerated. Had I been sleeping turned the other way, I would not have kids today. Fortunately, Linda didn't suffer any physical injury, though I'm sure that even now she doesn't sleep in first-floor motel rooms that border a street. She did manage to grab two sheets in the heat of things, and we were able to wrap them around our nakedness before the crowd gathered outside. As the motel room burst into flames, I struggled with E in my arms to wrench the door open and make our escape. I pleaded for someone in the gathering horde outside the room to take my dog, but no one would. They just stood and stared. When I weakened and fell against the door onto my blood-soaked sheet, E took off, and I spent two days searching for him after I got out of the hospital.

Though everything we owned was destroyed, including our money, I was billed for the motel accommodations and medical expenses. The Riverton paper pictured the scene on the front page the next day, and people sent me notes that were usually scrawled on the newspaper clipping. The messages welcomed my AIM ass to Wyoming. I couldn't help but wonder if that cowboy hadn't intentionally done that to us. I'd be surprised if it truly was a "freak accident," and I'd be a little relieved too because that would mean that such strange things just happen to people and that maybe my tendency toward self-importance sometimes still leads me to occasional slips into paranoia. I do know one thing for certain. I couldn't get a lawyer to help me. For no local lawyer was willing to risk his practice to help Indians then, and helping me get restitution for some of what Linda and I had lost in that "freak accident" would have been a professional risk. The explosion into our motel room my first night at Wind River proved one thing for sure: It was a sign that things could get ugly around there.

I was young and determined, though, and remained to become a teacher of the People; that is, until death threats became apparent, and the time became imminent. This was shortly after the books I taught from at the school were confiscated, and I was fired and banned from teaching, and the legionnaires came calling. My dismissal came right before my rented trailer burned to the ground. Those incidents were, more or less, the end of it, though Linda leaving me for a Shoshone man who called himself an AIM friend was probably the final torch to any ideals I may have had lingering on.

When my AIM friend would stop by the trailer to visit, I could vaguely hear my inner voice trying to tell me something, but I didn't want to really hear it, so I wouldn't listen to it. When I felt like I had had enough, I had my fateful talk with Uncle Nip on the telephone. I told him about making my "last stand" there, and he told me instead to "get out or die in a ditch." A couple of years later when the body of an Indian teacher and AIM activist, Anna Mae Aquash, was found in a ditch alongside a lonely South Dakota road, I understood more of what Uncle Nip was talking about.

My problems as a teacher began almost the day I officially arrived on the reservation to teach. When the white school director phoned me before I'd left Florida and informed me that I had to sign

130

a loyalty oath that the state of Wyoming required for new teaching certificates, I told him no. I told him that my loyalty lies with my people and to the land, not to a flag, not to the state of Wyoming, and certainly not to the United States. It was one of those things, however, that Uncle Nip would have strongly advised me to do. He would have said that signing such an oath was supporting the treaty rights of the People, that the Constitution states that treaty rights are "the supreme law of the land." Uncle Nip told me that signing the document to become certified to teach was one of those compromises in life that I would have to learn to make if I was to be a teacher of the People. Someone spared me that decision, however, and forged my name to the oath. Whomever it was, it was obviously someone who wanted me to teach at Wyoming Indian High School.

When I first arrived at the school, I was sort of blissed out at the idea of teaching my people and finally fulfilling what I had worked so hard in college to accomplish, and I didn't consider that the shadows I saw as a child on the island where I rode the door had now become the shadows of my own people. For as soon as I got to Wind River, I learned that the white school director who had hired me, and who was enthusiastic about having a certified Indian teacher on the faculty, was no longer there. And within a few weeks of living on the reservation and teaching at the high school, I started hearing through secondhand sources how some of the local Indians were making jokes about my hair. They cracked about cutting my braids off for a quarter a piece, though they never said so in my presence. For even on an Indian reservation back in the early Seventies, long hair, especially braided, was a sign of militancy and nonconformity. It was a sign of not letting go of the past.

The local Christians, Indian and white, called me an "outside agitator." They must have felt that people like me, with braids, a college education, and a semblance of Indian identity, were dangerous and would cause trouble. "He's gonna be a bad influence on the youth."

From their point of view, maybe they were right. My first official act as a teacher was to order books written by Indians or books written about Indians that were honest and treated the People with dignity. I ordered novels like *House Made of Dawn* and *The Way to Rainy Mountain*, Indian anthologies like *Literature of the American Indian*, autobiographies like *Black Elk Speaks* and *Lame Deer — Seeker of Visions*, and history books, like *Bury My Heart at Wounded Knee*. I figured that the best way to teach Indians to read was by giving them back the knowledge they'd been denied. The best way to teach them to think was to have them write about such things. And it worked.

In the beginning, and really all through the six months that we had classes together, there were some interesting times. Like when I first taught about the differences between the Judeo-Christian concept of God and the Native American concept of the Great Mystery. How else was I to begin an Indian literature class than the way I had learned? You see, I had come across something so good in my learning experience and had worked so hard to get into a position where I could share it that I guess I never really considered all the ramifications and repercussions of doing so. Besides, where else could I begin teaching the literature of the People without starting at the beginning itself, the Creation Accounts? In short, I did for my Indian students what Uncle Nip had done for me: I helped to give them the words that helped describe and explain the feelings that were Indian.

I wrote the word "god" on the board and defined it according to the dictionary that was available. "A god," I explained to my eleventh- and twelfth-grade Arapaho and Shoshone students, "has to have at least two characteristics in order to be a god: it must be supernatural and it must be immortal. The word itself is a generic term. Flower, for example, is a generic term like god. There are many flowers. And, according to Judeo-Christian beliefs, by definition, there are also many gods. God lacked the power to kill Lucifer because Lucifer was immortal, so God threw him out of heaven. It says so in the Bible." Then I'd write roses, daisies, lilies, and violets on the board. "What the Christians did was capitalize the letter G," and I'd cross out the small letter g, "and say there is only one and He is ours. That would be like saying that there are no more roses or daisies or lilies or violets, there is just one Flower," and I'd capitalize the F real big. I'd say, "Sorry, there are no more elms or maples or cedars or sabals, there is just Tree.

"The Judeo-Christian names for the First Cause are Elohim, Yahweh, and Jehovah; at least, those are the ones I know of. They're Hebrew names . . . Jewish names. From what I've heard, the true name of God was lost, but I'm not certain of that. Whatever the case, none of those names are Native American."

I'd then explain about how Native Americans, at the time the first white people came to this country, were every bit as monotheistic as our Judeo-Christian brothers. "It's just that your ancestors' concept of a First Cause was far more abstract than a man-like being who lived in heaven. Your people's concept of a First Cause was one of totality, that everything was a part of the whole.

"Imagine," I said, "that the moon exploded. And after that initial explosion others followed; each time more parts of the moon would shatter and disperse. Wouldn't all those parts, no matter how small or distant they were, still be a part of the moon? Well, that's the way your ancestors understood about something they called the Great Mystery. They didn't assign a sex to the Mystery either, like male or female. The sexual manifestations of the Mystery would be something like Father Sky and Mother Earth. Or Grandfather Sun and Grandmother Moon."

Then I'd go on and explain how the blood of the Indian flowed through the female's lines, but how the churches and government reversed that because their idea of a First Cause was a white man.

What really stirred things up on the reservation, though, was when I asked the students to go home and see if they could return to class with the original Arapaho and Shoshone names for the Great Mystery, or First Cause. And a few did. And there was a connection made then between the young and the old.

I have to laugh at the times when my students would confront the Mormons who consistently descended on the reservation seeking converts. An Arapaho girl asked the two Mormon missionaries what the name of their God was. When the Mormons shrugged their shoulders together and answered "God," a Shoshone boy explained that God is not a name. "God is a term," the young Shoshone said. I couldn't help but gloat and feel somewhat confident that what I was teaching was working to restore identity as well as basic academic skills.

Besides teaching literature and writing, I also taught mass media, which included publishing the school's newspaper, *Tribe Talk*. Our first issue blasted Columbus Day!

However, I think my most influential teaching, and the one that got me into the most trouble with the establishment, came in speech and drama. We started the Wyoming Indian High School Theatre. Both major performances that year were done before a standing-room-only crowd in the high school gym. We did skits on reservation life that were not only funny, but politically potent. We made the old people laugh and the Bureau of Indian Affairs cronies stew in their front-row hard-back metal chairs. We used terms in the performances like the Great Mystery and Mother Earth, and it must have terrified the BIA and tribal councils then. Their ideas and the ideas of progressive Indians till this day are to take what we can from the earth for profit. That means it's okay to violate her body

134   by drilling into her for oil and raping her for strip-mining projects. How can we call ourselves Indians, Native Americans, Arapahoes, or Shoshones if we no longer see ourselves as a part of this creation and no longer regard the earth as our mother? Yeah, these ideas surely must've been frightening for the progressive minds of government and private enterprise.

A lot happened in the seven or eight months that I taught at Wyoming Indian High School. I went to a lot of funerals, and I think that's what got to me most of all — the dying. Every weekend someone died in a car wreck or someone hung himself or someone blew his head off. I couldn't take the dying, and I think that some of me died a little each time a young Indian was put into a cold grave, for so many times, they were students I'd had in class just yesterday. Living at Wind River made me quit alcohol altogether for a while. Maybe Benjamin Franklin was on to something sick when he suggested that rum would be the best means to "extirpate the savages." And though I will occasionally have a drink and even indulge a bit now and again, I am careful, for I've seen some of the ways that alcohol can kill.

When my teaching certificate finally arrived, the new school director, a round and short, dark-skinned Indian in his late thirties who drank too much and had dark shifty eyes, made it clear he didn't want me teaching there. I posted the certificate on the school bulletin board with an AIM arrow painted through it. I was telling him and my white and Christian Shoshone teacher colleagues that I had had enough of their snobbery that excluded me from faculty meetings because I wasn't as qualified as they were in the eyes of the state to teach. I was saying to them all that I was fed up with their unsigned notes they'd stick in my school mailbox calling me "an eastern nigger" and "a satan worshiper" and "a communist" and "an outside agitator." My act of protest on behalf of my students carried a different meaning: "Hey," I was saying to them, "I did it. I got my degree and returned to help our people, and I didn't sacrifice my identity. You can do it too. You can do it and still remain an Indian. You don't have to become a white man to get a college degree."

▲ ▲ ▲

When Vince Lonewolf conducted a sweat lodge for me right after the Christmas break, he gave me something I've treasured all my life, my first sweat lodge experience, and one of the best sweat ceremonies I have ever participated in.

Some of the young Arapahoes and Shoshones, who were my students, had traveled into the hills to gather the wood so Vince could heat the rocks. They would only take the dead wood that the Wind River range provided. And they gathered much wood, for there were many rocks. Some of the old stones were jagged and much larger than a man's hand; others were smaller and rounder. They were all dark and heavy.

The women and girls did their part too. Like the Sky and the Earth, sex roles among the People are varied but equal. The women and girls who prepared the feast after the ceremony were as much respected for their role in the ceremony as the men and boys who gathered the wood, made the fire, and heated the stones. If there was anyone looking for something to do, he or she helped lay the blankets, sleeping bags, canvas, and hides over the beehive-shaped lodge. The lodge itself was bigger than any sweat lodge I've ever been in. Inside, layers of sweet sage carpeted the dirt floor; I would swear throughout my life that nothing ever smelled as wonderful as the inside of that lodge. Later on, during the ceremony itself, I dug my fingers through that thick carpet of sweet sage to feel even a hint of coolness and moisture from the earth.

The people crawled through the flap and moved to the left, sunwise, mostly naked, men and women, young and old, greeting the grandfather stones in the center as they entered. I stood outside, my turquoise towel wrapped around my waist. I had never been in a sweat lodge ceremony, and I didn't know some of the people who were there. That made me uncomfortable. And I guess I was scared.

So, I alone remained outside the lodge contemplating: I knew that the sweat lodge ceremony was an offering — a purification in the old tradition. I knew that if I was to walk the path of heart, that I would need such ceremonies along the way. I knew that such ceremonies belonged to the People and that their practices go back to antiquity. As I stood outside Lonewolf's lodge, though, I must admit that I wanted to leave . . . just get the hell out of there. After all, I reasoned, Uncle Nip and I used to sit in the Florida sun for long periods of time; we sweated that way. We didn't need a sweat lodge. There was no hot tropical sun in Wyoming, however, especially in winter, and I needed the purification. I felt too alone, and I was beginning to think that what the Christian Indians were saying about me was true. I was feeling like I had no purpose or place in the world.

Yet I remained there because of my love and respect for Vince Lonewolf, and because he let everyone know that he was holding this particular ceremony for me.

Everything I believed in seemed tested that wintry day. My religious ideas were surely being tested. I wasn't in a classroom now, reading ceremonial songs as poetry from our anthology. I was practicing the beliefs that inspired the songs and became the literature. I can remember standing almost naked outside the lodge in the cold thinking how easy it would be if I were a Christian. All I would have to do is sit in a church pew and pray. I could say Hail Marys and Our Fathers and that would do. No pain. That's how the Shadow People taught me.

But I was Indian, not Christian.

Outside Lonewolf's sweat lodge that day, I knew that if I was to continue to serve Mother Earth and the people and walk the Way that Uncle Nip had instructed, I would need the purification rituals and the prayers and the power that one shares and discovers in the sweat lodge.

Before the ceremony began, Vince asked me to sit by him. Vince was an elder with several beautiful children and a lovely Arapaho wife. Many residents at Wind River called him a medicine man. To sit by his side during such a ceremony was an honor. Vince befriended me because I stayed with his son once when the boy had been injured playing football after school one day. After he assured his teammates that he was okay, the young boy's knee buckled under him, and he fell getting on his bike. It was early autumn and I didn't know many people on the reservation. I stopped to help the boy, though, as I figured anyone would. But it was not so. The other teachers didn't seem concerned. Even the football coach had left for home without checking on his injured player. No one did. They left him on the ground. He was probably just an Indian to them. A student. Someone they weren't getting overtime to care for.

To me, leaving the boy stranded there at the bike rack was like reading how people in New York City step over the body of someone lying in the street without trying to help. Only this wasn't a big city. This was Wind River, an Indian reservation. What were Indian kids to these people? A paycheck? A place to teach because they weren't fit to teach anyplace else? For some of them I know that Indians were nothing more than a way to make a living in a world where otherwise they couldn't. They didn't know anything about Arapahoes or Shoshones. They didn't know anything about Indians. They never thought enough of the People to try and learn something either. They didn't even know how to say hello or greet someone in a native language. They didn't know the Indian history, their literature, their customs, their beliefs, their treaty rights — especially that. After school the Indian students became faceless beings to them as the teachers headed back to their houses in Riverton or nearby Lander.

I didn't know then, but that teenage boy who I managed to bring to the clinic that day was the son of a medicine man and one of the most respected Arapaho traditionals on the reservation. Doing this ceremony for me may have been Vince Lonewolf's way of giving notice to all that he supported this teacher, the one who cared for his son.

Vince understood youth too. I'm sure knowing what he did about Indian life, that he must have seen the fire that burned in me. Maybe looking at me was sometimes like looking back at himself. Vince recognized the link that I was or could be to the past, to the present, to the future. He recognized his own place and purpose in it all. He recognized the thread that separates the dream from the vision, the past from the present. He would temper the fire burning in me through the heat of those red hot stones because he didn't want that fire to burn out of control. And that could certainly happen to a young man like me. So, Vince would help weave a piece of the thread back into my life and help keep me whole.

Though the lodge door was still open, I could only imagine that to close it would mean the terror that comes from feeling totally cut off from what is familiar, and of course the pain from the heat and the strangeness of total darkness. If I remained outside the lodge, they would talk. They would say how those Indians from the South aren't tough. They would say that I was afraid.

And I felt my white blood at war with my Indian blood. I didn't want my Indian blood to lose.

When I crawled inside and took my place next to Vince, it felt like parts of my skin would slip away. Vince passed me a copper cup of spring water. I sipped it. Never had water tasted so cool and sweet. I could feel its entire journey toward my center. Nothing had ever tasted or felt so precious as the water from the copper cup that day. No doubt it is these kinds of rituals that remind our people how dependent we all are and how well-provided for we are in this life by the earth. Water. It is renewal. The copper cup traveled sunwise, and each person who crowded into the lodge that day sipped its life force.

When the door of the lodge closed, it was so dark that I could see nothing, even with my eyes opened. I felt as though I was a ghost or even a spirit, yet my body could feel the pain from the heat. And when I heard the crackle and hiss of the rocks as Vince poured the icy cold water over them, I thought that maybe I would die.

The heat exploded around me. It was more sudden and powerful in that way than the heat of the Florida sun at midday in the summer. The burning heat of the grandfather stones enveloped me and I prayed. As the poisons poured from my body and mind, my thoughts became silent words; the words became silent prayers: 'What is it that makes you Indian? Why do you feel the way you do about things? Why does anyone care for you? Why do you feel like you're failing? Where do you belong? What's the matter with you?' It was as if all I could see in my mind and feel with my heart was the pain of my life. It almost equaled the pain I was feeling from the intense heat of the grandfather stones. Almost.

Vince moved his hand along his side in the darkness until he located his turtle shell rattle. He picked it up and shook it rhythmically, then began singing in Arapaho; some of the men and women joined in the song. The sound of the rattle and the voices of the people filled the lodge. Though I didn't know the words, I sang too. Then the rattling and singing stopped, and the hissing steam exploded once again from the stones as Vince poured the icy water from the copper cup over them. I felt the depth of the heat in a fiery wet wind as Vince fanned me with an eagle's wing and spoke Arapaho words for my well-being. And all the while I felt as though I was peeling away, layer by layer. Snakes and cicadas and butterflies shed their skins and their shells and their superficial injuries go with them; so this is how humans do it. This is purification!

140

During that first round, others prayed aloud. One man started rambling about Jesus. How can he pray to Jesus in here? I wondered. By the third round, that man was gone. By the fifth, only a few of us remained. By the seventh round, there were three: Vince, Jimmy Lodge, and me. I was in strong company. Jimmy was one of the real AIM leaders on the reservation. That winter he had to bury his older brother who killed himself by blowing his head off with a shotgun. I wondered if other people can imagine how much Indians can hate the white man's world. When the door flap opened for the last time I saw Jimmy Lodge across from me. The hot mist swirled around us. He sat cross-legged, wet from sweat and glistening, his green eyes watching the fading glow of the old stones. Vince passed the copper cup of pure water, and it was shared by the three of us one last time. With each sip, I felt the life gifts of water and friendship pass through my heart and touch my center.

When I crawled out the door, it was like emerging from a womb in Mother Earth. I felt reborn. And as I stood outside the lodge in the icy cold air with Vince and Jimmy and with white steam from our bare bodies rising from us like clouds, I could see oil rigs in the distance pumping up and down and newer ones getting installed, and I could see the new government housing being constructed not far from the ridge where Vince had his sweat lodge. I could see the beams for the roof on the new school building being put into place by a crane, and I could see at least three different churches alongside the road below, where cars moved along like ants on the back of an asphalt snake whose many heads dwelled in the new BIA office building at Washakie. With just the three of us standing naked up there on the distant hill, it felt like we were at the center of the world. And it was good to feel that I was not alone. I felt like I did that day long ago when I rode the door out to the island and the dolphins gathered around me and helped me feel good about myself; Vince Lonewolf and Jimmy Lodge helped in the same way.

▲▲▲

Soon after the Christmas break, lots of things seemed to happen. First, there was the incident when I didn't allow the Riverton police to arrest an Indian student at school one day. I told them that federal law did not grant state or city police that type of jurisdiction on reservation land. Then, when I was returning from Cheyenne after a speaking engagement at the University of Wyoming, two of those same police blocked my entrance onto the reservation and arrested me for careless driving. It took all the money I had and could borrow to bail me out, but staying in jail in Riverton would have been far worse for me.

And there were the occasional verbal incidents with other teachers. I'd overhear them saying how unpleasant it was teaching Indians, and I would confront them. It was over something said like that, that I resorted to calling the new football coach a racist asshole in front of the Post Office where everyone on the Arapaho side of the reservation did their business, and could hear. I guess I was still harboring bad feelings too about the way he left Vince Lonewolf's son. I also called the school director an "apple" because he told me not to teach history and literature from the books I was using. He said that I was teaching hate and mumbled about me being a southern nigger.

At forty-four I can look back now and see that the shadows I saw then were not nearly quite as big as I imagined them to be. Though that, of course, is relevant to the moment of the experience . . . sort of like the cricket on my vision quest would show me. The bright hope of light among the shadows came from the Indian students at the school, and from men like Vince Lonewolf.

But the day some of the Wyoming Indian High School students turned the American flag upside down at the Post Office in Ethete was the day the spirit of oppression asserted itself with force.

That single act of "flag desecration" was all the proof the BIA and the flag-waving patriots of red or white persuasion needed. Whether the Indian students did it as a political act or as a prank, it didn't matter; it became a political act just the same, and it would be stated as such in an official school board letter posting the charges against me on the door of my rented trailer. The charge stated that the Indian students acted as a direct result of the hate and militancy that I had taught them.

Along with that indictment, I was written up for insubordination. That had to be the time I called the school director an apple and the football coach, who was also the history teacher, a racist asshole.

I was also written up for leaving school grounds without permission. That must have been the time when John Parks, the students, some AIM guys, and I borrowed the drivers' education car and went to Cheyenne and walked into the office of the governor of Wyoming and demanded that a traffic light be installed at the crossroads by the school. Since the tribal council failed to act, we did. "There have been many accidents at that crossroads," we told him. "Just that weekend a semi-truck, speeding like they always do through that section, killed a horse." The governor assured us that he was sorry he hadn't acted on the tribal council's request. He said that the money wasn't there, but that he figured he could find it somewhere. He also offered us a herd of buffalo.

Two weeks later the traffic light was installed. It was a real fancy one with push-button walk signs. And Jimmy Lodge was making arrangements for a herd of buffalo.

The school board and federal officials were not impressed. They also charged me with locking BIA evaluators out of my classroom, which was simply not true. They said that I nearly cost the school its federal funding for the next year. I explained to the director right after the incident that I would have really liked it if the BIA had come into my class and seen where the only certified Indian teacher there was forced to teach. I told him if they had come into my class, they would've seen how good it was to be Indian and how important it was to teach the white man's ways of reading and writing but to do it through the beauty, power, and truthfulness of the People's words. I would have liked that. And though they visited all the other classrooms that day, the BIA evaluators never did come out to the shop area and mechanics classroom where I taught Indian literature and history while John Parks was teaching shop and auto repair. The school's director steered the BIA clear of me.

John later described what went down the night of the closed school board meeting. Because he was the auto repair teacher, John had managed to get the keys that would allow him access to the meeting that night by saying he had to work late on someone's car. He stayed inside the school and overheard the meeting between the new Indian school board, the school director, and BIA officials. John told me that the BIA offered to fund the school entirely the following year, and to finish the construction of the new building on one condition: Gabriel Horn must not teach there again.

I didn't see my trailer burning in the night because I was on my way back to Florida, as Uncle Nip had told me I should if I wanted to live a long-enough life to fulfill some of its purpose. I heard by way of the moccasin telegraph that there had been a party at the trailer just after I left and that there was a lot of drinking and that's how it burned down. I also heard that the VFW legionnaires had returned to "punish me" for the upside-down flag incident and, not finding me home, they burned down the trailer.

But another way I heard the story told — the one that I liked the most — was that some of my students, the same ones who turned the flag upside down, were the ones who really burned the trailer down. The students said they did it so no one else would live there; they said no one else could take my place.

CHAPTER 15

IN THE BEGINNING . . .

A FTER WIND RIVER and the long, hot summer that followed on the shore of the Gulf of Mexico, I headed for the
place where AIM was born, Minneapolis, Minnesota. Though I
had sought a vision in the old way on the Gulf Coast of Florida,
I did not receive one. I did manage to gain a stronger sense of purpose though. So when the chance came for me to head up to Minneapolis and become directly involved with the American Indian
Movement, I took it. I figured that if I was going to be allowed to
teach my people anywhere, then it would have to be in the newly
founded AIM Survival School, Heart of the Earth.

I taught there for nearly two years when I met someone
who would become part of the rest of my life. I met Simone. Ironically, she would tell me later how, when she was just a young girl,
the native leaders of the American Indian community would often
gather over hot coffee in her mom's kitchen in Minneapolis, and
that it was there, in her mom's kitchen, that the idea for AIM was
conceived and the movement was born.

Some things are not coincidence.

How does one describe the love of a lifetime?

In the beginning there was everything. There were the strong times of intense passion between two lovers. There were the peaceful moments of ceremony and prayer that we shared with the people of The Way. There were nights of quiet thought on the starry shores of Hidden Beach, and autumn afternoons in the colored leaves on the banks of the wide Mississippi. There were feasts and drumming with the children and the old ones. There was the joy of marriages and names for new lives. There was the pain and the anguish spent over the graves of friends and in circles of families when death came, unexpected and violent. There were political incidents of tremendous stress and times when the needs of the People came first. There were the ghost dance dreams and the ceremonies among the ghosts. And there were the ancestors and the star people who guided us along The Way.

And always, there was the Pipe.

Leaning over the railing of the second-floor balcony of the Indian Center, I watched the young Indian woman with long, crow-black hair and listened to the singing syllables that gave meaning to my world. Her voice carried up to the great cedar rafters of the Center like a loon's call rising in morning mists over the water; the words floated into my heart. She was speaking to people who came to tour the Indian Center and who came to hear about something they had wanted to believe still existed in this world. She introduced them to life as the Indian artist sees it, through art and color and symbols and dreams.

Her knowledge reached past her nineteen years as she spoke; her hair reached down her back. It fell, long and luxurious, to the curve of her waist. . . . I listened to her words, but I could not take my eyes from her hair, her silky, crow-black hair that parted across one shoulder and over her breast.

Though I saw her as the Ojibway beauty she was, I made no advances toward her. Maybe I didn't want to ruin what already felt good to me. Maybe some kind of spirit-knowing through the destiny of our meeting would allow me the patience to wait for her mother Elaine to introduce us. Or maybe I was so taken by her that just to watch and to listen to her was enough for me; I desired nothing more. So I watched her and was content to follow her tours at the Center each day from my position on the second floor, listening.

One morning I was sitting at a desk in the library of the Indian Center, and she walked in with her mother. Elaine introduced us and left.

I watched her eyes glance at my braids brushing against the black printed words before me. As I struggled to see through the darkness of their meaning and contemplated the magnitude of the event that the words described, she came over. As if drawn to the same spot, Simone stood on one side of me, scanning the newspaper I had been reading. We studied it quietly together, focusing on the latest Viking pictures of Mars and the crimson rock and desert and the orange horizon of another new world.

I told her that it was no coincidence the spacecraft that landed on Mars was called the Viking. "It's history repeating itself," I said. "They'll do to that world what they did to this one, and their new spaceships will still reflect their old wooden-ships mentality."

She sat next to me. "You made me nervous when I gave my tours," she said. "I thought that if I were to say something wrong you'd be down for sure from your second-balcony perch to tell me that I didn't know what I was talking about, but you didn't do that."

I moved the newspaper that pictured Mars toward her. "I liked hearing your voice . . . that's why I stayed up there . . . to listen. I'm sorry. I didn't realize I was making you uncomfortable. I just enjoyed listening to you." Then I considered how insensitive I was and apologized again.

When our eyes embraced for the first time, there was that pause that comes when the eyes do speak. It was as if we were meeting again.

We had lunch at the Dairy Queen that first day of September, 1975, and talked about books. I never met an Indian woman who read as much as Simone did. She told me about the times she used to skip school at Holy Rosary and hide in her grandma's garage, reading books. We both laughed when she described how the nuns would warn her mother that this was a dangerous sign.

I discovered I was nearly ten years older than she was. I had just turned twenty-nine that summer; she was nineteen.

Every day I woke up wanting to see her. She told me later on that she had felt the same. She said that she didn't really want that feeling in her life. I said that I had reached the same place.

After Linda and I went our separate ways, I didn't date for a while. It took some time before I wanted to go out with anyone, and when I did ask a woman out it was probably because in some way she reminded me of Linda. Then, after a year had passed, I had a dream about her, and in the dream I severed any ties left from that relationship. It was that simple. In the dream I actually remember cutting the threads away, freeing myself from the web I had been entangled in. When I woke from that dream I was free of my love for Linda. It was that simple, yes, but it took me a year to prepare for such a dream.

The Indian women I began meeting and dating in Minnesota were beautiful women, and they were usually sensitive and smart and passionate. But after unhappy endings to our relationships, I became a recluse of a kind. I figured that I was married, more or less, to the pipe and that my destiny would be fulfilled without a mate or children. I also came to realize that broken hearts were as painful to give as to receive, and that dating me would no doubt lead to one or the other. Yet, from nearly 2,000 miles away, there were

Uncle Nip's letters urging me to find someone, because he said I was getting too old to have children, for children would need a dad with enough vitality to play with them and help raise them. His advice confused me to some extent because sometimes I think maybe I tried to make a woman love me when probably she didn't, and once she did, I stopped loving her. I was trying to find love with my head, not with my heart. I was trying to see which Indian woman would logically make a good mate for me. It didn't work.

Nip's advice, however, would not go without having some impact on my love life, for it was such advice that enabled me to allow Simone into my life so easily. Because of all he taught me about the qualities of a woman of the People, I would have no conflict between wanting her as a mate and my responsibilities to the People and ways of the pipe.

But, before I met her, I had finally concluded that unless I had that special feeling for a woman that comes from loving her, that comes from the heart, I shouldn't marry again. Maybe it was meant to be this way, I thought . . . that I shouldn't ever marry. I didn't realize then that to grow spiritually in the way of the pipe I carried would include the experience of a loving wife and children. That would make me a whole man. You see, the round circular bowl of the pipe I kept had that extension. That extension usually means that only a man who has a family keeps such a pipe.

A few hours after her mom had introduced us at the Indian Center and we had shared lunch at the Dairy Queen, Simone and I went down to the Mississippi. We talked more about books and even discussed Indian politics as we walked the difficult path to a special place where I had, on occasion, held sunrise ceremonies on the west bank with the students and other teachers of the Heart of the Earth. I explained to her that those little ceremonies were real special times when some of the teachers would smoke the pipe with the students and greet the rising sun with the pipe and the drum.

I described watching Ana, the Ojibway language and culture teacher, singing a beautiful song in Ojibway while holding the pipe up as the sun rose big and yellow over the treeline on the east bank of the river. I can almost smell the bacon, eggs, and potatoes cooking over the open fire, and I can still see in my memory the Heart of the Earth students standing in line to get their breakfast after the ceremony and then sitting on the river bank scattered like an Indian camp along the great river's shore.

As Simone and I descended deeper into the ravine of many colored leaves, we would occasionally grab hold of a smaller elm or maple to keep from falling off the narrow trail or going down it too fast. We talked a little more about Mars. I reiterated my fears about how they would soon do to that planet what they've done to the earth.

She agreed. And she described to me how her father and she had just come out of the Franklin Avenue Theatre after seeing the sci-fi horror film Soylent Green. She said that they both stood hand-in-hand staring up at the moon. "Just think, my girl," her dad had said, while their eyes were fixed on the white moon above the city, "humans are up there right now."

Simone described how quiet their walk home that night was and how "ominous" it felt to look up at the moon and know that the white man was really there.

And as we dropped farther into the earth, we pointed out the beauty around us also. She said how cold she felt it was, though, on that first day of September. We both shared our disappointment that autumn had come quickly that year, and that it was seemingly all ready to leave, for the sky had grown grey and a light snow had begun falling, almost like a drizzle at times, then it would change and only flakes floated down from the grey, white and wet and cold.

I started talking about tribal enrollment and what I thought was a conspiracy to legislate Indians out of existence. I said that I had learned in my two years teaching there that so many Indian children who were born and grew up in the city were not being enrolled. I said that less than half my students at the AIM school were enrolled.

"The fewer tribally enrolled Indians there are," she responded, "the less justification the white man needs to allow Indians a large land base, or someday, needs to allow us any land base at all."

I explained that the ideas Uncle Nip had taught me about being Indian were so opposed to that way of thinking. "He taught me that to be an Indian had far more to do with belief than a percent of blood. 'It's in your heart!' he'd say. 'It's how you live your life.'"

Simone paused as we reached Minnehaha Creek, a small winding creek that trickled that time of year into the Mississippi. She gazed down and picked up a stone. "It took me till this year to figure out why some of my own brothers and sisters weren't on the Red Lake rolls and I was," she said. "They changed the blood quantum to mean only those Ojibways born of parents from that reservation. My father was from Red Lake. My mother was from White Earth."

"Paper genocide is what it is. That's how Indians are going to disappear first. I have a friend who lives in Brazil. He told me that in the minds of the people who live in that country, Indians already don't exist."

Simone clutched the stone she'd been holding.

We headed farther down the winding path that followed the creek toward the river. I don't recall what we said after that or if we spoke at all the rest of the way. I only remember the feeling that I had being with her was like nothing I'd ever felt. I don't recall wanting her; I just remember how I loved being with her and how beautiful she was. Seeing her ahead of me walking down a trail once traveled by her ancestors seemed so right.

Autumn colors were still there at the river. The treeline on the east bank was incredible. Leaves fell on us. It was cold. We sat

together on the drier sand under a huge elm looking out at the
swiftly moving water.

"Do you think dreams are important?" she asked.

"I can't imagine a life without them," I said. "But I think
there are different kinds of dreams. . . . Some can't be ignored."

"Do you think they're real . . . that they tell us the future?"

"I think they're a reality in and of themselves and very much
a part of life. Yes, I do think they can tell us the future, or at least
guide us through it." I reflected silently on some of my dreams.

She drew a circle in the sand between our legs.

She told me some time later that she was thinking about the
dream she'd had about me a few nights before that day down by
the river. . . .

"How could I have told you that I dreamed we made love?"

In that grey and colorful autumn afternoon, while Mars was
being the next new-world victim to be explored, Simone and the
cold and wide Mississippi moved in their own destiny, emerging
from the northernmost regions of this turtle continent only to
merge with me and the warm waters of the Gulf of Mexico far
away. And almost without our knowing, we flowed with the
energy that comes from living in the wheel of life, for like the river
water, we too would be always.

THE VISION THAT LEADS TO PLACES LIKE SISSETON

T WO WEEKS AFTER autumn snow fell with leaves on the banks of the Mississippi, I headed for Sisseton, South Dakota, carrying the pipe. It wasn't the first time I'd left someone I loved behind, but leaving Simone then was like no other feeling I would ever have. In just a short while Simone had already become an anchor in my life. She would be the one I would always return to, even from my dreams. She would be the one who would forever connect me to the real beauty of my life.

And as I passed the cottonwoods that lined parts of the road leading through western Minnesota into South Dakota, I realized that meeting Simone had changed my life and that I truly loved that young woman with the long, crow-black hair. And for the first time, the love I felt for her . . . felt right. It was a love born out of two independent people with no need to use or manipulate others. It was love that destiny, if not Simone's mom, had already decided.

I was being transported to Sisseton by no other than Cactus Jack in his invisible green Gremlin. Cactus was a smart man of Lebanese descent who was in his mid-forties, and a man who seemed to have a beard even after he shaved, which is why the People called him Cactus. He had shunned the idea of chasing money to feel powerful and decided, instead, to become a part of the Indian movement that was stirring in the country then. He seemed delightfully challenged now, transporting me to a place where I was warned not to go.

Word had it that the tribal chairman had declared a death sentence for AIM people on his reservation. Though I was heading there with the pipe on an invitation from the traditional Sioux faction who lived there, and though my only affiliation with AIM at the time was as a teacher at the Red School House, the other AIM survival school in St. Paul, I was as much of a threat as a band of militants might have been. For I was carrying something that represented the old ways, the grass-roots ways that had much to do about being sovereign, about being respectful of Mother Earth, and about identity.

Once I traveled up to a Canadian reserve with a few of the elders, warriors, and young women of the Red School House. Our purpose for going into Canada was to help the Indians on that reservation deal with the alarming number of teenage suicides being committed there. The director of the Red School House told us before we left on that snowy November night that the Canadian Mounties would try and stop us. He said that he was told that any AIM people from the United States would be shot should they step foot on a Canadian reserve. The others from the tiny AIM school in St. Paul and I went to Canada anyway and helped to reestablish the power of the traditional ways and traditional people by conducting sweat ceremonies with the traditionally minded Indians from there and smoking the pipe with them deep in the woods around a half-moon shaped mound while a strong fire heated the stones for the sweat lodge and the stars danced and moved above. The Mounties never showed.

Now I was on my way to Sisseton, to be with my Santee friends and to help them rekindle the fire of the old ways. No warning would keep me from that.

Besides, I had to go, for this way I would be living a vision the way that it came to me when I fell from exhaustion onto my couch late one wintery evening. . . .

I remember that the air was damp and still outside my tiny house in Minneapolis. The house was on a narrow street lined on both sides by old elms. On the side opposite where I lived was Powderhorn Park. The park had high rolling hills that sloped down into a small lake. It must have always been a sacred place, for it was a very pretty place that even affected the white people who came there because they had left it alone and turned it into a city park. And that sacredness and sense of place and my state of mind must have set the moment into motion, and the vision came.

It was a vision that, nearly two years earlier, I had made my quest for. For nearly four full days and nights I had fasted and prayed, and cried out into the Mystery in my anguish and in my search for purpose and self-worth. I was defeated and desperate and angry then, and I had drawn my circle there on the shore of a tiny island under a hot Florida sun with the hope of finding some meaning in my life, some sense of purpose or direction in order to go on.

Insights came to me then. Dreams disturbed me. Identity strengthened in me. But the vision never came.

Instead, two years later, under a full and cold Minnesota moon, the vision came. . . .

It was an especially hard and cold winter, even by Minnesota standards. And there was no circle etched in the frozen crusty snow outside except the one created by the ring of hills and elms across the street at Powderhorn. And though I had not time to eat that day nor the day before, or I had simply forgotten to eat, I was not fasting. And I was not filled with despair and desperation either; I was

154

only very tired. I'd been teaching young Indians from kindergarten to high school at Heart of the Earth all day, and that night I'd been teaching adults in the city library. I did this day after day. I taught reading and writing through the books and ideas that reflected the truth about the People and the truth about the history of this land. I was also making preparations to bring the pipe into Stillwater, so I was especially exhausted when I came through the door and fell into the couch that night. I had hardly enough energy to greet my dog E. I remember that my mind was so tired and that my eyes hardly remained opened, yet they were opened when the room changed and reality transcended into vision.

I cannot describe in its entirety what happened to me that night, for that would reveal something of myself that my enemies could use against me. The words written and told by the wise ones must guide me now, for their advice was for a man not to reveal his vision, not entirely, for that would make him vulnerable. Yet there are those things I wish to tell because they show how a man is indeed guided by a vision and how lost a man can be without one.

Old men tell of their great visions because they are old and will soon be joining the Mystery. For them, there is little their enemies can do that can outweigh the importance of revealing the guiding force of their lives to those who wish to know. Maybe, in some way, it is how they keep their visions alive, by recording them in books as the literature of the People. Though I am not an old man, I have lived a full life, and there are aspects of my vision that I have fulfilled, so telling parts of my vision that I choose to tell may not affect what I've already done. Revealing aspects of the power of that night cannot take what I have accomplished away by my enemies and the enemies of the People. Still, I will reveal parts of what happened to me that night so it can be further seen how important a vision is and how it compelled me to live my life and to go to places like Sisseton. . . .

It was like a cloud of light had silently exploded in the room and streams of mists had suddenly swept in and enveloped me. And in such white and quiet space stood a grandfatherly man, who resembled more a being of light than a man. He was wrapped in a blood-red robe. His hair was the color of starlight. His eyes were black and penetrating.

Now I knew I wasn't dreaming, for I do not recall falling asleep, yet I had no sense of fear at what I was seeing. Instead, I too seemed to explode, only not with light but with incredible awe.

Without sound as I knew it, the spirit-being told me to turn around and to look. When he motioned with his eyes in a specific direction for me to see, I turned and saw. . . .

Human-like forms, who seemed to be the representatives of the different earthly human races, all appeared dead, not just like in body death, though, but dead as in spirit death too. I saw that they had drank something from a golden cup that had poisoned their spirit and killed them.

I then saw an Indian among the other races who was not dead but dying. As I watched him gasp for breath, I began gasping too, for the Indian I was watching had become as one with me. Our struggled breathing became synchronized. And as I felt the last life-breath about to leave us both, I was turned in yet another direction and another being was before me.

She appeared to be a woman-spirit who seemed angry and anguished. Her age was impossible to determine. She seemed as ancient and as timeless as the earth.

She began speaking so fast that my mind could barely comprehend that hers was a message about language. Through the rapidity of her thoughts, she made me understand how the Word has been misused. She spoke of man-made laws and things I could barely understand . . . things that all related to words and human waste and words and human greed and words and human destruction of the land. Words and deceit. Words and manipulations. Half-truths and lies. Words that demean and belittle. Words and trees. Words and vibrations. Somehow she managed to tell me all this in the time it takes a falling leaf to touch the earth in autumn. And this is some of what she told me by sometimes angry gestures and by the language that was understood faster than sound can be heard.

I was turned again in another direction, and this time the grandfather spirit-being spoke to me, again not using familiar sounds, but spirit ones, and everything he said was very clear and distinct. I would one day wonder if this was the language of the spirits who travel from the stars and into the dreams and visions of the children of the earth.

Now this ancient man-like being of light who stood before me held out a book for me to see and motioned for me to look. And when I did, what I saw was magnificent. Its cover was the stars, and peering into it as I did I could glimpse the universe. The old spirit-being of light, wrapped in a robe of red, spoke to me about the stars and pointed to a particular place among them. And when he finished, the book of stars became a living pipe.

That was, in part, the vision of my life. It was the vision Uncle Nip had urged me to seek, the one that I had fasted and cried for on the Island-Where-The-Great-Turtles-Nest, but had never received, the one which came to me then in my little Minneapolis house as unexpectedly and as abruptly as my boyhood vision had on another island in the Gulf of Mexico, where the evening star had danced and where the morning star enticed me. "The vision will come," Uncle Nip had told me, "when we're ready."

And the vision that would guide me throughout my adult life would not come when I was not ready in the white heat of a blazing Florida sun. It would come out of the starry mists under the white cold of a Minnesota moon. It would not come to me on a tropical island set in the Gulf of Mexico, but in a tiny urban house in Minneapolis across from a city park. And it would help me to define the thread that exists between the vision and the dream, a thread that separates the two the way the winding Mississippi appears from space to separate the shell of the great turtle's back as the river winds across the continent. It would help me define the thread that separates the past from the present.

This was the vision I would follow into Canada, into Still-water, and into the Sisseton Indian reservation in the autumn of 1976, despite the warnings to stay away.

THE NAMINGS
AT SISSETON

W HEN CACTUS JACK and I arrived on the reservation, we
headed unnoticed straight to the house of the Santee elder
who defied the tribal chairman's threats against the ceremony. The
old one's wife Rosalyn and her daughter Maggie greeted us at the
door and invited us inside. When I first saw the old man he was
sitting in the small living room in a cushy, dark blue chair with his
back to the window. What hair still remained on his head was
white and thin. Though his nose was straight and sharp, his grey
eyes, set just above protruding cheekbones, were dim and blurred.
And though he was sunk into the soft cushion of the chair, I could
tell that the old one was very tall, for the height of his knees was
greater than the height of the arms of the chair. It turned out that
his name, the one he was passing on to his great-grandson that
day, was Stands Tall.

"I got shot up pretty bad in the first world war," he said as
I sat down in the couch across from him. His voice was raspy, but
clear. "They nearly gave me up for dead. I needed a complete
blood transfusion if I was to live." He leaned forward, raised his
one arm, and pointed to a place where the wound was located on

his left side. "You know, if it wasn't for some generous white man,

I wouldn't be here today."

I laughed. What a great story! In the brief silence that followed, I began to wonder about the length of this man's life . . . the things he'd seen. World War I. World War II. And why was he telling me this story about blood?

"So," the old one continued, leaning back in the chair and smiling, "when the tribal chairman asked me to fill out some form about how much Indian blood I have, so that I could run for office, I tell him, why, I got none. I haven't got a drop of Indian blood in me."

Stands Tall and I enjoyed the laughs that the story provided. We enjoyed the unspoken idea of what it means to be Indian. And the time between the words felt good.

"They asked you to come because we've got no one here with a pipe. My kids told me about you . . . how you teach the truth."

I listened as he spoke and then I felt the need to explain that his grandchildren tried to get a Sioux medicine man, but that no one could come. "That was the first thing I asked them when they invited me," I said.

"We asked you," is all he said.

At a quick glance it was plain to see that Stands Tall and Rosalyn weren't rich people by the white man's standards. They had not accumulated many things or much money in their years of living The Way, but they were rich in spirit and love, and they made sure that they shared some of that Native wealth and love with me.

There was something very right about being there. It is as though all hearts were one, and nothing could break that connection. There was also something pure about this, something the Christians wouldn't understand when they tried so hard to change the Indian. It was the thing that made the People who they were and keeps them who they are. I felt real good about being where I was. I felt a harmony that only a man who follows a vision can feel, and there is no feeling like it on the earth.

Rosalyn gave me the most beautiful star quilt I'd ever seen. She and the other women of her family made it for me. It was their way of expressing appreciation . . . through their art and through their own connections to the stars and to me.

Stands Tall and Rosalyn had two beautiful daughters and several grandchildren. The daughters and their women relatives would cook the finest feast that day. The grandchildren and their friends would assist in preparing the place for the ceremony and would gather the wood for the fires.

As the sun rose high in a cloudless sky, I followed the children and some of the other adults, who joined us at the house, back into the hills to where other traditionals lived. We headed far away with the pipe for the naming, only Stands Tall couldn't make the trip. He was too old, so he said that he would watch it from the house. Before I walked out the door I turned to him one last time and saw him still sitting in the old cushy chair with his back against the window. His eyes were closed. He seemed to be already watching.

About a hundred Indians, young and old, were gathered back in the hills to welcome us. Soon, we were sitting on the open earth in a great circle. Old men sang on the old drum. Eagles squealed and circled above. And in the gentle power of it all, Stands Tall passed his name on to his great-grandson through the pipe. His wife Rosalyn held it above her head and called out his name so that the whole world would know that this was now her great-grandson's name. And another elder woman, small and beautiful, also passed on a name that day. She, too, stood before her grandson and held the pipe to the Four Directions. "Sacred Place," she cried in Sioux as the eagles watched, circling above. "Sacred Place. Sacred Place. Sacred Place."

162

When she handed the pipe back to me, I held it high, like she did. With its eagle and owl feathers twirling in the wind, I addressed Wakan-Tanka and smoked. Then I passed it in the direction of the sun, and each man and woman and child smoked and prayed for these two young Indian boys, while eagles soared above, and the drum of the old men pounded the heartbeat of the earth. The pipe never went out.

When the ceremony was over, several elders approached me. They formed a small circle around me, and one by one they each waited to shake my hand, saying thank you in either Sioux or English as they did. When they told me that their name was Eastman, I recognized the sound immediately, for Charles Eastman wrote several books on the Dakota at the turn of the nineteenth century, all ones that I had read and felt especially close to. The old people who gathered around me told me that not since their great-uncle had died had they ever heard a person address Wakan-Tanka as the Great Mystery. They each shook my hand again, saying that this was the first time a pipe had been used this way at Sisseton in many years. I thanked them too, saying that through the books and hearts of Indians like their uncle, Dr. Charles Eastman, I learned about the Great Mystery.

And it felt like my vision was truly alive and that another circle had been completed.

That night under countless stars one of the traditional families set up a huge tipi on one of the hills. Inside that wonderful lodge a fire burned strong and around it were all these faces of Indians from the past, the present, and the future. Some were old, some were young, some were snuggled in the arms of loving relatives, and all anticipated the stories of the things that we believe as Indians that I had been invited to tell. I remember talking about the Great Mystery and how wonderful it was to be an Indian — how it was the most wonderful thing in the world.

Cactus Jack and I left the Sisseton reservation early the next morning as a blanket of clouds moved in with a wave of cold Canadian air. Even as we drove through the reservation toward the state road that would take us into Minnesota, it was as if the tribal chairman and his tribal police force did not exist. Or maybe our green Gremlin really was invisible. And as we turned onto the paved state road and left the reservation I wondered if our Santee friends would be okay. Something inside me told me they would. And Cactus and I agreed that yesterday may have been the warmest day that fall and that winter would probably be coming early this year. This time, as I watched the bare cottonwoods as we traveled into Minnesota, I had a better understanding of my purpose in this Great Mystery, for I was seeing through the People and the pipe that I and the visions I had as a boy and a young man were truly one.

When I arrived in Minneapolis, I found Simone sweeping out the dust that had collected in my small house since I'd been gone. Seeing her there in a world that would no longer be the same without her, I hugged and held onto her, and I told her that I loved her.

That night we made love under the stars of heaven, wrapped in the loving quilt of stars I was given in Sisseton.

CHAPTER 18

CEREMONY AMONG
THE GHOST DANCERS

T HE GHOST DANCE shirts and dresses came from everywhere: attics of old farmhouses, basements of churches, and
from shelves and boxes of museum storerooms. They were
brought together for a fall exhibit at the Minneapolis Institute of
Arts in 1976. It had been eighty-six years since the wearers of these
magical things last danced and sang to roll up the world and make
it new again. Whatever would bind Simone and I together during
this time would bind us for the rest of our lives.

Simone was a researcher and lecturer for this first and last
exhibit of the American Indian Ghost Dance Movement. There
were about a hundred shirts and dresses on display. They were suspended on black hangers attached to black wooden platforms in a
room that was black. Track lights above the area of the exhibit enabled patrons to read the small plaques underneath each article of
clothing. The tribes and names of the owners were printed there.
Some of the shirts and dresses came from Wounded Knee. Some
were torn by bullets shot from US Army guns and stained by the
blood of the Indian ghost dancers.

A few of the shirts and dresses, mainly Kiowa and Comanche, were buckskin. They were decorated with shells and quills and intricate beadwork designs. The burlap shirts belonged mostly to the Lakota wearers. They had no buckskin left. They had no buffalo robes to paint their dreams on. The animals were all dead or chased away by the pioneers, settlers, soldiers, gold rushers, homesteaders, train riders, sportsmen, outlaws, and waves of immigrants who swept into Indian country in a human flood. The birds were nearly all gone. The trees were disappearing.

Instead of the soft skin of the deer or the strength of buffalo hides against their flesh, the Lakota made shirts and leggings and even dresses of hasty dream pictures and magic symbols of the moon and the stars and feathers of crows and eagles on US Government-issued potato sacks. But sometimes out of poverty and desperation comes hope. It may have been only a burning cinder in the hearts of the People until the Ghost Dance Movement. Then hope became a fire that spread from Indian nation to Indian nation. Its teachings, ignited in 1890 by the vision of the Paiute Indian Wovoka, and by the needs of those times, united the hearts of Indians of many tribes into one more attempt at saving Mother Earth and themselves.

The movement was a religion of non-violence; yet, as the People became more desperate, some misconstrued its teachings in defense of their homeland. New and worried white settlers demanded the army put an end to religious gatherings of Indians, especially those who did not practice Christianity. And end it the army did in the bloody 1890 massacre of hundreds of unarmed Lakota men, women, and children and their friends and relatives from other nations at Wounded Knee, South Dakota.

When I first entered the Ghost Dance exhibit with my students from the Red School House in St. Paul, it was like entering another world. It was as if we entered another dimension of time and ghosts and memories. It didn't matter what tribe you were. You were here to touch the past, to honor the ghosts. One by one I watched the students find the shirts of their ancestors. Though being there among the shirts and dresses was a magical experience for everyone, not all the kids had ancestors who were ghost dancers. But some of them were truly drawn to certain articles. It was as if they were called to them, and then they'd say, "Quick! Come here! This shirt belongs to my great uncle!" Or, "This is my great-grandfather's shirt. Look! It has holes in it where the bullets went." One Lakota girl whose last name was Little Wound sat beneath a particular shirt for a long time. I looked up the owner's name in the catalog, since there was no plaque below it. I approached her respectfully and sat beside her. "This shirt," I told her, "belonged to a man named Little Wound."

Whenever Indians attended the exhibit, the room of shirts and dresses became unusually crowded. I observed white people occasionally. They would enter the exhibit, circle a few of the items, and as if whirled around and spun away, many would leave as quickly as they appeared.

Since she was there every day at the exhibit, Simone would especially notice unusual occurrences around the ghost dance items, especially the nights when we held ceremonies. We always waited until the museum was closed. The curators and guards would allow us to stay. They would leave us alone with the lights out, a lit candle glowing against the void of blackness, and the shirts and dresses.

Sitting in a circle within the circle of ghost dance clothes, we held the pipe and prayed and contemplated the ghosts with Old Man Bill and Simone's mom Elaine and the others who came. Like the movement itself, Indians of different tribes would sit and pray together for our Mother Earth and our people, especially the ancestors. That was the visible power of the Ghost Dance religion. And what we believed united us all.

At any time, there were never more than fifteen people, yet our circle would always be crowded. The room would be alive with   **167** movement and people. They would join us as hazy forms and faceless beings. We would pass the Great Mystery pipe and watch the fringe on their dresses sway, the crow feathers on their shirts twirl in the stillness.

One night after such a ceremony I commented about something I observed to Old Man Bill. Bill was an Ojibway elder who was responsible for saving in writing much of the Ojibway beliefs and stories. He would often visit the survival schools and talk about philosophical things. I don't really know how old he was, but he told us stories going back to the beginning of the twentieth century. He told us stories about the missionaries and what they and other white people did to him in church and government schools. Old Man Bill was one of the few elders who wore his hair long, usually in a thin silvery ponytail, and he was the one who told me once that "you could tell a man's wisdom by the length of his braids."

"Bill," I said, as we walked out of the darkened ceremonial room and as I observed the many people trailing off ahead of us down the corridor of the Institute, "a lot of people came tonight."

Bill glanced up through his thick glasses and nodded.

Later on, when all the participants of the small ceremony sat together at a local restaurant, we squeezed into two tables. It was then that I asked, "Where are the others?"

That question and the awareness that there were indeed many others with us in the ceremony that night seemed to hit us all at once. We sat quietly and ate.

That was some of the magic of the ghost dancers and some of the power that their shirts and dresses yet possessed.

At home, wrapped in the star quilt from Sisseton, Simone and I would dream ghost dance dreams. As we slept together, we would dream of the stars. Loving voices would speak to us, and they would teach us. "Guard your love," the voices said to me. "Because it is love,

168

there will be those who will seek to destroy it, to destroy you for having such love. Protect your love . . . for it is beautiful, and there will be those who seek to destroy what is beautiful. . . . Be careful with those you choose to allow in your circle and in the circle of your children to come.

"Come with us to the stars now. See the earth! See the sun!"

Simone remembers being taken past the moon and seeing me on the other side. She recalled seeing the sun and the stars . . . the stars!

I kept moving, though, into the galaxy. When I saw the sun become an indiscernible light in a spiral ocean of countless lights, I was frightened and did not want to go farther. Next thing I knew, I was sitting up in bed with Simone, who was telling me about the voices that spoke to her.

One night I was taken into the clouds and taught a sacred song to sing to the Four Directions.

And, on another night, Simone had a dream of a loon emerging from the water and singing what she knew to be her name.

For both of us, that time of the Ghost Dance exhibit was filled with dreams and dream images.

I believe our connection to the ghost dancers was most special. It connected us spiritually to each other. I better understood Chief Seattle's words too, when he said that the dead are not powerless. It was their support and guidance that enabled our relationship to have a strong foundation. And, like individuals who need balance between the physical and spiritual aspects of their existence, so do relationships. I also believe these ghost dancers were well aware of the magic in the stars. It was evident in the designs on their shirts and dresses. They traveled like we did. They did, indeed, use the powers of the Word, belief, music, and dance to roll the world up and make it beautiful again.

That is the power and the beauty of what was given to them, and to us.

THE CROWS
AT FALLEN TIMBERS

"THE ELM TREES are dying," Simone said to me, having just read the headlines in the *Minneapolis Star and Tribune*. "They say that it came from Europe." She put down the paper and looked at me. "It's another one of those diseases they've brought here. Only it doesn't kill Indians; it kills trees."

I told her that I read somewhere that the Iroquois believe that the elms are the source of power for the protectors of the earth. Their dying was not a good sign.

In early autumn of 1976, it was plain to see that the elm trees in Minnesota were losing their battle against yet another sickness introduced in America from across the great water. At the end of October in this first year of our lives together, Simone and I left the bare and sick elms of Minnesota. We left them with prayers that they may rest, be cleansed, and be strengthened by the coming cold as we headed east, toward the Onondaga Nation. Onondaga is sort of like the capital of the Iroquois Six Nations. It's located on a small area of land about 800 miles east of Minneapolis, just outside Syracuse, New York.

170

The director of the Red School House had asked me if I would go there to help the Onondagas in their own conflict with the white man's educational system.

I had smoked the pipe with Onondaga representatives a year earlier in the basement of the Red School in St. Paul. I had my give-away at that time too. It all happened the night before the "Walk For Survival," which was a national gathering of Indians who, through the walk, would help bring attention to the masses of our pathetic economic state. It was also a way for the students to raise money, having people pledge something like a dime for every mile a student walked.

Among those Indians who went on "the Walk" was Will Sampson. Will was an actor who had recently worked alongside Jack Nicholson in the famous film, "One Flew Over the Cuckoo's Nest." It's best said that he's the first Indian actor in memory not to be stereotyped. Will was there in the basement of the Red School House the night before "the Walk." He was there with the rest of us to pray with the pipe. He was also there to help heal himself.

I can clearly remember that night in the basement of the Red School House, and I can clearly picture Will Sampson's long and heavy body as he sat cross-legged and shirtless before the medicine man who prayed in front of him with the pipe. Those of us who were there formed the circle around them and sang for Will Samp-son's strength and well-being. He seemed like a humble man with a native heart. It felt to me that his heart was as big as he was a man. I don't know for certain, but I think that maybe what was making Will Sampson feel the need to get healed that night was the very thing that, years later, would finally kill him.

The next day, when the "Walk For Survival" began, I was asked to say the words that would begin such a journey. I can remember the great circle of people that enclosed me as I spoke to the heavens and to the earth. I appealed to the powers of the Four

Directions to help the People on their journey, and I kissed Mother Earth and said that the People were doing this because they loved her and were determined to pass on that love to future generations. When this was done the great procession began. And standing tall and at the head of the long unwinding serpent of people was Will Sampson. Alongside him was the Red School House director, and behind him were the students and teachers from the AIM schools, the elders from Onondaga, lots of Indian children, me, and the rest of the several hundred Indians and other people who came from many nations to walk from St. Paul to Minneapolis — the long way.

I hadn't gone far before a tall, muscular white man with blond hair, dead blue eyes, and a dingy beard approached me and sneered in my face. "How much Indian are you?"

I'd seen his look before at other Indian gatherings and I'd sure see it again in my life. His type appears out of nowhere and confronts you and makes you mad by saying something that he knows is provocative. That's his purpose: to force a fight, create a disturbance, and somehow discredit any of the good that would be going on.

"Fuck you," I replied. The words seemed to fly out of my mouth. "Indians don't come in parts."

He lunged towards me and appeared as though he was about to start a fight when suddenly he was confronted by Red School House students, AIM warriors, and Onondaga elders. The blond man with the dingy beard and cold blue eyes cowered back and disappeared into the crowd.

I spent the day walking with the people from Onondaga. I felt good when they thanked me for the beautiful things I gave to them at my give-away the night before. I felt good when they smiled and asked me to stay with them on the walk.

▲ ▲ ▲

Now, with Simone alongside me, we were heading east in my 1969 Mustang toward the Onondaga Nation. I was hoping that maybe I could discover some connection to my own Indian past, the one not tied to Florida. It's true that the Onondagas have an alligator dance, and it's true they traded extensively with Indians from everywhere, yet how did I tie into all this? This I wondered many nights. Was it all a childhood fantasy that I conjured up in Catholic school, or was the woman real, the one with dark hair who fastened a tiny gold charm to my neck the shape of a horn when I was just a baby, and told me not to forget my name, and told me about Onondaga and my ties to that place?

Uncle Nip had always told Simone and I to give the children, even while they were in her womb, the words, that in time they may grow to understand their meaning. I wondered then if that mysterious woman had been the one who gave me the word Onondaga when I was a baby, when I couldn't understand its meaning. I wondered what I would discover there in Onondaga. I reminded myself that it didn't matter if I discovered anything there or if I would gain any knowledge of my dim past. What mattered was that I had something to give.

As we rode in the Mustang down through the Dells of Wisconsin and through the man-made monster octopus of Chicago, we suddenly became two natives who felt like two salmon heading upstream against a steady flow of people, machines, and pollution. Having lived and worked among Indians for so long, it felt especially lonely when we didn't see any more Indians once we left our small Minneapolis community. All we saw were white people and black people, people occupying a land that belonged to the ancestors and still felt as though it belonged to us.

"There are as many of the whites as there are leaves on the trees." That's the way Black Hawk described their numbers when he returned to his Sac people after trying to negotiate an honorable treaty with the white man in the East. The way it felt to Black Hawk then was the way it felt to us as we traveled on.

Outside of Chicago, just past Calumet Highway, Simone tied a goose feather onto the Four Directions' symbol that we hung from the rearview mirror. She had made it out of pipe cleaners and blue thread that we'd picked up in a five-and-dime store along the way. It was an appropriate symbol for good luck on a long journey. Now a goose feather twirled from its center as our guide and drew our attention to a sign that led us off the main road to the monument commemorating the Battle of Fallen Timbers.

We were in Indiana, in a little two-acre park located in the middle of highways angling in every direction, heading toward Ohio.

"Ohio," I muttered to Simone as we pulled the car over and got out. "Ray Fadden said it was an Iroquois word and that it means beautiful waters."

I took the pipe from the back seat and carried it as Simone and I walked up to the twenty-foot statue of General Anthony Wayne who defeated, with his army, a united Indian force led by Tecumtha. The Indians were determined to resist the white man's invasion of the Ohio Valley. Under the giant statue that towered over us, we read the words asserting General Wayne's defeat of the Indian army, and how his soldiers had opened up the valley and made it a free and safe place for Americans to settle. It gave no mention of the Native warriors who died protecting their country from the mass invasion nor of their surviving families who were evicted to make room for the new transplant Americans. It gave no mention how Tecumtha was shot again and again yet managed to move back and forth among his warriors and, with blood pouring from his mouth, encouraged them to defend their country.

There was, however, a large rock there. It was about five feet tall and rested a few yards away from the left side of the sword-waving general. On the rock was a plaque that stated that this was the spot where Indians made offerings to the Great Spirit.

I put the bowl of the pipe and its stem together and filled it with a pinch of tobacco.

It was dusk and the sky was grey; the air was cold and damp. It created the kind of chill that goes through your bones. There were a few leafless trees, probably oaks, that seemed like skeletons standing and watching. A light snow began falling, and I wondered if it might not cleanse this place somewhat. I lit the pipe and addressed the Four Directions and the Earth and the Sky and the Great Mystery. I addressed the ghosts of the people, and thanked them for defending this country with their lives. I vowed never to surrender it. I felt their Orenda and the power of the place being absorbed by the pipe. This is why I took it out, I thought, to gather the power for the good of the People and the land.

Simone stood near and watched the snowy grey sky suddenly thicken with the black of crows. Their numbers were more than we could count. It might have been frightening to anyone else, maybe even to us had we not been traveling in the Wheel, but now . . . now their presence was more like an honoring, like an acknowledgment.

The crows descended all around us, and perched quietly and ominously on the statue of General Wayne, who called the Native American people savages before he killed them and stole their country.

The crows clustered silently on bare branches of leafless trees and on the rock where I held the pipe. They even gathered on the car. They seemed to be everywhere. It was as if the Ghost Dance Movement had returned from the other world, and the crows were saying to us that we were not alone. In all this shit, we were not alone! I flashed on the images of crows drawn on ghost dance shirts and their black feathers twirling in the stillness of the museum on those magical nights of ceremony.

I flashed on the nightmare that had befallen the Indian people, and we stayed there until dark among the crows at Fallen Timbers.

At Fallen Timbers Simone and I shared many thoughts about the irony of the monument and its location. "In the middle of all that junk," she said, "we shared a sense of history."

Somehow, in making this journey east together and seeing a few of the other great lakes, we had a sense of place — especially for Simone, who had no intellectual way of knowing that she was on an ancient route once taken by her ancestors who migrated from the east towards the great lakes' region thousands of years ago.

I can recall her talking in the car that night as the road turned into a black void ahead and the snow fell like white streams. She expressed her disbelief that the white man's history of the place gave no mention of Tecumtha and his efforts. The monument honored only the white soldiers — as though no Indian warrior had died there. "One should get used to it," she said, "but it still gets to me. You think that Tecumtha's spirit was there in the middle of all that and you remember what he said about protecting the land; and you could see from the place that it was evident how ugly the white man is."

Gradually the snow stopped falling as we traveled farther east, and then it began to rain, and the rain finally quit. The air turned warmer. As we crossed the New York State line at dawn, we began our second autumn. Uncle Nip once told me that autumn is the season when the power of change is everywhere. Now I was traveling with my new love through two autumns, and our lives would experience the change as powerfully as the colorful trees in the Seneca Mountains.

IN THE MYSTERY

S IMONE AND I stopped at Cataraugus and met the Fishers. We
talked about things as they are on the reservations while they
fed us. How ironic that these "savages," as Benjamin Franklin and
the rest of the colonizers referred to the Senecas, would be so
generous with strangers. The Fishers didn't know us, but they
treated us as though they did. And though it was obvious by their
humble surroundings that they didn't have much, they shared
with us what they could.

The cemetery at Cataraugus seemed timeless. Though it was
an Indian graveyard, there were crosses at many gravesites. The two
young men and their father who had taken Simone and me to the
cemetery led us to the grave where I was asked to smoke the pipe.
There was no cross over it, just the engraved name of Ellie Fisher
on a small grey block of weathered stone. The two young men
and their father understood that I had come at the request of their
niece back in Minneapolis when she learned that I would be
traveling in this part of the country. She explained to me that her
grandmother was a traditional Seneca woman but was buried as a
Christian. She asked me to smoke the pipe over her grave.

Simone stood somewhat apart from me and the two men. She said that she had watched them watch me as I smoked. "The respect and look on their faces was indescribable. And you . . . your face changed also."

She said that as she watched the smoke lift from the pipe, she felt connected to everything, to the People especially, in a way she had never felt. Leaves of red and yellow rained down around us as I prayed with the pipe for peace: peace for this woman's niece who felt the importance of this ritual and closing of a circle; peace for this woman's ghost and for the return of her spirit back to the Great Mystery and her goodness back to her family and her people.

Simone would one day describe the way she felt at that moment. "It was as though my future flashed before my eyes: husband, kids, family. Seeing you with the pipe among the autumn colors in the cemetery of Cataraugus, I knew that this was for real."

Hazy forms shimmered in the afternoon sunlight slanting through the colorful trees and shining on the mist that rose from the earth. Simone would catch a glimpse of movement here and there among the shadows. She knew she was among the ghosts again. She could hear them. Somehow, in the slight wind that stirred the leaves on the highest limbs, in their soft murmuring, she could hear them inside her head, and she knew that from then on there was no turning back. She had arrived at that point in her life when there was no turning back.

▲▲▲

We each would remember that day at the Cataraugus cemetery many years later, because people don't forget death.

I knew that one day Uncle Nip would die. I just didn't want to believe it would ever happen. It was worse than when my dog E died. Carises was still a baby, yet E had seen me through a couple of marriages and got to see my children. He lived to be eighteen years old. That's old for any dog! But I still keep his ashes near me, hoping the day will come when they'll be given back with mine to Mother Earth. In my period of deep mourning, Uncle Nip explained that I was to mourn for my loss, not for E. . . . E was with the Mystery. "Animals teach us how to die, Kid." That's what Uncle Nip had told me then. I found solace in finding E's black dog hair around the house even months after he died. I found solace in the clouds where I would see his face.

Where would I find solace now?

Simone and the children stood over Uncle's grave, staring at the earth. The urn was before me, filled with his ashes. With so many Indian graves robbed for scientific research, anthropological studies, or museum curiosity collections, Uncle Nip chose cremation.

Traditionals like him wanted assurances that their bodies would return to Mother Earth, who nourished them all their lives, and that their gravesites would remain a place to meditate for those who loved them, a place to visit and remember the past. The body's return to Mother Earth is the Indian people's small but sacred way of giving back some of what they take from her. Cremation was the only way Uncle Nip could be assured that this would happen.

Death was a shadow that came to Simone and me early that winter of '87. It stood in the bedroom one night, watching us. It stood, a deep, black shadow in the darkness of the room. It would come again later that same season while Elaine lay dying of cancer.

But Uncle Nip's death was sudden. The news struck early on New Year's morning. "Nip's gone," is all Simone said, and I shook and heaved and cried.

Uncle died in his sleep of a heart attack after we had watched the sun trail lengthen a few days earlier in the Gulf of Mexico while the children played around us. It was Peace Day, the day Christians call Christmas. It was the last time Simone and I and the children would see Uncle Nip in his body. There was one point when we were watching the sunset that I said something about how it seemed like each time we were together it was even better than the last time. Nip said it was because those times I was referring to were becoming fewer.

Uncle Nip had told me when I was practically still a boy that he was living on borrowed time anyway. He said that after forty-four years, any American Indian man is, and that I would be too one day.

"When you get to the bridge of death," Uncle Nip told the children once, "you have to jump onto the great serpent's head. He takes you to the other side."

He had them practice, like in a game, making their final jumps at the bridge. One by one, they'd take their turns in the back-yard among the ferns and between the palms. First, Ihasha would hold the shovel, which served as the head of the great serpent, while Calusa, with her long, fawn legs springing her high and strong, landed squarely on it. Then, she'd hold the shovel for Carises.

His short, powerful brown legs would take off at the precise moment, only to miss and fall over.

"Calusa moved the shovel, Uncle."

"Then Calusa's teaching you to time your jump," Nip replied. "It's in the timing, Little Buffalo-Calf. Death is not a timely thing. You must be ready to say, 'It's a good day to die!' Don't take the jump for granted, ever. That serpent can always move his head. If you miss, you get washed away by the rushing waters and never join the others across the river."

Carises tried again, and once again Calusa moved the shovel. This time he managed to land briefly on the head before he fell over. Uncle Nip laughed under the cool shadow of a sabal.

"I missed again, Uncle."

"You must practice, Little Buffalo. You must practice."

Uncle Nip wrote a story about it called "The Bridge." It was published in *South Dakota Review* and won a literary award to top it off. It was the last story Uncle Nip wrote before he jumped.

Though we all felt certain he'd make the jump, we worried
that his earthly commitments could hold him back. He knew the
children would need him. They were his heart's delight. But he had
taught Simone and me all he could about being good parents; the
kids would do okay.

None of us wanted to be the ones to keep our uncle from his
journey, nor allow the earthly things to prevent his jump at the
bridge, so we were careful in our mourning.

There was a strong gust across the old graveyard where we
stood with Uncle's ashes. It came from the south with a sudden
blast of warm air. The sun came out from behind the cloud blanket
that covered the sky on that January day. We could feel the spirit-
presence of Uncle Nip all around the grave. I felt it pour into me, and
I could hear the ghost voice consoling me. . . .

"When you're born, kid, you take a cup of spirit from the
Mystery for your life. You live your days for the good of the People
and the earth, and you fill your cup with goodness. This way, when
it's time for you to die, all that goodness pours back into those you
love; and the spirit, which has increased in power, returns to the
Mystery like a drop of rain in the ocean, to be a part of all things
once again, recycled, and used for the coming generations. . . .
There is no death," he'd say, "only the Great Change."

Ihasha and I lifted the heavy urn and placed it down in
the hole.

Simone recognized her responsibility to the children and
knew this was a time of teaching, even as she agonized over the loss.
While placing one hand gently on Calusa's shoulder, she held the
little hand of Carises in her other; and, speaking softly, her voice
penetrated the darkness of their sorrow, like the loon's sound
penetrates the darkness of the night. "Children, do you remember
what Uncle said about not being selfish at death?"

Ihasha quickly responded and turned from the grave. "He
said the body becomes food for Mother Earth."

"Yes, and the spirit becomes one with the Mystery."

I fell to my knees. Tears dammed in my eyes until they finally **181** trickled down my cheeks and ran in a continuous stream. I tried to stop them, but I could not stop them. There was a flood of anguish flowing from my heart, and I could not stop the tears flowing from my eyes and falling on the sacred earth below. Then I could hear the ghost voice of Uncle Nip again. This time it was telling me that it was okay to express my grief, just as long as I knew that I was crying for my loss, not for him; "Uncle's in the Mystery."

"Come, children," I said, motioning them towards the grave. "Help Dad give Uncle's body back to Mother Earth."

One by one they too fell on their knees and helped me push the sandy earth over the ashes with their small hands. I wondered if Nip's ghost and spirit could see us, especially the loving children, being brave in belief and returning his ashes to the land.

"This is why the land is sacred to our people, children," Simone said, wiping tears away with her fingers. "The land is sacred because generations of our people have been given back to this land; it is where your body comes from. Your people have become the land itself."

"Thank you, Mother Earth," I said, weeping. "You have sustained Uncle Nip's life . . . and ours. And we thank you."

We stood at the fresh grave: Simone, me, and the children. . . . It had been eleven years after Simone and I stood at the grave in Cataraugus where she was given a glimpse into her future. . . . It was just as she felt it then among the ghosts and spirits of colorful autumn leaves and graves of Cataraugus.

Simone recalled that day at the Seneca cemetery with great affection. "As we left Cataraugus in fall color and many leaves, I thought of our children," she said. "I thought if I was to have any, you were the one I'd have them with."

The dead are not powerless.

IN THE HILLS
OF ONONDAGA

A S WE TRAVELED in the Mustang south and east along America's modern highways, we moved in the spirit of the old land on an ancestral path that helped make us more aware of ourselves in hard and wonderful ways. And we moved closer to understanding each other in a world that used to teach that understanding between people was necessary before there could be a lasting love. When we arrived in Onondaga, we were especially blessed. For there among the people and the hills, we would understand even more about who we were and why we were here in this place . . . in this world.

As we stood in the doorway of a tiny house nestled in a valley of brightly colored forests and clear flowing streams, there was a pleasant crowing sound and then the welcoming words of an Onondaga grandmother. "Come in and get homely," she said. She was seated near the old wood stove.

When Simone and I stepped inside, we stepped into an old and familiar world. We sat and dined with this Iroquois grandmother and many other relatives in her extended family, including her grandson who was one of the Onondaga chiefs. We feasted on

Iroquois cuisine of hominy and corn and potatoes and venison. There was hot, buttery fry bread. There was pumpkin pie. And in this small and lovely home, a lamp light glowed on beaded belts that draped over low log rafters and on colorful feathers that filled painted vases. And the pungent scent of burning cedar emanated from the old wood stove, lifting the warmth of quiet laughter and good Indian conversation. And this small and lovely home would become a symbol of a kind of how simple and good life was and still can be. Of all the things that would seem ephemeral to Simone and me as we traveled together across modern America, one thing was still certain and was clearly evident in that small and lovely home of the Onondaga grandmother who welcomed us: the white man did not bring these things of life and love to our people. They were already here and well-established and were among the few things that the white man had not yet taken all away.

We were nearly a thousand miles from Minnesota, more than a thousand miles from Florida, and Simone and I felt like we had arrived home . . . home . . . in another place on the back of the great turtle island we call our country.

The grandmother who shared her gifts of food that nourished our bodies also shared her gift of wisdom that would nourish our spirit and our minds. After everyone had met us, eaten and left, she spoke privately and strongly about identity and nationalism.

"We're no Christians here," she said, feeding the old wood stove a few more pieces of dried wood. "We grandmothers and clan mothers had our chiefs give eviction notices to all those around here who think themselves Christians and want to practice their religion here in Onondaga." She picked up an iron rod and poked at the wood; the fire flared. "And we told all those who considered themselves Americans of the United States to leave too. We told them that this land was preserved by our ancestors for Onondagas."

184

She closed the stove door, leaned back in the wooden chair she was sitting in, and looked up at Simone. I wondered if she was seeing aspects of herself in Simone. For I learned from Uncle Nip that age has a funny kind of clarity when it comes to memory. Not always able to recall the events that started today, some old people, like the Onondaga woman who sat across from us, were able to look at a young maiden like Simone and remember years ago just as if it were yesterday. I was sure that she could see the same youthful uncertainty in Simone that she had felt when she was nineteen and thinking about marrying a man whose name she told us was Warren Benjamin. She was watching Simone and talking about her own youthful doubts of spending the rest of her life with Warren. And while she talked and kept glancing at Simone, I became suddenly aware that Simone could be having those same feelings about me. I wondered too if maybe it was the same kind of uncertainty the grandmother still felt, now that Warren was dead and knowing that she must go on without him. It's the kind of uncertainty, perhaps, that a woman feels about life, knowing that everything must come to an end, and the kind of anxiousness that always exists in the eyes of some women who tend to live life to the fullest because this awareness makes life that much more precious to them. And then the elderly woman's soft gaze fell upon me, for she must have seen that same look in my eyes that she'd seen in her husband back then. It was a look she said she saw in only a few men, but it was one that never died because she told us she could still see Warren with her eyes closed. I could tell she could see that look now with her eyes open.

"We told the people that if they wanted to be Christians," she repeated, "then be Christians outside Onondaga. If you want to be an American, go be an American out there in the United States. This land is for Onondagas." And she smiled again and added, "and for Indians like the two of you."

She stood and shuffled to the table where Simone had gathered our coffee cups. "We're having a lot of problems at the school," she said, "but I'm sure you know that. Halloween is just one of them. Do you know how upset the grandmothers and grandfathers were last year when the American school pressured the Indian children to wear masks for fun and for scarin' people? The idea that they'd do it again this year just can't be tolerated. Wearing masks is something the Iroquois only do after their dreams instruct them."

As if her years and the burden of responsibility she carried around as a grandmother weighed too heavily on her, she sat at the table and sort of slumped wearily, yet she never lost her sense of dignity. That was like an aura around her. She had every right to be tired, I thought, for she had prepared a wonderful meal for her guests and articulated the philosophy of her traditional people. She kept a fine fire glowing in the old wood stove and then struck deeper into the heart of the Onondagas' concerns about their children's education. Her silvery white hair gleamed in the soft light as she continued to talk about the school and how it affected the community. She talked about how repulsed the grandmothers and grandfathers were at the desecration of pumpkins on Halloween. "To the people," she said, "pumpkins are food. They're a gift of Mother Earth. Last year we found them smashed along the road leading into the nation. We just can't take it anymore . . . the children are our future. If they desecrate what it is to be Onondaga . . . then we'll disappear. . . .

"Which is why you're here," she said, looking at me. "You've come to help keep this from happening. We'll start our own school if that's what it takes."

I felt humbled and right about being there. I felt good about listening to Uncle Nip's advice when he told me about how I could come to Onondaga, but only when I had something to give. Maybe now I've something to give.

That night I met with the elders and discussed the reason I was sent there by the American Indian Movement schools — to help the Onondagas start their own Indian school and, in the meantime, to make the American school already there better at meeting the needs of the children of that community and Indian nation.

Before I started speaking, I was nervous. I was about to address the Onondaga sachems and elders and wise mothers. Then one of the chiefs made a bet with one of the more serious-looking women who just sat down that he could make her smile. She glanced up at him and shook her head. She denied that he could, but she was smiling when she said it.

Soon the Onondagas explained to me how difficult it was to create changes within the white man's public school that was located on the reservation. They said that they were impressed when they had come to Minnesota and visited the Red School House. They said that maybe they could start a school like that there in Onondaga.

I listened to their concerns. I listened to the origin of the words and knew that they were coming from their hearts. I knew that they were already setting changes into motion.

I spoke first about Wind River. I told them about my experiences there and did not omit my own flaws of youth, which would from time to time still emerge. I talked to them about the importance of our people's literature, and how using it helps Indian children to read and write. How it helps unite Indian people in a common way. I explained how the BIA Indians confiscated the Indian literature and history books when the Indian school board allowed the BIA to take control. I spoke about money and how it usually became the central issue of Indian education. I explained that this was how the BIA gained control of that reservation school in the first place.

"I can understand that your children deserve a nice school, at least as nice as the colonizers have in their communities, but having a nice modern school building can be like a pretty sea shell, very beautiful to look at but hollow inside." I explained how new build- 187 ings for classrooms became more important than what was taught in the old ones. I talked about how a few people, Indian people, got powerful positions because they did the bidding of the BIA. I said that this was the ultimate act of stealing our basic human rights.

I also told the elders that night at Onondaga about the hard times at some of the AIM schools and how I often taught in the cold basement of an apartment in a Minneapolis housing project. I told them how the funding for the schools would barely trickle in to the teachers and the kids. I told the elders how Heart of the Earth seemed to split apart after we successfully acquired a new building and how accusations would be made by one Indian against another.

I told them in Onondaga that night that what my wise uncle had told me once was true: We can be our own worst enemy, "even worse than the men who pointed guns at me and the children," I said. And I told them about the petty adult jealousies that inevitably creep into organizations and boards of directors once the funding is established . . . how the behavior of the adults can wind up hurting the children in the end. "It's the power plays," I said. "One group pitted against another. It's the squabbling you hear. The kids pick up on that. So, beware. Not only will the white school system be out to stop you because you're taking money out of their schools for every Indian child who comes to your school, but our own people can destroy the school from within. And that's really what the government wants. There's only one way of avoiding this self-inflicted genocide. . . .

"Always," I implored, "keep the children in mind, above all things. Give them the books of knowledge and understanding that help to teach them how to be human as well as how to read. Even if their teachers are white, they can provide the children with the books of the people, and through the books, they can help teach the children how to read and write in the white man's language but still express themselves as Indians." And I wished my words could have had the power to make this happen, but I knew such a condition would be up to them.

The meeting lasted till late that night. By the time I got upstairs where we were staying, I figured that Simone would have gone to bed, but I was wrong. She was at a desk by the window reading. She said that she was waiting to hear how everything went and that she wanted to talk.

"Tonight you spoke with the people," she said, closing the book and looking over at me. "I didn't hear what you said, yet I could hear, like I hear you now. Your voice still fills my ears from today. You put things so black and white. There's no grey for you. . . . I was brought up in that grey space and I know I can't live it. Yet it's what I want. I know some people call it fence-walking. I had always thought it best to walk the fence and avoid the conflict that comes from making decisions — this way or that way. But I see now that that is not the way to live."

She stood and stepped away from the desk where she had been reading and gazed out the window. She was wearing a long pink T-shirt decorated with quetzal birds. It hung nearly to her knees. Her black hair fell down her back. I recall now how truly beautiful she was to me then and how wonderful it felt to set my eyes upon her as she stood, looking into the darkness and seeing her own reflection.

"So at long last it comes to the place I knew it would," she continued, *"how to be Indian."* She pressed her face to the cool glass pane. "As we travel I see what the white man has done to the land, to the people, and I have a sense of the strength it takes to survive that stuff with any beauty or pride intact. Nearly 500 years later and I still see that strength of beauty alive in the people . . . like the grandmother who greeted us and cooked for us. She is so strong in her identity; with such women among the people, there is still hope. . . . Can I be a woman like her?"

"Be who you are, Simone."

"You speak in truths," she said, taking herself away from the window and leaning her back against the wall near it. "Such truth touches one's heart and mind. It is inescapable. . . . It only remains for me to act. You perceive the world more radically — perhaps I have yet the naivete of youth and need more years to become convinced that you should be radical. And, on the other hand, I may well be a coward.

"You say, 'Live your experiences as an Indian . . . experience your people and then make a choice.' I've not felt the urge to choose until now . . . maybe because I've not lived your commitment."

That night we snuggled close together in bed and dreamed powerful dreams — she about someone . . . a voice that spoke to her in Ojibway . . . and about a loon. I dreamed about the stars . . . a star traveler, star people.

She said she dreamed also of the ghost dance and the river: walking on the plain, there were only a few of us . . . and coming to the river where we were to cross. We saw that it was huge . . . much wider than even the Missouri . . . and at the river bank we came to a deserted house and we went in. . . . She said that all the white people were dead and that she was surprised, and an old man was there and she asked, "Grandfather, why?" And he said, "They are dust; they had no ears." And as he said that, Simone says she watched as all the white people crumbled and blew away.

Simone says that we gathered with the people outside and sang. "Then I was coming through the stars," she said, "and past the moon which was huge and white . . . and then I woke."

The next morning on a hill above Onondaga we looked at the land and saw its beauty and power, and as we went for a drive we were reminded that there is so little left that is ours. . . . We saw the beauty of that land and felt a sense of wonder — the land has power. The hills surround you and roll in such beautiful color. . . .

The haze cloaks them in purple and makes the reds and golds stand
out even more. . . .

▲▲▲

The word has much power too as it rings on the land! The
following evening a meeting was called at the reservation's public
school. I told Simone that probably a handful of people would show
up, since everyone must've felt that they had heard everything I had
to say. As we neared the school, though, I saw all the cars parked
along the road. "There must be something big going on tonight,"
I said. "Look at all the cars!"

As it turned out, most of Onondaga seemed to be there at the
school that night, and all the teachers who were required to come
were there too.

As if a voice spoke from within me, my words to the teachers
just wouldn't stop. They were all white — I mean their attitude
. . . their way of looking like this was just some meeting they were
obliged to attend. No wonder the people were concerned and
wanted to start their own school. When I spoke of the circle, I tried
to get them to form one. It was very difficult for them. I talked about
teaching the way of the circle.

An old man standing behind me said, "The teachers don't
know how to make a circle."

"You must understand," I said, "that it's not just a form our
uncle is talking about; it is a way, a natural thing, and it has power.
Many things will naturally follow — if you begin with an understanding of the circle."

Simone said afterwards that she was having a hard time seeing how they — the whites — were going to be able to make the
school go because they know so little of the history and literature
of the people and will have a lot of research to do; at this point the
focus seemed to be on surreptitiously un-indoctrinating the children

without the State School Board saying: "Hey! You must teach that
this way. . . ."

My presence there that night was directed at getting the
teachers to think about truth. The truth of where they come from
and where they are. Ofttimes they will concede about the history
of the People and say: "Well, it was blood and guts but, however. . . ." So what you have are not total lies — only half-truths
that are still nothing, worthless. They say or think, "Oh, but they
are so young to know that stuff. . . ." When are you too young to
know truth?

Glossed-over history does us no good.

I explained to these teachers of our people what I observed
just walking through their school. "When I walked into this school
tonight, I noticed that you had some Happy Halloween poster greeting us as we came in, and there was another one just above it that
praised God and country. I also observed that each classroom had
an American flag in it, and that the desks were all set in rows. There
is not a circle in this whole school! Before I came into this meeting,
I stopped by some of the classrooms and didn't find one Indian
book, or anything hanging from the walls that would indicate that
Indians even lived here. May I remind the teachers in this room of
their responsibility and their place in this world. This is Onondaga,
not the United States of America. You are in Onondaga now.

"You must first understand the truth here . . . that these are
Native American children you are teaching. They have a unique culture that is indigenous to this land, and one that does not condone
the wearing of masks for the sake of scaring people and for amusement. Ghosts and spirits are manifestations and ideas that these children are taught to respect.

"You must also, beginning tomorrow, take down every
American flag in this school. You are not in the United States now.
You are in Onondaga. And that billboard at the entrance of the

school . . . that's the first thing the kids see of this place every morning. It must be changed to reflect who they are and what they believe. Replace it with something about the circle of life."

▲ ▲ ▲

That night Simone told me she was having a hard time going to sleep because of the discussion we'd had the night before, when we talked about the way to be an Indian. I suggested that she try and get some sleep . . . that perhaps the spirits would send her a dream to help her understand.

Simone awoke the next morning at first light and said that she dreamed someone told her that she would receive a feather and a song to help.

That day, one of the Onondaga chiefs gave us two eagle feathers, and she was named "Loon Song" at the creek near sundown. . . .

She sat at the edge of the rushing creek among the hills of Onondaga. Wearing faded jeans and a Mayan shirt of embroidered quetzal birds and flowers, she was gathering small round stones. Around her neck was a necklace she had made of silver beads and chunks of turquoise. It glistened on her ivory brown skin. Her long, silky-black hair draped over porcupine-quill earrings and brushed the thin, silver bracelet on her wrist. She was about to place the last stone in the circle she had formed with the others.

I had just been in the woods where Hyonwatha once began his quest. This was over a thousand years ago. Now I had just smoked there. It was also the place where Deganawida once spoke of peace beneath the pines, and love between the People of Five Nations. This too was over a thousand years ago. Yet the spirit of Orenda, the collective spirit of the ancestors that comes out of the land and out of the Mystery, was with me then. What was most important, though, was that the Orenda of the place, like other sacred places I'd been, was with the pipe.

Squatting before her, I cradled the pipe and looked into the mystery of her black, almond eyes. "The loon singing is your name," I said. "When the loon surfaced in the water of your dream, the singing was your name. Do you see? You are the manifestation of the loon's song in your dream. You are the song, as visible as the breath of my words are in this . . . blue, autumn air."

I turned toward the woods and the place where I'd just come from and then back to her. "While a blanket of wind had covered me in silence, I felt the flowing water of the creek inside me. I could feel the Orenda speaking your name, Simone . . . and the name it spoke was Loon Song, Loon Song. I can hear it in my mind as plainly as the rushing water. And I suddenly felt transformed. I heard these words in the water, Simone . . . in the Orenda of the water. I heard them in the forests.

"I do not think to name you, but only bring to you these words to help give meaning to your dream."

Her dark eyes seemed to meditate for a moment on the small round stone she still held in her hand. The moon rose behind her. The creek sang alongside her. Autumn leaves rained through the fading sunlight. She glanced at me and smiled, and then gazed at the stones beneath her. Gently, she placed the one she held in her hand with the others upon the ground, and the circle was complete.

▲▲▲

Early the next evening, we met with some elders and parents and lots of kids in the basement of the public school there in Onondaga. I brought the pipe. In our quiet and snug circle, I talked to the children about how important it was to know our history, and to keep our beliefs in the Great Mystery and the Circle of Life alive. I talked about the pipe and about the books that they needed: *Lame Deer*, *Black Elk Speaks*, *The Education of Little Tree*, *Bury My Heart at Wounded Knee*, *The Way to Rainy Mountain*, and many, many more.

"This is the literature and history of all our people," I said. "Fill this
place with books of truth!"

And we discussed Halloween and how upset the grandmothers and grandfathers were that the public schools encouraged
and pressured the children to wear masks, something Iroquois only
do after their dreams instruct them. We talked about how repulsed
the grandmothers and grandfathers were at the desecration of
pumpkins, a food staple and gift of Mother Earth to the People. We
spoke about all these things in the presence of the pipe, which rested
by my side on its white rabbit furs.

The next day, some of the Onondaga and Mohawk boys took
me down into one of the False Face caves where we smoked for the
People and the Earth. In the deep dark crevice of our Mother, we sent
strong words into the Mystery for the spirits who lived there.

That day I went into the elementary school where I had
addressed the teachers. I met more of the students there and talked
more personally with the administrators and the teachers. Generally
speaking, they did cooperate. Some of the teachers actually had
arranged the students' desks in circles. As a matter of fact, in the
whole school I noticed only one classroom where the American
flag remained. I could tell by the posters on the wall and the books
on the shelves that it was a social studies and American history
classroom. Though there was no one in it, the door was left open,
and I simply walked in, removed the flag, rolled it up, and placed it
respectfully on the teacher's desk with a brief note. I wrote that I
understood how difficult it was for him to remove his country's flag
from the room, but that I had done it for him.

The following morning I visited with the Faithkeeper of
Onondaga. She was also a clan mother who reflected generations of
Iroquois beauty and dignity. She was round and loving like the
earth. Her hair was corn-silk white and silver like the moon. She
was teaching an Indian culture class in the basement of the grade

194

school. She asked me if I would come and say some words to the children.

It was quite a visit. They shared their Indian projects with me and enjoyed touching my braids. They looked at me and studied me, and I winked and smiled back. Why is it, I thought, that I have such love for these children? The love is so strong, it fills me to the point that it hurts. It hurts because I want so much for them. It hurts because I see in them the potential of that new Indian nation, and I see it so often untapped or abused. Being with these kids and this clan mother that morning made me more determined than ever to live my vision.

I described to the children, the clan mother, and the two Indian teacher-aides what Fallen Timbers was like and, of course, the crows. I told them about the huge statue to honor General Wayne and his troops and how the crows gathered on it. I described how horrible the place was with super-highways going every which way. I told them about the rock where I stood smoking the pipe and how the plaque beneath it read that the Indians had offered their prayers with tobacco on that spot, and I reminded them that many of our native people had died to protect Mother Earth and this country from the destruction of the land that I saw there. I explained how Tecumtha, the great Shawnee leader who believed in the unity of all tribes, was killed in that battle, protecting his country and the earth. How the American soldiers shot Tecumtha again and again, but the soldiers could still hear Tecumtha's war cry, rallying his people to never surrender.

The children sat wide-eyed and listened.

"Observe your elders and your clan mothers, children," I told them. "See in their faces all the past generations who never surrendered your country and your culture. Never."

That afternoon I also visited the high school, which was off the reservation. I got to meet more of the Indian teenagers there.

They were small in numbers, yet they were strong of heart. I told them about the books. I gave the leader of their group a list of books that they should insist be put in the school library. And I met a white teacher who said that she would be there to support them.

On the last day, one of the elder chiefs and his wife invited Simone and me for lunch. It was wonderful to share that last afternoon with them, and get a glimpse of ourselves in years to come. They too lived in a small house tucked in the woods and embraced by the hills. It seemed what was left of the Onondaga Nation was still embraced and protected by those hills. And as old as the old people were to us then, their eyes sparkled with love that was still there, a love that had enabled our people to endure one of the greatest acts of aggression in the history of this world.

When we were about to leave, she handed us a roll of bills that they had collected to help us on our journey.

"I can't take anything from my people," I said as Simone stood by my side. "This is how I was taught. I did not come here to take; I came here to give. As it stands, we have much love to take back. Besides, we'll make it to Minnesota. But, would you give this money to the high school kids, so that they can start buying books? I'd like that."

They said that they would.

While riding away, we decided to stop one last time to thank the land and the ghosts and the spirit of the place for helping, and to say words of strength for the People. We pulled the Mustang to the side of the road and walked into the woods and made our prayers that the People would continue.

CHAPTER 22

DOVE CREST
AND THE PRINCESS

T HE MUSTANG HUMMED up the winding road through the autumn-painted Berkshires of Massachusetts. I glanced over at Simone. She was reading from the book *Lame Deer*, peeking up every now and then, so she wouldn't miss the beauty of the mountains as we went. It was as though, in the Way of the Mystery, we were riding on the back of a great earth serpent, connecting what once was to what is next.

As we approached the coast, Simone put the book aside. She had never seen the ocean. While we stood on the rocky Rhode Island shore, her long Indian hair whipped in the wet wind as she stared out at the great, grey water. Here time, like the sea, has neither a beginning nor an end; it is all an ongoing part of the Mystery. In nineteen circles of seasons, she had never seen Atlantic waves nor felt Atlantic chill.

The water lapped at her feet; she bent down and touched it. She carried its salty tang to her lips on a shell. I imagined she was feeling our primordial beginnings. She was sensing her tribal knowing that came from countless generations of living The Way on this land. She was being blessed by this saltwater womb of

Mother Earth and by the energy that would keep her own womb fertile and strong. Gazing out at the ocean's grey, rolling vastness, her eyes reflected the wonder of it all: how it once separated worlds of people, worlds apart.

The Ojibway migration began here, not across a frozen arctic sea as she'd been taught in the white man's schools. Standing here, on this shore, Loon Song knew she was not a descendant of early immigrants to this Turtle Island continent. That whole Bering Strait theory was a white man's creation probably conceived to justify the white man's coming here and taking this land. So many white people who believe in this theory have said to us, "We came here just like you did, so we have just as much of a right to this land as you." Facts don't fully support the Bering Strait theory. They never will. For Simone's people have always been here. The Algonquins of the Northeast, the Narragansets and the Wampanoags, know this. They evolved here in America and grew as a People on this land.

When we arrived in their community of Dove Crest, we entered a Narraganset paradise, that is, if paradise can be defined by the beauty of the land and a people's ability to live in harmony with it. Leaving the Mustang in the gravel parking lot, we stood as if in the center of the world and sort of spun around just staring. There it all was, like I had described to her: the popular American Indian restaurant, with its basement bar where wild times and liquid memories had their days, and the big white house where the Doves, Fair Flower and her husband Roaring Bull, lived with the elder Princess Red Wing. And, of course, there was the trading post that the Princess operated. Across from the trading post was the Tomaquag Indian Museum. Alongside the old log building that stored the ancient wares and ways was the grassy knoll and open meadow where the ceremonies and pow wows took place on every full moon, for every season. It was here that Red Wing led her people in the ways of her ancestors, thanking the Earth and the Moon and

the Sun and the Rain and all of Manitou, the Great Mystery, for the
foods of life that made the People strong.

Several times a week, school children would empty out of
yellow buses and scamper and scramble up the incline to the welcoming smile of a "real Indian Princess." There, she would teach
and tell the stories that helped them understand the natural world
they lived in a little better, stories that made them understand themselves and the Indian even more. Soon, she'd have them dancing and
singing like natives to the beat of her grandmother drum, the drum
Red Wing would one day, before she died, pass to my daughter
Calusa. "This is the drum I have kept," she explained to Calusa,
"but now I'm too old and will be passing soon. Now I know you've
seen your brothers beat their sticks on the warrior's drum when you
could not. I know how this made me feel when I was a girl. Then
my grandmother gave me this drum. She told me like I'm telling
you now, that songs of war are sung on the warrior's drum; you
should not touch it. That would interfere with its purpose to invoke
death and yours to create life, so keep this grandmother drum and
take care of her, Calusa. Sing on her for your people and for Mother
Earth. Should your brothers ask you to use the drum for these reasons, only you may grant that permission."

There was no beating of Red Wing's grandmother drum that
day along the grassy knoll as Simone and I walked toward the creek
that splashed through the woods bordering this pretty place. There
was only the familiar beating of our native Indian hearts along the
quiet path. Hearing the gentle rush of water ahead, I recalled earlier
visits to Dove Crest and the times I had smoked the pipe alongside
the creek in the morning rays of sunlight. While I held it high, I
remember seeing the dew drops on colored leaves transform themselves into glistening diamonds, decorating the trees. At times they
even seemed to me like countless crystals, each with its own special
gift of spirit and life, each with an insight. So as the mists of the

earth would warm and settle, I would squat by the creek, cradling the pipe closer, as if it brought me closer to the Mystery of where I began. I would imagine feeling the ghosts of the people around me, and I would feel humbled by their presence, imagined or not, until I felt the sun melt the mists all away.

Simone and I stayed there for a while by the pretty waters flowing, and then we headed for the trading post where Princess Red Wing was. All along the path we sensed and felt the spirit of this peaceful place; it was everywhere, and we were everywhere in it.

When we reached the trading post door, Simone stood somewhat nervously behind me. When I opened it and stepped inside, my eyes adjusted quickly to the dimmer light and fixed on the birch-bark scroll over the back door that opened into Princess Red Wing's study. It was still there, just as I remembered. Inscribed on it were the names of Red Wing's family. I pointed to it. "There I am," I said, smiling. "See, Simone? White Deer." Indeed! I thought. There I am.

Seeing my name recorded in that way meant that I belonged. It was proof I had a family. I guess one could say that having my name included on Red Wing's family scroll allowed me a sense of identity. I would need such tangible acceptance of who I was in this white man's world that requires legal documents and papers to prove who and what we are. That inscription on the birch-bark scroll allowed me a sense of legitimacy. It was something she and my uncles wanted for me, something they each gave to me because they loved me and understood.

Simone gazed up at the scroll over the door and squeezed my arm. "Yes, I see it," she whispered. "I see your name."

▲▲▲

It was set into motion very late one night, when the currents of air were still, and the power of silence was deep. Nippawanock had a vision. It happened at the table in the room in Florida where he sat grading papers while a cup of coffee cooled in front of him. His hands helped to support his weary head, and his eyes rested closed when the magical singing began, "and the walls of the room fell away," Uncle Nip described. Within a mist that somehow manifested out of the Mystery, a white deer came singing. The sacred deer was singing my name. The song he was singing was my name.

So, behind Nip's house in Florida, we passed the old, black stone pipe as Princess Red Wing was summoned to introduce me to the Universe. This happened the night after I received my college degree. "Through this pipe the People live," Red Wing said, pointing it towards the evening sky. "Through this pipe, the Indian prays to the four quarters of the universe and to Manitou."

The particular pipe she held was kept by the uncles, but it was presented to them by Red Wing. Among all the experiences it shared with the People, it was for Red Wing a most special pipe: It was her marriage pipe. On that early spring night in the backyard of my old uncle's house, it became my naming pipe as well. With both hands, she held it high and called out my new name in the language of the People: "Skanondeh Galaga," she said to the stars, again and again. "Skanondeh Galaga. . . ."

"White Deer . . ." Uncle Nip would respond each time, "White Deer."

They repeated this until it became an incantation to each of the Four Directions and to the Sky and to the Earth. They called out my name on the pipe to the mighty sun, and to all living things of the land, great and small, to the trees and the plants, to the flowing streams and seas, to all the nations of the air and waters, and to the greater winds and lesser ones. And the evening star danced in the West all the while like I remember seeing it as a boy. They prayed that I would ascend the four hills of life and travel beyond where the ancestors lived. Then Uncle Nip pierced our fingers until our blood appeared, and he bound our hands together with strips of red Pima cotton, and we mixed our blood in the presence of the pipe and we made our vows of love and loyalty in this way.

▲▲▲

When Princess Red Wing emerged from the back room of the trading post and opened the door over which the scroll hung, she saw me and glowed with excitement and happy surprise, and she embraced me. She was as old and as beautiful as she was every time I remembered seeing her. Bent over from age, her hug was nevertheless as strong as it always had been. Stepping back, she smiled and acknowledged Simone. Her magnified eyes twinkled behind her wire-framed glasses as she put out her hand and took Simone's.

My stomach churned. This was my godmother. Red Wing was one of the most special people in my life, so bringing Simone here had to be a sign that Simone was, indeed, the special one. I had taken Simone to Onondaga; now we were in Dove Crest with the woman who bestowed my name upon me. Red Wing was more than a godmother, more than a grandmother. Our ties were greater than blood; they were bonds made on the pipe in the Mystery. We were spirit family now, and we always would be.

"Princess Red Wing," I stammered, "this is Simone. She's Ojibway. She's . . . my . . . girlfriend?" Did that sound awkward! Girlfriend? I hadn't said that word since I was a teenager. But what else could I say? And it was that word that kept Simone and I from sleeping together while we stayed at Dove Crest. It was that word and the nights we slept apart that caused us to look more deeply into what truly was happening to our lives and what it was like to sleep without the other.

"You can stay in my study, Grandson," insisted the Princess. "I'll take Simone up to my room. She'll be very comfortable there. If you were married, then I would take the study, or you could even have the small apartment over the museum."

The possibilities were endless; some I'd already heard from the grandmothers at Onondaga. Married? I repeated the idea to myself. **203** I'd marry Simone. Would she marry me? Wasn't this trip through two autumns an elopement of sorts, the kind they had back when a young Indian couple simply set up house together? I could feel the loving concern of the People urging us to do what was right.

That first night I stayed with Red Wing while she beaded. It was an unforgettable time.

Anyone who ever knew Red Wing knew she was for real. She was, indeed, the direct descendant of the Massasoit Osamekun and his two sons, Wamsutta and Metacomet. That blood she shared with me. They were the ones who greeted the Pilgrims as "brothers" on these shores. They helped them through that first winter.

Oh, I had heard the stories before! They were not the ones I learned in the schools of shadow people. Red Wing and the uncles told me how the white man came to these fertile shores, deformed, weak, and dying, loaded with rum and righteousness, but starving for sustenance of spirit and love. First, they came as disease-infested slavers. Then, as religious zealots and bigots. I was told how they said they wanted only a place to spread their blankets. How they twisted the sacredness of language. How the kind Massasoit Osamekun died disillusioned. How poison and humiliation killed his oldest son Wamsutta. How these hungry, desperate and transplanted humans from across the great water became insolent and bold. How they took and kept taking. How Metacomet's stirring orations rallied the Native People to fight the first war on this turtle island against the invaders from Europe.

I was told how the early colonists slaughtered Red Wing's ancestors in their sleep, quartering the body of Metacomet and severing his head. I learned how, for twenty-seven years, it was impaled on a spike and displayed in a glass case in the quaint Pilgrim town of Plymouth. Oh, I knew the stories of these timidly portrayed little folks, who countless kids play on Thanksgiving Day, with their nifty Pilgrim hats and cute Pilgrim bonnets. They may have called Metacomet "King Philip of Pokanoket" because they feared his power and his influence, but they butchered him just the same. Like one of their transplanted pigs, they butchered a man they called a king.

In spite of all that had happened, Red Wing tried to show the white man how he could still grow. She told the stories of the desperate Pilgrim Governor Bradford and the tolerant religious leader, Roger Williams. She told the stories of the past to all those she would ever address as a spokesperson for her people. Whether speaking at a conference in Geneva or as a guest speaker at the United Nations, she always tried to raise the consciousness of people. But what truly fascinated me when I was young was how she could still refer to the white man as brother. With all she knew, with all her people had been through, she called the white man brother!

I understand more about these things now than I did during that year of two autumns. I had much to learn from Red Wing, and while Simone was sleeping alone upstairs that first night at Dove Crest, Red Wing and I stayed up very late.

I never knew that Red Wing was nearly banished because she stood up to the elders during the early part of this century and said that we must write down our language and our stories, or our traditions and the truths would be lost. "It's forbidden!" they said. I never knew that even her peers conspired against her. They assaulted her character and threatened her welfare. They questioned her identity. That's why she cherished the scroll, and why she inscribed my name upon it. She knew something about such needs that I was not yet aware of.

Regardless of what her elders said or her peers did to try and stop her, Red Wing did what she believed was right. She wrote

down all she could and recorded the stories that give origin to identity. She wrote them down and suffered for it for many years. She
even recorded the language. Then the old ones died; one by one the
Narraganset stories and the Wampanoag language and their ceremonies died with them. Their children's children and the children of
her peers would know little of the things that keep a people strong
had it not been for the written word of Princess Red Wing and her
courage to save what she could.

This I learned that first night while she beaded symbols for
her new headband. "But whatever else you must know, White
Deer, know that we must never quarrel among ourselves in the face
of the white man. We do our disagreeing behind the wigwam's
door. When we appear before him, we must appear as one."

The next morning I stood by the creek at dawn, gazing at the
crystals of light formed on the dewy earth by the rising sun. Red
Wing does not hate the white man, I thought. She considers him
a "brother." She regards him as a relative who has never been trained
in The Way. She sees him like a younger brother who is still evolv-
ing and still frightened of all he can't comprehend.

I wondered if maybe Red Wing was too forgiving because
she became a Christian some time back, even though she'd never
talk to me about that, and even though it was something she separated from being Indian. I kept thinking; the creek kept splashing.

She spent her life teaching the white man and his children
and even those among her own people who came to share his civilized fears and confusions. She taught them truths about the past,
and she taught them about love. She reminded them of their commitments to Mother Earth and to the future generations. She spent
her life doing this. Whether as an Indian or a Christian, she
reaffirmed our spiritual ties to each other and to nature. She instilled
in her audiences, old and young, the need to live in peace. She
instructed the Indian boys on the importance of seeking visions

from Manitou. She reminded the Indian girls of their indigenous independence and beauty.

Here I stood by this flowing creek once again, holding the red stone Great Mystery pipe and thinking all this . . . thinking how, after nearly 500 years of genocide and greed, the creek's joyful energy, like Red Wing's words of truth, still sings like music through the land. The beauty of the People and the earth, however fragile and small, has endured!

My words carried in the smoke that early morning at Dove Crest, words that would help me draw from this beautiful place all that it has to teach, that I too may grow in Beauty's Way for the People and the Earth. That I too may help the beauty of the People to endure.

Later that morning, after Simone and I toured the Tomaquag Indian Museum and shared the stories woven into the baskets and painted on the pottery, Red Wing gave us directions to the Great Swamp. This was the site of the last Indian resistance to colonization in the area of the United States now called, understandably, New England. It lies deep in the woods where a straight, black-top road leads to a huge, black monument erected in honor of the English colonists who "defeated a united Indian force."

The Great Swamp was the place where hundreds of tired and starving Indians, mostly women and children, were killed before sunrise that day by the sternly devoted Christian newcomers from across the very sea that Simone had first seen the day we arrived at Dove Crest. They came over and finally surrounded what was left of the People after the smallpox-ridden slavers had ventured through this country a year or so before the Pilgrims. They surrounded the People at the Great Swamp and killed them all, including the great King Metacomet himself.

In my anguish I recalled that day of horror when the sun rose unwelcome above the horizon. Its light cast only shadows through the torn trees and on the devastation of the Great Swamp. Whatever remained alive must have heard only the gurgling cries of hungry babies writhing in the dark red mire near their dead fallen mothers. There was no smoke from the Indian's pipe to greet the sun that day, no scent of Indian tobacco, only the smoke and burning smell of the white man's guns. There was no song on the drum for the sun that day, not even the beating of happy hearts. There was no melody of flute to accompany the birds, no music of laughing children, no prayers to Manitou; there were only the words of thanksgiving to a new God and Savior, for helping to send the red devils back to hell where they belonged.

Princess Red Wing knew what path we were on in this great Wheel of Life. She knew we had to go there, to the Great Swamp, just like she had to. Looking back, I'm sure we reminded Red Wing very much of herself, when she was young and newly in love with her handsome Tama husband. The youthful fire of the heart must have burned in her in much the same way she was seeing the flames in me, in the same way I now see that fire in the eyes of other children. Perhaps it is a flame passed on in the genes. Perhaps it is that tiny spark of the Mystery that still holds passion for life.

Before we left for the Great Swamp, Red Wing untied her headband and gave it to me. "Your braids have grown longer," she said. I think she was telling me in the way of the elders that I had matured. I stared at the beaded band in my hands. It was her naming headband, the one that tells the story of her origin in beaded symbols: Princess Red Wing of the Seven Crescents of the Royal House of Pokanoket. It was the headband she had worn for most of her life. I tied it on, and I could feel the power of her love and experience encircling my brain and forever my thoughts.

With the sun high over the peaceful, pretty place the Narragansets and Wampanoags called Dove Crest, Simone and I rode the Mustang back down the colorful, tree-lined road that took us there.

When a school bus passed with wide-eyed kids of all colors peering out, it made me think about the love Princess Red Wing had for all people, especially the children. I thought about this small Indian sanctuary as all that remained of King Philip's nation, whose boundaries once extended between the Berkshires and the sea. I thought about how much Indians have in common with the birds and the animals and the trees these days. I thought about the crows gathering ahead.

TIES TO THE PAST

L IKE A SACHEM in the old tradition, contemplating some aspect of the Great Mystery, Carises sat in the front yard with his back against a palm tree. The long fronds above him swept over him and shaded him from a warm winter sun. Standing alongside him, like a sentry from the ghost world, was the young crow his sister Calusa had raised. He's called Quoth. You don't often see kids seven years old quietly contemplating things by themselves these days, but there Carises was, his long dark hair and the black feathers of the crow being tousled by a strong southeasterly wind.

Carises is the darkest of our three children. When he was old enough to talk, he would often surprise us by asking questions about the extinct people he was named for, the Carises. His first phrases and complete thoughts were ideas expressed about where these people lived and how they died.

I can remember that during Simone's pregnancy with Carises, Uncle Nip had researched the people called the Carises. From all the books Nip read, and from that special way he had of understanding things through dreams and contemplation, he discovered some very interesting characteristics about these extinct people. Through Uncle Nip, Carises would not only understand something very special about the people he was named for, but he would learn about Carises, the boy that he was as well.

One night when the moonlight shone bright through the dream wheel that hung from the window just above his crib, Carises gazed up at Simone and told her that his mother and father used to live in California — and that Carises had died at thirty-seven after being sick a long time. He said that he had died among tall trees while looking out at the ocean.

Strangely, this was what Uncle Nip had learned through his research: that the Carises did, in fact, live in California, and that they were decimated by the white man's guns and diseases. Nip also learned something much more. The Carises people formed two groups, probably large enough to consider each a separate tribe. One lived on the coast of northern California, thriving and developing there for, perhaps, forty thousand years. They lived not far away from present day Sunnyvale, the location where skeletal remains of some of the oldest Homo sapiens in the world were found — that is, some of the oldest remains of fully modern humans.

Uncle Nip also discovered in his research on the Carises people that they not only occupied an expanse of territory on the northern California coast, but that the other tribe, or group, lived among the giant redwoods in the northern California mountains. Though they were both Carises, they developed apart and somewhat differently. The ones who lived on the coast were, probably, what some contemporaries would call pacifists — they rejected violence. But the Carises people who lived in the mountains among the redwoods were different. They were what modern sociologists might call militants, a kind of people who would be willing to fight if the occasion warranted such conduct.

While Carises sat with his back against the palm in the front yard with Quoth, Simone and I joined him.

Placing our arms around Carises and our kisses on his soft and brown chubby cheeks, we took turns greeting him.

"Hey, Crispy Critter," Simone said. He smiled at the sound of his pet name. He's grown to see his brownness as beautiful and a part of the nature of this land. "What are you thinking about?"

"I'm thinking about what Dad told me about the Carises people. I'm thinking about what Uncle Nip said about them bein' pacifists and militants."

I glanced at Simone and she at me. Those were impressive words for a seven-year-old to remember after hearing them but a few times a while back, and the very idea that he remembered them at all was intriguing, though Uncle Nip had always taught us to tell them the words — that in time they'll learn their meanings.

Then Simone seemed to recall something important that we had forgotten to tell him. "Carises," she said, "Dad never got to finish what Uncle Nip had said about you because soon after we had this conversation with him, Uncle died. He'd made the Great Change before he got a chance to tell you the most important part about what he learned. And after his death, well, I guess Dad and I forgot to tell you." A warm gust whipped around us, stirring the fronds above and settling still among us, as if it chose to stop and listen. It was as though we had watched it as it moved through the fronds and settled near us.

"What Uncle Nip said about you, Carises," Simone continued, "is very special. He said that you'd live to be the embodiment of both. This means that Uncle Nip believed you would be the blend of the Carises people, both pacifist and militant. He meant that you will never start a fight. You'll only fight when, and if, it's absolutely necessary. You're a protector, Carises, not a destroyer. Those are his words."

Carises smiled, acknowledging the words, and rested his head on his mother's shoulder. He understood that he was loved by those living, and not living. Simone kissed him again, this time on the head; and she hugged him again too, and she held onto his small, brown hand. Quoth cawed and took wing, circled, cawed again, and flew away.

"Can you feel him?" Carises asked, sighing and taking in a deep breath of sweet air.

"Who?" I asked.

"Uncle Nip. That's why I'm sitting out here. Can't you just feel him, Dad?"

And I could. I could feel Uncle Nip in the air, and it reminded me so strongly of that day when Simone and I arrived at the Great Swamp and we could feel the presence of the People.

▲▲▲

It happened on our journey through two autumns, several years before Carises would be born. We could feel the people then. We could feel them everywhere. The tall dark statue that stood in memory of colonial power at the park's entrance stood as a symbolic reminder of the military might and aggression used to usurp another people's country. But there was no beauty there in such an image. And there was no power, at least, not in the spiritual sense and meaning of the word "power."

Instead, the beauty was there in the quiet woods and the power could be felt in the air, which was still when we reached the site of the massacre, but now and then a gust would whip the colored leaves still clinging to their trees and blow many more to the ground. Their fall hues made the woods appear sun-drenched yellow and gold and earth-red rust and brown.

Everywhere were trees. They rose out of a fertile dark muck and mire, and seemed to luxuriate in the warmth of that Indian summer day in autumn.

The ruffled feathers of many crows quivered in the autumn wind as they perched on the boughs of bare limbs. The big birds stood mysterious in their blackness. They seemed to be everywhere, observing our presence.

Neither Simone nor I spoke a word. There was nothing that needed saying. We simply walked with the Pipe that I carried in my arms among the trees. Even with the crows perched all around, there was no sharp caw to pierce the silence. I can only figure that they must have perceived the two people walking below them were not beings of danger or a threat to this place where the spirits of dead leaves and people dwelled. I even wondered if the crows might not be, in some way, the very spirits of the people who had died here, the ones whose true story must be told. I wondered too if they could even be the messengers of those people who traveled from the ghost world through the dimensions of past and present. I thought about the crow feathers that twirled on the ghost-dance shirts in the still air that night we smoked with Old Man Bill and the others in the Minneapolis Institute of Arts.

Our hair that day in the Great Swamp was like the feathers of the crows above us. It was dark in this yellow place, dark like the moist earth, dark like the night. And, in such darkness, there is that essence of mystery, that essence of hope that arises out of the moist earth and the night like new life and stars.

And it occurred to me that day when we smoked at the Great Swamp that we had been on a pilgrimage of sorts. . . . Fallen Timbers and Tecumtha . . . now Metacomet . . . and always the crows. We came to pray for strength and wisdom and to thank our ancestors for that which we have already received from them . . . the legacy of their word. . . . And it occurs to the mind that they had organized the final resistance to the colonizers. . . . Surely all these journeys and musings would come together as we traveled the land and saw, and felt in our blood, in our genes, our ties to the land.

And we thought of the peacemaker and The Great Law . . . the times then and what is now. . . . We thought of creation accounts and migration accounts . . . of how the original people, in the midst of five hundred years of indoctrination under the force and the depression of sheer numbers of "them," have survived and are attempting to make it good for our children. . . . Surely this says something . . . for our power as a people, as a nation, and the will we have to survive.

Simone remarked on our way back towards the car that she had heard a Palestinian ask, "When have they ever stopped being colonizers?"

On that day I know that we both felt that these people from another land hadn't.

"They are not comfortable here in America," she said. "They haven't yet become residents on the earth. They don't share our sense of beauty." We could see by their cities and pollution that they never became one with this land — they have never really "lived" here. . . .

The caves at Onondaga, those crevices that go deep into the body of the earth, are where spirits of the false-face beings dwell. Their purpose is healing. From there I sensed the idea of emergence — how needed they are in this world that has grown sick. I sensed the idea of emergence all around me — the Navajo account — the Zuni — the Hopi — the Kiowa. As we traveled we sensed more and more that we did in some form emerge from this earth. Our migration and creation stories do not tell of Asian descent — they tell us we came from here, from this land.

And as we traveled we talked about the original people and the original cosmology. They are profound indeed!

Simone and I agreed that we had gained innate understandings from that trip, yet we still had trouble putting them together and seeing our place in it all. But we realized we were growing, learning, seeking . . . and that we were doing this together.

Occasionally, Simone would say that she could glimpse an understanding or insight, but then they seemed fleeting, ephemeral.

And as these "flashes in the dark happened," we both could feel the need to be teaching again and nurturing all those other sparks. . . .

Yes, I had smoked the pipe among the crows at Fallen Timbers and among the graves at Cataraugus. I smoked it among the ancient hills and forests of Onondaga, and now I smoked it again, this time with Simone among the crows at the Great Swamp. Together we'd once again feel the Orenda of the land. This time it would rise from the earth and surge through our whole being. We could feel the goodness of the People in the wind, just like Carises would that day in the future under the palm with his mother and me, recollecting things that are, as Uncle Nip would say, simply of the Mystery.

THE DREAM

O N THE WAY BACK to Minnesota, Simone and I talked and got excited and exchanged ideas. Together we could see how the literature of the People truly supported the history, and how the poetry reinforces and reflects the understandings of the People. "Everything's related," Simone said, looking up from reading *Lame Deer.* "Everything's within the circle of life, and equal."

Simone told me that she had also realized that she had gained as great an understanding of history as do the ones who profess to teach it. She said that she had experienced the irony and the profoundness of this history.

"Sometimes," she said, "I become frightened by the clarity."

We stopped by Onondaga after the day at the Great Swamp. We spent one more day there. We spent one more day becoming more in harmony with the beauty of the hills and the land. We spent one more day giving ourselves up to them and concentrating on them, trying to remember, and trying to understand.

After we left Onondaga, Simone would recall the beauty of the Berkshires and say how overwhelmed she was by the knowledge that this land is ours . . . that it all belongs to our people and to us by extension.

I said that I felt that way too, and that for me, "It's like something I remember . . . from a long time ago."

That night we stayed in Canada, and something happened to me. What did occur would once again make it so difficult for me to find the thread that separates the vision and the dream.

What a dream it was! What memory had been evoked?

The images remain. . . . And the feelings . . . they will never leave. Even now as I tell the story about the innocents I killed, the feelings return and they are real. . . .

▲ ▲ ▲

The soldiers were on our trail, so I led the small band of our people across the stream that cut through the side of a familiar mountain. It was an early autumn for the people and the land. It was cold. The sun had nearly set. I took a winding path where the spirits of dead leaves rose in a mist from the ground around my legs and the legs of those who followed. We traveled to where the path ended at a deserted cabin tucked away in a meadow where corn stalks stood bent and dying or dead and heavy from the unharvested and rotting cobs. I recall thinking how much like the corn we have always been.

The soldiers were coming fast, but the People were weak. It was so cold that I shivered in the dream. Some of the people were near starvation. The soldiers pursued us like angry wasps.

One of the women was pregnant. We had to stop in the cabin while the baby could be born. The soldiers drew closer. If we stayed, we understood that we would all be killed. We had to move on. I'd begun urging the People out the door when the woman who was pregnant suddenly gave birth to a child with no name. It was as silent an act as day turning into night. She could not go on. She was bleeding to death. The other females in the small band were either too young or too old. There was no milk for the child with no name. No one could help. If we left her and the baby behind, we feared that the soldiers would do horrible things. We had learned what the soldiers did to women.

She begged me to kill her and the baby in order to save the rest from the soldiers.

I told the others to leave . . . quickly. I was alone with her and the newborn. With her face drawn and determined, she squeezed my arm with all the strength that was left in her. "Please," she implored.

A crow cawed loudly and flew across the path that led to the cabin. He was a dark shadow fleeting across the cold grey sky.

The soldiers were approaching.

I pressed the face of the infant to my chest. It died to the beating of my heart, never opening its eyes, still attached to the cord that bound him to his mother.

Turning to the young woman who lay in her own blood on the hardwood floor of the cabin near the crimson placenta that had enabled her baby to live, I drew my steel knife. And then the man I dreamed I was ended it all. It was a powerful force she may never have felt. Though her body collapsed from the blow, she seemed dead already. The knife that was deep in her chest only stopped her heart from beating.

I awoke crying and sat heaving at the edge of the bed. My hands were over my face. I stood against the wall of the motel room and, still sobbing, I turned to Simone. I said that I would always fight them. I would always fight the white man. If I had to be born back again and live a whole lifetime just for the chance to fight them once, then I would do it. That was my vow when I killed the woman and her baby.

That was the dream that made it so hard to live the vision all these years. The thread that separates the two is so fine. Yet, as the elders had said, there is a difference between the dream and the vision.

Past lives. Ghosts. Spirits. Powers of the day and the night. Forces in the wind. Beings who dwell among the stars. In a universe that is incomprehensible, I've come to believe that anything is possible because it's all a part of an ongoing Mystery that we all share.

▲▲▲

We followed the Canadian highways west heading back on a path Old Man Bill would tell us later was the exact route the Ojibways took before they settled in the forests and along the shores of Gitchie Gumme, the Great Lake now called Superior.

Being in Canada didn't do much, though, to help alleviate the feeling of oppression that comes when an Indian sees so many strangers and so much of what "they've" done. Canada was never a haven for Indians to find sanctuary, as it was for young Americans who were fleeing the draft and the Vietnam War.

I hear the Metis and the Mohawks are the ones to tell you about Canada's treatment of our Native people. It was, for certain, no refuge for AIM leader Leonard Peltier, who fled there to escape the United States justice system.

Snow fell most of the way back, and I had the uneasy feeling that we were being followed some of the way. Maybe it was that inner voice, but I felt something oppressive about to happen, something ominous and unavoidable.

It was late at night and I'd been driving in the snow-streaked darkness for several hours. Simone was asleep as we approached the summit of the hill we'd been climbing for several miles, and for what seemed like a long time. As soon as the Mustang reached the top, the entire area of the sky ahead suddenly illuminated. As we headed toward the light, I got confused and had that strange sensation that I'd somehow tripped back in time and fell through again.

WE WILL REMEMBER . . .

T HE BLINDING HEADLIGHTS and spotlights of the police
cruisers burst the dark South Dakota night and blasted
through the windows of the church. I took cover with the children
of Heart of the Earth behind the cinder block walls and quickly
assembled make-shift barriers.

Out from the darkness behind the light-shattered night,
malicious men in uniforms jeered and tormented. "Send out the
squaws, and we'll let you go."

"Bring out the red pussy. . . . "

Then came the shots from their guns, momentarily aimed
in the air, and then the mock war-whooping from their mouths.
They seemed to be having the same kind of fun Redskins football
fans have on any given autumn Sunday at Robert F. Kennedy
Memorial Stadium. It was the same kind of fun the Cleveland
Indians baseball fans have cheering the image of Chief Wahoo
around the bases. Only these were officers of white American law
in Rapid City, South Dakota, and their mocking war-whoops
were not those of sports fans. Though they too were having fun
at the expense of the Indian, their kind of fun was different and

deadly. It was darker and more sinister in nature, because the game they played was not football or baseball, but life and death. And the genocide they threatened to inflict was not cultural, but physical.

We were four adults, two men — a young aide and me — and two women. In our care were about forty students from the survival school, ranging from eight years old to about sixteen. We had just arrived in Rapid City after a long bus ride from Minneapolis. For any Indian associated with AIM at that time, the state of South Dakota was a monster that devoured Indians. It was 1974. We were in Rapid City, in the monster's jaws, to support the newly founded We Will Remember Survival School and attend the first American Indian Movement Survival School Conference. We stayed the night in a Catholic church on a hill way above the city. We were totally cut off from the Indian leaders and men below; it was the perfect place for malevolent cops to harass and threaten us.

Among the older students were the warrior boys who had stood with me at gunpoint that frigid night in Minneapolis after our school had been ransacked. True to their nature, and without any of the adults knowing, two of them managed to slip outside the church and get a better look at what we were up against. They were excited and breathing hard when they returned.

"They got lots a guns, Gabe!"

"And they're yellin' about squaws and pussy."

"Yeah, they're saying a lot of real dirty stuff. This one cop car got this gun that's as big as the dashboard."

"They got huge guns."

Impressed by their abilities to scout the situation without being seen, I couldn't help but commend their acts of courage and skill. My concern for their well-being, however, balanced any glorification. "It was a brave thing that you did, but don't do it again without checking with us first. We don't want you dead."

I turned to the school's director, who had just pulled up behind me. I considered the worst, and I saw that concern reflected in her dark brown eyes. Elaine was a very proud Ojibway woman. She stood about five feet, four inches. She was lean, not thin. Her face was as fair and pretty as a moon flower. In her mid-twenties, she was a dedicated worker for the People. As pretty as she was, she had no mate. It was the same with almost all of us who worked in the survival schools those early years. Most of us were more caught up in our people's survival than in finding a mate. There was little to our personal lives. In order to teach or administrate in any of the survival schools back then, dedication and strength were requirements, and they had to flow with our ability to adapt. These were essential characteristics for any teacher or director. Elaine could never have survived those early years at Heart of the Earth had she none of these.

She had a college degree and was officially certified to run a school, but she was in a situation that college didn't prepare her for.

"This could be really bad, Elaine." We both knew from the harshness of the voices barking behind the bright headlights that the situation was bad.

We stood behind the wall in the hallway for cover. The folded fingers of her hands pressed against her pale lips as she contemplated the possible horror that might await us all. "Don't they know these are kids?" The muffled crashing and scraping sounds of tables being dragged across the floor and chairs turning over and shoved against the doors made it all more real to her. Then, more shouts and whooping from outside. More shots.

Scott, an eleven-year-old Lakota boy with brown, waist-long braids, and one of the older students, a fourteen-year-old Ojibway we called BJ, scooched up to us at the same time. They told us that they had just returned from the back of the church. "They're on the roof! You could hear 'em runnin' around up there!"

Elaine's lips tightened. "Damn it!" she said behind clenched teeth. "Where are our AIM leaders now?"

We smiled. It was as though she'd made a joke. They were in town staying in motels. Another gunshot shredded the humorous moment, and we became serious again.

"Is there any way to reach AIM on the phone?" she asked.

I shook my head slowly. "I don't think so . . . unless you know where any of them are staying."

"No. Besides, it wouldn't matter. They'd bust them as soon as they left. Maybe that's the whole idea behind this . . . to draw them up here."

"Or us out there," I added. "Look, why don't we try and get someone on the phone . . . anyone . . . before they bust in here? One of these kids is likely to get killed. They're slipping in and out. One of them's gonna get hurt."

Ana, the Ojibway culture and language teacher at the school, joined us in the hallway. Ana was in her mid-forties. Once a heavy drinker, she was the daughter of a well-known medicine man who had died some years earlier. What he had taught Ana about language, culture, and herbs, though, she would use to teach the Indian students at Heart of the Earth, and her job would also help to give her a sense of purpose and help keep her out of the bars on Franklin Avenue. And though Ana's drinking would cause her to fall too many times back on the avenue and eventually cost her the job she was so good at, that night under the gun in South Dakota there wasn't a better person than she to be with the kids. It was times like this, more often than not, that brought the best out in our people. It makes me sometimes wonder if that's not the most significant purpose of struggles in this life, to either break you or bring out the best in you.

Elaine and I edged over to the phone and squatted there behind the wall, deciding who to call. She looked at Ana. "How are the kids?" she asked.

"They're okay. The older ones are watchin' out for the younger ones." Ana paused, looked at me, then back at Elaine. "What'll we do?"

Again the shouts and the pounding on the roof. More shots, and our flinches.

"I'm gonna call the goddamned governor!" I said. "I'll call the goddamned head of the state police. I'll get someone to know what's goin' on up here." I knew something had to be done soon. The abominations outside could blast in at any moment or a shot could stray and strike one of the kids. An invincible will had suddenly suppressed any fear for my own well-being. I was not going to let these kids or any of our people get hurt or killed. To be without fear for my own welfare was a force in itself, to love one's people that much I believe is at the core of the native heart. But I wondered too if other Indians who had been killed recently had not felt the same as I did then.

Ana returned to the children, and Elaine stayed with me while I picked up the phone. It still worked!

Elaine and I took turns making calls as I had to go off with the boys and investigate the dark, isolated areas of the church where the kids would hear an occasional slam against a door or roof. We kept the place as dark as we could so not to be seen by the enemy outside, who would appear like shadows moving across the bright lights of their cruisers.

Seeing us scrambling low from room to room, carrying table legs for weapons, must've been a sight for the little ones huddled in a small classroom that was attached to the church. They were huddled in a long line with Ana behind the wall and barricade. Their little round faces and alert dark eyes appeared calm, yet they were fully aware of the imminent danger outside. These are Indian kids, I thought. And racial memory serves them well. It would serve us all well that night.

I don't know how many calls were made, but we finally got somebody out of bed. It might have been the lieutenant governor, I'm not sure. I do know it was someone high up in government though. What I do recollect was telling him that unless these heavily armed police outside this church were called off, there could be a slaughter. At that time, I wasn't alone in feeling this way. Elaine and Ana and the older students all knew the history of this land well. It's been a living and unchanged history ever since the Spaniards landed on San Salvador and the first American immigrants discovered gold in the Black Hills; only now it's not gold alone that drives their descendants crazy and allows them to inflict and tolerate abuse of Native people. It's uranium and coal and oil and the trees, and the economic profit generated from these "natural resources" that makes the white man, or any man who does not love the earth, so aggressively dangerous and threatening to those of us who do.

You see, beneath the surface of Native American lands are huge deposits of coal and uranium. On some reservations there are still mountains covered with trees. What true history has taught us about the white man's presence in this country is simple: What he wants, if he can't get it legally, he'll take. Or he'll manipulate the system so he can declare it his right to take what does not belong to him. This is what the "divine right of kings" was all about. This is what was behind the concept of Manifest Destiny. This is what the white man did with his religion, and this is what he does with his government.

To the Indian, the flag of the United States is not a unifying symbol at all, but rather a symbol that represents the white man's philosophy. As Uncle Nip once wrote, "Some see the stars as unfettered aspirations, the bars as confining reality." What the white man does is make the system work for him because he created the system, and the system is him. Even Henry David Thoreau in his

226   famous essay, "Civil Disobedience," called the American army a tool of government. That army can be the South Dakota State Police; it can be the Rapid City Police; it can be the F.B.I. agents who were there; it can even be the justice system that tried and convicted Indians like Leonard Peltier.

And what the white man has created is a society very different from the native and natural ones that existed here in America before he came. Indian societies were not divided into the haves and the have nots. You could not go into an Indian village or town and find a section of the town for the rich and a section for the poor. As Princess Red Wing once said, "Why, an Indian would be ashamed to have enough food in his lodge for his family yet allow the family in the lodge next to him to go hungry."

We taught the kids in the AIM survival schools that money can buy you just about anything, including your land back, but it cannot buy your integrity, your dignity, and certainly not your identity. So the reason why the Heart of the Earth or Red School House or We Will Remember schools were so threatening, and why the standing army of the United States attempted to terrorize even little kids that night in South Dakota, is basically because we instilled a sense of pride in Indian identity, and that identity binds us to our Mother Earth and allows us to be responsible citizens of this planet because she is our mother and every life form on her is our relative. We taught them that we all share an equal importance in this universe that we call the Great Holy Mystery. Such is our way and that cannot change either. If it does, and Indians regard the land as a resource to exploit for material gain, and violate the body of our mother with oil drills, radiation contamination, and strip mining, and cut the life out of trees growing old for profit, then those Indians may be monetarily better off for a time, but really they will be dead. As Luther Standing Bear said, ". . . though he [the Indian] walk crowded streets, he will, in truth, be dead."

In the late night hours, we heard the engines of the police cruisers outside cranking up. And just as suddenly as they burst their bigotry into our lives, they were gone. The church darkened, and all eyes inside peeked above the window sills and piled-up furniture. With owl eyes, we watched the crimson taillights of their cruisers head back down the hill. They were like drops of unspilled blood.

CROSSING BORDERS

T HEN I FOUND MYSELF following the taillights at some distance ahead as my beloved Simone stirred next to me.

I explained to her as she rubbed her tired eyes that the bright
cluster of lights in front of us seemed to come out of nowhere, and
that for an instant I couldn't remember where I was. As I drove
toward the light, Simone lowered the sleeping bag she had cuddled
into and sat up. She said that we must have reached the U.S. border
station. The snow was still falling and the wind still gusting when
we pulled under the pavilion's lights and into the station.

I stopped at the booth where I was supposed to, and two
American border guards with rifles stepped in front of the car. At
that point we were made to get out at gunpoint while they
insisted we were running guns for AIM and that I was Russell
Means. Our greatest fear was for the pipe I had wrapped in the
back seat. We knew that if they found it they could think it was
a rifle and take it out. There was no telling what they'd do to the
pipe once they found it.

I had heard what they did at Crow Dog's place — everyone
affiliated with AIM had. We heard that the feds went into his

home in South Dakota and smashed religious articles and took others. Medicine bags were opened, and their contents dumped onto the floor. Like thieves of spirit, the men of the government and white man's law acted like the Spaniards I saw on the island when I was a boy. Maybe this was their kind of racial memory.

What little traffic there was coming through the gate had to be detoured around us. Soon, there were only a few cars that slowly rolled under the roof and the bright lights. I'd glance at the cranked heads inside of them and see the eyes, staring at us through foggy windows. Then the cars would skid and fishtail away, tire chains crunching and rattling beneath them as they headed south into the snowy black night of Minnesota, where we wanted to go.

After they went through the contents of the trunk, one of the guards poked his head through the car window. He stayed there for what seemed to both of us like a long time before he straightened and walked over to us.

A third guard inside the station, who I had not seen, pushed the door open and stepped into the bitter night. As he leaned over the steps into the blowing snowy wind in his big grey coat, he shouted, "Are you Leonard Peltier?"

"No, I'm not Leonard Peltier. . . . I'm not carrying weapons. I'm a teacher. This is my wife."

All three guards, shielding themselves behind their baseball-type caps and furry nylon collars, stared at us and each other, like they were disappointed and didn't know what to do. The one by the station door stared the longest; then he turned and, struggling against the door, finally managed to open it wide enough to step back inside the station.

The guard who stood nearest me kept his rifle aimed at my chest as he said that they had information that we crossed the border in New York.

I turned my head and looked into his blue eyes. They were

cold and stoic. I'd seen eyes like his before. I'd seen them in the men who held guns at my head the night Heart of the Earth was invaded. I'd seen that cold blue in the eyes of F.B.I. agents whose job it was to infiltrate and disrupt AIM functions.

He demanded my license.

"I'm a teacher," I repeated, as he examined it. Then, as if to defy any sense of reason, I had to add that this was our country and that we should be free to travel in our own country.

"It sure doesn't look that way at the present moment now, does it?" he responded. "And don't give me that rhetoric. I'm a Native American. I was born in this country. We go back three generations."

The roof over the border station rattled as if something outside of us had become angry. The roof seemed like it would be torn away. No longer did it provide even the slightest protection from the blowing snow and bitter wind. The roof had suddenly become threatening. It made the two guards feel vulnerable and insecure even as they held their weapons close. The station door opened and the head of the man inside peeked out, turned, and looked upward. His eyes scanned the rattling roof. He didn't like what he saw. Then I could see him, through the window, on the telephone. The two guards looked at each other, then above. They seemed suddenly bent by the arctic cold, and they stepped back away from the car and Simone and me before breaking for the station door.

The power of three hundred horses surged forward on the icy road, as Simone and I slid across the border, and, like a snowy blur, disappeared into the wintry night of Ojibway country.

For two hours I drove the Mustang in second and third gears through a white, freezing night, sometimes blindly through the snow. Simone, bundled up in a sleeping bag, stared ahead. Her voice kept me focused. Her words kept my mind from sleep. We were hungry and very tired. Had we taken the money we were offered in Onondaga, we could get a room and put up for the night. But we had to keep going.

Finally, the snow stopped, and I shifted into fourth. We flew the rest of the way back to the Twin Cities in the dark without the snow. We were like owls in the night.

By the time we swooped down I-90 through St. Paul and over the Mississippi River into Minneapolis, we were running on empty. It was about three in the morning when we finally got home. It had been a wondrous journey through two autumns. Now, winter was coming on strong. And winter, especially in Indian country, usually means a lot of death.

THE SPIRIT JOURNEY
AND THE PIPE

WHEN THE FLORIDA AUTUMN gives way to winter, the warm afternoons spent lazily in the hammock become brisk, wintry walks on a barren beach. During a cold front we sometimes bundle up in sweaters or wrap ourselves in blankets; then, barefooted, Simone and I and the children head up and down the shore, often stopping to examine pretty shells or to sift the sand for scattered sharks' teeth or old pottery shards. We search through the sea grasses, poking sticks of driftwood into the soft wet clumps that washed up on the beach, or we simply pause, like a ritual of acknowledgment for the Mystery of life that created all this, and say thank you. The unusually crisp and salty air cuffs our faces and fills our senses and helps us maintain our connection, not only to the land, but to the elements as well. We sometimes stand into the wind and watch the waves of the clean, clear water break into cold white crystals of foam that caress our feet as we wade through tidepools warmed by the sun. And beyond the whitewater we might even see dolphins or pilot whales, spraying and rising high enough to be seen, greeted, and appreciated.

And that peculiar feeling that comes to me every fall, that feeling of being back in time, usually gives way to that winter feeling of wanting to be close with the things and the people that I love, drawing in life's energies and keeping quiet . . . being still . . . and listening. We call the winter solstice and that time around Christmas, Peace-time.

Winter brings to mind all these things, and yet. . . .

Perhaps it was my first year teaching at Wind River that makes me so aware of death during the winter months. Maybe it was all those funerals I remember, the ones where the old and the too-young-to-die were buried. Perhaps it's because that didn't change when I was a teacher in AIM or worked at the Indian Center in Minneapolis as the cultural arts director. Perhaps winter seems like a time of dying to me because everyone I've loved as family has died in winter's presence. I know that in the great Circle of Life that is a purpose of winter, though; it's another part of the balance.

It seems like just a few years ago, when my wife Simone was only thirty-one, that her mother, Elaine Stately, or Woman-Who-Sweeps-Away-With-The-Crane's-Wing, died of cancer. She was fifty years old. Two years before her death, she went to the Indian Health Board in Minneapolis to see one of the doctors there. She told him she was feeling some pain and discomfort in her abdomen and was diagnosed with a kidney infection. She took her medicine as prescribed but the pain continued. A year later the pain had become so severe that she had to go to General Hospital. Her death came less than a year after that, after she was diagnosed as having cancer.

Her death did not come quickly nor easily. It was a slow and horrible death through a long bitter winter, yet it must have given her spirit-power a chance to gather itself, so when it finally did make its contribution into the Mystery, there was plenty enough power there for the next generation. That is what Uncle Nip had told me

234

the traditional Indian believed. That is the way I understood it. When we are born, it's like taking a cup of spirit out of the gene pool of life that the Mystery provides. We must pour that cup back when we die, like a drop of rain that falls back into the ocean where it originated, except that the drop of spirit we take into this world should increase in size. It can do this if we become closer to the spiritual things of life rather than the material. That way we put back more than we came in with. This assures each generation of enough spirit-power to be born spiritually strong, with innate understandings and knowledge.

The key idea, according to the way Uncle Nip described it, is to fill our cups with goodness. That way, when we die, all that goodness pours back into the Mystery and into those we love. A slow death by cancer is not a choice of death anyone would make, but for Simone's mother, it allowed the spirit of her life to fill up with even more goodness. It allowed Elaine the time to make arrangements to be buried like an Indian, and to make her jump at the bridge and her journey on the trail of stars a smooth one.

Uncle Nip, who learned of Elaine's cancer shortly before his final and fatal heart attack that same winter, told Simone that all mothers must die. "Ihasha and Carises and Calusa's mother will die too some day. How well you handle your mother's death is an indication to them how you want them to handle yours." And he told her that if Elaine had lived long enough to see, enjoy, and influence her grandchildren, then she had been truly blessed with life. He told Elaine the last time they were together that whatever she had done in her life, she did right by Simone.

I tried to console my mother-in-law with the idea of death. I said that Nip had already made the Great Change. I said that the city summers were going to be extremely hot and uncomfortable in the coming years. I said the pollution and violence would just get worse. "It would hurt you too much to see what will happen,

Elaine." I told her that Mother Earth was changing so fast and so quickly that maybe it would be better if she didn't see the changes. "Maybe you can help your children and your grandchildren more from the other side, Elaine. Maybe you can help us all better from the other side." I also said that I would care for her daughter Simone as long as I lived, and that I would raise our children to be Indian, and that she could be assured she was part of a genetic line that would not stop being Indian. Like the sense of accomplishment that comes at the end of a man's life who knows he has fulfilled his vision, Elaine had fulfilled her primary purpose also. She was, indeed, a progenitor of the race.

And though her death was horribly slow, she was able to have moments of clear recollections and vivid memories, like when she and her younger brother and sister were still kids, living up on the White Earth reservation. One day they were walking home across a meadow together when it started to rain. They headed toward a cluster of trees when suddenly the sky became very bright. But the brightness was not caused by the sun through a patch in the clouds. It came from something circular and white, like a star that floated momentarily above their wide and startled eyes. And then, the rain changed into flowers of all colors pouring down on them.

Even when she heaved and groaned with pain, she knew she was still alive and with her children, and she clung to every minute of every day. And Simone never faltered in her love or devotion to her mother. She cleaned the bedpans, delicately massaged the tiny body, issued the drugs that kept her mom relatively pain-free and fed, and cleared the black tarry substance from her mother's throat when she was too weak to cough it up — that black hideous goo from nicotine and tar that coated her throat like resin.

And in the end, it was Simone who encouraged her mom to make the jump into the Great Change. The day before she died, though, Elaine would go to the bathroom on her own. She would clean herself and insist that she wanted to go for a walk with Simone and the grandchildren. Had the icy sidewalks of urban Minneapolis been easier to travel upon, and had the bottles of liquid food and morphine dangling from the pole attached to her bed been transportable, Simone would have taken her mom on that last walk.

A slow death enabled Simone to be there, and to hold her fragile, shriveled mother in her arms in much the same way as her mom probably held her. However, the woman lying in her daughter's arms then was not stirring with new life; it was an emaciated body that was holding the spirit captive. Simone whispered one final time, "Let go, Mom. Let go. . . ." And Elaine died, hearing those words and the soft voices of her grandchildren playing quietly in the kitchen, the same kitchen where AIM had been conceived, the same kitchen where feasts were prepared for the pipe. And for a moment after her death, Elaine's body radiated with beauty, and the room glowed. . . . Then, the stark cold reality of cancer and the dark days ahead. . . .

Hundreds of people passed through her home to say goodbye those last few weeks before she died. Hundreds more came to her wake at the Little Earth Indian housing project that she struggled so vehemently to keep in Indian control. Others came representing the National Indian Youth Olympics, which Elaine's efforts made a reality for city Indian kids. There were former Indian prisoners from Stillwater who smoked the pipe with Elaine, and who lingered near the wall of the gym at Little Earth where her body lay. The mayor of Minneapolis came, and other representatives of government came who had benefitted from her wisdom. AIM people were there, and because of her dedication to the dignity of her people, they would name their new office the Elaine Stately Peacekeepers Center and AIM Patrol.

At her gravesite, she requested that her daughters Rebecca and Simone read the great oration of Chief Seattle. Some said it was too political. Her children read it just the same — Elaine's life among the People had been political, so why not her death? She was buried in the hard winter ground of White Earth in the presence of a sacred pipe. These days, that's a political statement, for it says to all that even in death, Elaine Stately, Woman-Who-Sweeps-Away-With-The-Crane's-Wing, chose to be Indian.

She was not alone. . . .

▲ ▲ ▲

The big house where Simone and I first lived in Minneapolis, and the one we returned to after our journey through two autumns, was located on one of the sloping hills overlooking Lake Calhoun. It was a land that the Dakota author, Charles Eastman, described as once belonging to his people before they were evicted, and before the lake became too polluted to swim in on hot summer days and the creeks that fed the lake became unfit to drink.

Some of the Dakota people survived Little Crow's War and escaped the executions at Mankato and the forced marches through the southern Minnesota town of New Ulm, where its citizens gathered in hate-filled mobs to throw rocks at the Indian people who were shackled up and paraded like circus animals in cages through the town, and where such hate could allow a Dakota baby to be torn from its mother's arms and smashed to death alongside the road. Yes, some of the Dakotas survived, refusing to surrender their lands at Shakopee and Prairie Island in southern Minnesota, and at Sisseton, in eastern South Dakota. These then became their reservations. And though the Dakota no longer thrived on the shores of Lake Calhoun, I would often sit on one of its sloping hills and imagine them still there.

Late at night, or just before dawn, I used to stand among the great elms and address the ghosts who still loved their land. It's one way of making peace with a place. I have, through the quiet that belongs to those hours, longed to hear the voices of all the happy Indian children who used to play there. And I have imagined the excitement that emanated from the great summer lacrosse games when the women would sing and the men would compete and the drums would pound.

I also stood there and watched Peter Smith, a thirteen-year-old Ojibway student from the Red School House, take the pipe out on the frozen lake and pray one night under the stars. As the oldest boy in a family of seven children, he was faced with the decision of whether or not to remove the life support system from his mother. She was lying brain dead in a downtown hospital. His older sister discovered her in bed at home, lying in her own blood. Her brain had hemorrhaged from a blow to the head, a blow delivered by an intoxicated man in a bar a few nights earlier. Peter was on the frozen lake with the pipe because he was forced to make the decision that none of his adult relatives would. Instead, just outside the door of the hospital chapel, they sat sullen and somber with a Catholic priest. The priest told them, "Her life is in God's hands now."

In the meantime, the spirit of the ancestors was flowing through Peter's hands as he prayed with the pipe out on the lake. The spirit of the People was everywhere. It was above him in the stars. It was in his visible breath, rising in the smoke with his prayers in the cold winter air. Whether Dakota or Ojibway, the spirit of the People and the land were with him because they are all part of the Mystery and the earth, and therefore a part of him. The pipe connected all this with the words Peter prayed. It connected the experiences of the land to the spirit journey along the stars.

Later that night, I went with Peter to the hospital and stood waiting while he visited with his mother. The room she lay in was stark, and a machine pumped air into her lungs.

Before first light, I sat with Peter and his brothers and sisters in a circle on the floor in the dark and quiet chapel of the hospital.

One by one, their friends and teachers from the AIM schools trickled in to lend the kids support and consolation. The adult relatives remained outside. Over the pipe, the children inside the tiny chapel took their turns talking. They were teary eyed and terribly burdened. They were brave. When it was all said, they decided to let their mom go. That decision was smoked on the pipe.

▲ ▲ ▲

A similar fate descended on another Indian family during that winter, the winter of '76. This time it involved the death of a Red School House teacher. There are those who were close to him who believed he was murdered because he had evidence that state and local Indian education money wasn't really going where it was supposed to go, and he was about to make it publicly known. Others say he was simply killed by a hit-and-run driver after his car broke down in the middle of nowhere. Yet, when the scene was actually investigated, such a strike appeared more deliberate than accidental. Until his killer is found, maybe we'll never know. I do know that after Anna Mae Aquash's body was discovered frozen alongside a deserted South Dakota road, the feds said the cause of her death was "exposure." Only after her body was exhumed under court order and a bullet was found lodged in the back of her head was it called murder. Both of these teachers were young and very bright, and both had strong Indian identities.

Though he was struck down by a car and left to die alongside a lonely road just outside Stillwater, he didn't die there. A male nurse, returning from a late-night shift at a St. Paul hospital, noticed the mangled and bleeding body and managed to get him to a hospital.

The Indian teacher's mother asked me to bring the pipe.

For weeks he struggled for life, never really gaining it all back, but all the while building up his spirit power, a power that couldn't have been greater even had he been allowed to grow old. His leg, at the hip, was severed at the scene. He lost so much blood and had so many internal injuries that the doctors even wondered how he stayed alive. When we smoked the pipe together for the last time, he gazed at something behind me and managed to barely raise his hand enough to point. He tried speaking, but his voice was low and raspy, and I had to bend close to hear. He told me a beautiful woman stood behind me holding a bundle. He said that she would watch over me. It was one of the last conscious moments of his life. It was one of the most important moments in mine.

A few days later, a blood clot lodged in his brain. Oh, the respirator would pump breath into him, but his mother, his father, and all his handsome and beautiful brothers and sisters knew that life was not something defined by technology. He fought the warrior's fight for his life. Now he should die like one. They came together, with other close relatives, as young Peter Smith and his family once had. They smoked and prayed on the pipe; and, in four days time, they let their son, their brother, their cousin, their uncle, and their friend . . . go. They did not leave the decision "in God's hands," as the shadow people of the church had advised. Being Indian and believing we are a part of the Great Mystery means assuming responsibility for our lives and the decisions that go along with living, and even dying, in this world. Indians seek guidance from those aspects of the Mystery that can help us in times of need; but in the end, life and the decisions that go with it are ours.

While the machines allowing him to stay unnaturally in this world were being shut down, a thunder storm swept over the city. We shut the lights off in the room, and I sang with the pipe in my arms as he died, for it was once upon a time that an Indian had been born into this world with song, and he would leave this world with song also. His mom and I went outside. Another clap of thunder. I had seen that losing a mother or father or uncle or aunt can be so hard and difficult for the young to accept. Losing a child is unimaginable. There were no words that could describe how either of us felt then as we walked in the rain outside the hospital, except that we knew that the spirit of his life had just departed with the Thunderbeings, and that we could feel him everywhere.

Through all the torment and emotional suffering, these Indian people remained true to their beliefs and close to the pipe. That's why I cringe when I see living pipes abused and disrespected, when I see them used as curios and exhibited in local, state, and national museums, when I see price tags on them at weekend spiritual gatherings so someone can buy one and pray to a Judeo-Christian concept of God with it, and not to the Great Mystery. I've seen pipes displayed in the windows of local head shops.

An Indian teacher was killed, and he believed in the Indian way, the way of the pipe on his death bed. What greater force is there than death to evoke our true beliefs? He smoked his prayers to the Great Holy Mystery on his own death bed. This was the spirit power this young man had. He was an Indian teacher who was a spark of hope for the future of his people, but he was not defeated, even in his death, from teaching identity.

Such identity is tied to our beliefs in the pipe, for the pipe allows our words to the Great Mystery to become physical. It connects us to earth and sky, like our DNA or our genetic code. We are people of the earth whose ties are also to the stars. We are people of the pipe whose teachings are of the Mystery.

His death that winter was followed by a spring that saw his sister give birth. She named her child after her courageous brother who died letting everyone know what he left this world believing in.

▲▲▲

During that winter of dying, a stranger came traveling with friends. Her experience with the pipe had a powerful impact upon her. . . .

No one rose early that morning; it was snowing heavily and our friends from Sisseton were sleeping over. Even the little children slept late.

But, like slumbering sparrows stir in warm niches on cold mornings, we were all suddenly moving at once. Simone and Roland's wife Marie were making coffee. Carolyn was helping her younger daughter Sara with the children. One child, an infant girl, was Sara's; the other, about two years old and in diapers too, was Roland's son. I remembered seeing them at the naming ceremony in Sisseton. The girl had rested quietly during the ceremony in her mother's arms while the pipe touched her lips. The little boy sat with his dad in the circle of loving friends and relatives that day. When the pipe came to him, he opened his tiny mouth and blew into the stem. I would, later in life, see my own children do this, staring wide-eyed while making strong puffs of smoke rise from the bowl, sometimes even from their lips.

Two more people emerged from a sleeping bag in the corner of the room. They were Roland's younger brother and his brother's wife. I remembered seeing them at the ceremony in Sisseton also. One by one, all of us awoke and engaged in soft and separate conversations. This was tipi living. One room, yet everyone had some semblance of privacy.

I guess I was simply laying back enjoying the early morning stirrings when I suddenly felt something there that shouldn't be, like an uncomfortable presence in the room.

I glanced over my shoulder and looked about, searching for what it was that had so abruptly made me uncomfortable, but I didn't know what I was looking for, until I noticed a woman. She was kneeling on a sleeping bag behind the table with her eyes closed. Her blonde hair was cropped short, just above her shoulders. I watched her through the wooden chairs. Black rosary beads dangled from her folded hands. Her lips moved but no sound came from them. Roland must have seen the glare in my eyes. He touched my arm.

"I had to take her along. They wouldn't take no for an answer."

He motioned with his eyes, and I knew that "they" meant his in-laws.

"She says she wants to know the Indian ways. . . . Muriel thought that takin' her to the pow wow this weekend and stayin' here would help her to learn them. You see, they're building a new Catholic church at Sisseton. She's a nun. They have a new priest there now who's telling the people that the white man's god and Wakan-Tanka are the same. He's telling 'em that the pipe and the Bible are the same. He's even put a pipe on his altar, with a beaded bag for it, no less!

"Anyway, this nun, Sister Mary Margaret, she can't understand why we don't go to church. She says our beliefs are not any different than hers. Well, when she hears we're coming to the pow wow at the Indian Center and would see you here in Minneapolis, she asked to come. She heard about the naming ceremony. She also heard we would be smoking the pipe here, so she asks the priest first if it would be all right. He must've given her permission. I don't know. She shows up yesterday morning as we were about to leave. I said, 'No, she can't come!' But they won't tell the sister no."

I pressed my fist to my lips and released a long breath through my nostrils. My eyes squinted as they focused more keenly on the praying nun. I nodded. "Okay, Roland. Okay." I said it, but how was I to deal with a nun's participation in a pipe ceremony? That's what it was coming to. They would ask this of me tonight. I didn't fully understand why they did this. They know how I feel about Christianity. They heard me say on the pipe that God and the Great Mystery can't be mixed! I didn't know what else to say to Roland. I understood his situation. He needed me to help them to understand this. Just by saying the words was not enough. I didn't

know what to do. Already I could feel our beliefs, and the wisdom of our traditions, being tested again.

It was yet another winter and the owl had come to me in my dreams. I understood that something was going to die.

Before the ceremony that night, I wondered who would watch the children. Besides the little ones from Sisseton, there were a few more who were brought by other Indians who felt the need to be there. I suggested that Sister Mary Margaret put herself to some usefulness and offer to watch the children upstairs. This way, all the Indian men and women linked by common belief could be together in the ceremony downstairs.

That was not how it was to be, however.

Sister Mary Margaret wanted to participate in that ceremony, and nothing short of forbidding her would change her mind. It's true that I resented her being there, especially when she refused to take care of the children. But, everyone had made their choices: Carolyn had suggested she could come, and then had presented her to Roland. Roland made the decision whether or not to say "no" back in Sisseton. Even Sara, who said she'd take care of the kids in order that Sister Mary Margaret could participate, made a decision. It was up to me now.

"Sister, it would be so good if you'd watch the children tonight during the ceremony." I had hoped that maybe she just didn't get it and, after being asked directly by me, she'd see where she could be of value, and offer to help in that way.

"But I've come all this way for the ceremony," she pleaded.

Carolyn joined us.

"Sister, you've got to understand that I'm the keeper of the pipe we'll be using for the ceremony. It's my responsibility to pro-tect it. We address no other concept on the pipe other than the Great Mystery. To us, that's the concept that binds all things and makes

all things of equal value and importance. Sister, do you see? The
sum total of all things living simultaneously together is the Great
Mystery. That's what we address through the pipe, the sum total of
all things that always was, and will always be."

Her blue eyes gleamed, and I searched them. They seemed
like fragile, colored glass.

"Sister, do you see? The Great Mystery, for the Indian, is like
the first thought manifested, and the breath it took to make that
thought carried the parts of the whole into the void. It's all still
expanding from that breath. Can you see why a man-like being
who created the universe can't be? Not for the Indian. Can you see
why, for us, nothing stays the same — all things change? Because
even the universe is forever moving, expanding and contracting. It's
like the breathing of the Mystery. It's like the Mystery's heart
beating. Each breath, each beat, the pulse of a quasar — an
eternity. . . ."

I paused and measured the meaning of my words. Had I said
enough? I didn't want to get lost in explanation, yet I felt that what
I had said didn't faze her. My words had not even penetrated the
glimmering blue eyes. I resolved to become more direct. "You cannot pray to God on this pipe, Sister. I can't allow that, for God is not
a name for such a concept. God is an idea of man as the Creator.
Who we are as Native Americans sprang forth from our understanding of the Mystery. Can you pray to the Great Mystery, Sister? Can
you address the oneness of all things, male and female? If you can't,
that's okay; we respect your belief and thank you for respecting
ours. . . . Now, will you watch the children?"

She smiled, clasped her hands to her lips, and nodded. "I
understand what you're saying," she said, "and that is the concept
I'll pray to."

I talked to Simone about my dilemma; she understood. If I
forbade the nun from participating in the ceremony, even though

246

she agreed to the stipulations set before her, it would not be right. The people from Sisseton would accept the decision, but it wasn't what they needed to help them understand why the nun shouldn't participate. On the other hand, who was I to make such a decision? At least, that's the way I was thinking then. "Let the pipe take care of it," Simone advised. "You've explained it to all of them. You can't do much else."

Her words echoed in my mind in the quiet time before the ceremony. It was late when we finally began. We waited for that moment in the world when peace permeates a place. When everything seems resting or asleep. It didn't matter what time it was; it just had to be peaceful. We found that time of night when the chance of disturbance is cut to its very lowest. It is a time when the spirit-beings come and help us and hear our prayers.

That's the way it was then, at that moment when the sticks and strips of dried cedar ignited and popped, releasing into the circle of people its sweet scent in little puffs of swirling smoke. I touched the fire with a thick braid of sweetgrass, bathing the bowl and the stem and me in its cleansing swirling smoke. "Let no bad or angry thoughts linger in our hearts and minds now," I said. "Let the fragrance of cedar and sweetgrass fill us with a sense of peace."

As each person in the circle used the cleansing smoke this way, I placed the bowl and stem of the pipe together. "It is alive," I whispered, working a pinch of tobacco and red willow into the shallow bowl. "The Great Mystery pipe is alive."

There were about twenty of us in all. Simone sat to my right, next to her was Sister Mary Margaret. Next to the sister was Roland. The pipe would travel toward them from my left.

Before I took an ember from the fire and placed it in the bowl, I spoke more about the Great Mystery and explained the different symbols attached to the pipe. Some of these were as old as the pipe; they were gifts to the pipe. They draw the spirits and the powers of the spirit-beings to the pipe as we pray. My words of explanation were not groping attempts for Sister Mary to find rea- sons to leave; I was just allowing her, or anyone else, the chance to do what they felt was right and respectful. If they did not believe in these powers and this way of seeing things, then they could dismiss themselves before we smoked.

"People have smoked from this pipe on their death beds," I continued. "It has been present at births and burials. The names of the People have been called out on this pipe. It has been smoked by Indian men in prison. Some have committed themselves to marriage on this pipe. Many of us have held it and cried for understanding.

"Work with it as it travels the circle. Speak your prayers on it. It will travel to your center."

There was nothing else for me to say. The rest was between the pipe and each person.

Time is of the Mystery, especially during such a ceremony are we aware of this. As the pipe is prayed with and addressed and passed from human to human, little is experienced from our everyday reality. It takes us to another dimension. I shook the rattle that would accompany the pipe around the circle. It shot spirit lights all around. Like flickering stars, the little lights darted and flashed and disappeared before our eyes and before the pipe. Their energy filled the circle. This is what those ancestors of the stars knew, and that's why we keep such things alive today. Such a ceremony is a connection to those ancient ones. As the pipe is presented, it binds us to all things, to all our relations. It takes our words directly to the Great Mystery, to the First Cause of All That Is. The power that flows through the stem into us connects that part of us that is spirit, that is the Mystery within all of us. And the pipe burned strong that night as it was handed to Roland, who prayed in Lakota to Wakan-Tanka. I could glimpse the big puffs of smoke rising in rings above him.

248   Then, he handed it to Sister Mary Margaret. "All my relations," he said in Sioux, and he let it go.

The sister held the pipe for some time, and I wondered if it
might not go out if she didn't work with it. I could feel her apparent
and sudden confusion. She was confronting her beliefs. Everyone
remained still and quiet and waiting. Then she said the word that
would explode her idea of the world forever. She said the one word
that everyone would hear, and everyone, from that moment on in
that circle, would know for the rest of their lives the truth of the
Great Mystery pipe. In that moment, Sister Mary Margaret bowed
her head and said, "Father."

The oneness was violated.

The instant that word was uttered, it felt as though we were
riding in a spacecraft that was out of control. A vital source of
power, the fire in the center, was suddenly turning cold.

Every dog in the neighborhood barked wildly, some
viciously; others howled like wolves. All the children upstairs with
Sara began crying at the same time the dogs began barking and
howling. We could hear Sara running frantically above us, trying to
comfort the children and keep them quiet. Everything was chaos.

And out of the chaos Sister Mary Margaret trembled; "I can't
do it. I can't do it," she said, glancing up at the faces of the
astounded Indians. We could barely hear her voice above the barking dogs and wailing infants. "I can't give up my God," she said,
shaking and crying. "I couldn't give up my God!" She handed the
pipe to Simone. "It's out anyway," she quivered. "It went out. . . ."

The moment Simone held the pipe, it was like someone
turned a switch; everything was quiet again. Simone described it
later as one of those pauses between space and time — a teaching
place — a sacred place. The dogs stopped barking; the children
made no sounds. A calm fell over the ceremonial circle. We had
regained control of our craft. As all eyes gazed at the pipe in

Simone's hands, its stem pressed to her lips, there was no glow from the bowl, no smoke rising. It was out. But, regardless of what was, Simone didn't stop smoking, and we didn't stop wanting the pipe to stay lit. I picked up the rattle and shook it fast and hard. The spirit lights shot out, leaving silver-white streaks across the circle of people, who were now determined and resolute.

With all our hearts, we wanted to see the smoke rise from the pipe one more time. Never had I felt such intensity. The rattle shook powerfully in my hand, and the spirit-lights resembling stars shot across the room. We implored the pipe to complete our circle. Simone prayed, and we prayed. Then, a tiny puff of smoke rose and swirled upwards from the bowl. And another, much stronger one, and then the center glowed. When she handed the pipe to me, I thanked it and the Mystery. And I thanked Simone. Inhaling the smoke deeply, I felt it touch my center. The feelings came from the deepest part of me. My thoughts became words rising in puffs of smoke.

The circle was complete.

We sang to the pipe that night and held it high above our heads as we passed it once again around the circle. The song was an incantation without words, sounds that evoked feelings. The feelings were so strong, the people wept and smiled and celebrated. I reached over with my hand and held Simone's. For a moment after the singing there was a wonderful quiet. It was that magic of silence that Uncle Nip had once told me about . . . that magic of silence in which the unspoken rests.

▲ ▲ ▲

Months later, I met an AIM friend from Sisseton, who was at the ceremony that night in Minneapolis, and I inquired about Sister Mary Margaret. I asked about the impact of the new Catholic church on the reservation. He explained that the sister went back to

Sisseton, but was never quite the same after the ceremony. She became a recluse, incapable of performing any tasks for the church, insisting that "the Indians be left to their own gods." He said that the church sent Sister Mary Margaret back East, apparently on some sort of retreat.

As for my friends from Sisseton and their relationship to the church? Last I heard they represented a strong traditional faction on the reservation, and Roland was running for tribal office. I also heard that the pipe was taken from the church alter.

Word on the moccasin telegraph claimed that the traditionals planned their Sundance that summer up in the hills. It was to happen on the site where the descendants of Charles Eastman sat with us all and smoked the names of the People on the Great Mystery pipe.

MEDICINE —
IN A BAD WAY

I WAS ALONE.

When I heard the medicine man speaking Ojibway to me, I thought I was having the kind of dream one has before the spirit and ghost separate from the body. I didn't understand the words of the ancient language he was speaking, but I could feel the sounds, and they anchored me.

When his old hand brushed against my burning forehead, I was afraid I would wake, and the pain would still be there, and I would still be alive. I wanted to stay sleeping on the edge of death. In a dream stage, at least, the severity of the pain was lessened. I did not want to hear the voice urging me to consciousness; but I couldn't keep the vibrations from my ears, and the pain exploded in my brain. The figure of the old man above me blurred, disappeared, and blurred, until my eyes struggled against my will and finally remained opened. Dim light filtered through.

"This medicine man's from Canada." The voice was Ana's.

Alongside her was my dog E. With muscles tensed and black ears pulled back, he growled, low and serious. Though he'd met Ana before, the unwelcoming sounds E was making in his language were directed at her.

"How are you doin'?"

"Ana . . . Elaine. . . ." I tried to raise my head but couldn't. E growled again at Ana, and she told him to stop. He laid by her chair; his eyes fixed on her. I muttered for him to settle down, puzzled at his behavior. I saw Elaine, the director of Heart of the Earth, sitting in a chair opposite the couch where I was laying. And I wondered if I had been that close to making the Great Change that I never heard him barking when they entered.

The old man began speaking again. In my half-dream state, I understood the urgency in his voice. Geez, I thought, I'm on the couch. I guess I never made it to bed. Where did I put my clothes? I felt another blanket fall gently on me. For the past few weeks, I had been suffering from horrible headaches. They went beyond any type of pain relief. They went beyond whatever medicine I took for migraines. I had been to the Indian clinic earlier in the week. After an hour of convincing the young doctor that I was not hung over, and after refusing to allow myself to be admitted to the University Hospital for a CAT scan and possible "exploratory brain surgery," I got a shot of Demerol. Though it allowed me some relief, by the time I got home, it returned. This time the pain was even worse than it had been.

As of that morning, I couldn't remember getting ready for work. I just remember the pain became too much, and I wanted to die. It was sharp and piercing, stabbing into the area of the third eye, just above the bridge of my nose. It also penetrated the occipital bone in the back of my head. By the time the medicine man had arrived that night, it had crippled me. It had driven me to near insanity, and I was willing myself to die.

"The old man says that you must sit up."

"I don't think I can, Ana. . . . I don't think . . . I can."

"Come on," Elaine urged. "You can do it."

Ana instructed me to do what the old man told me. "You've got to sit up, and then he'll help you."

They each took an arm and pulled. I groaned. The very old man was now before me.

Ana sat in a chair behind him. "This man will not speak English," she explained. "He's over a hundred years old. In the ceremony at my place tonight, there was a red light that appeared above my father's drum. Everyone saw it. The medicine man starts singing, and the light moves. He looks into the light and says there's a young Indian with braids who needs help, and that we must go to him. We look around, and you're not there. We all knew it was you in the light."

It felt good knowing that people cared enough to come and help. Knowing they knew of my ordeal with pain helped lift some of it from me, and I felt stronger.

He placed his one hand behind my head, and the other he used to work the area between my eyes with his fingers. He pressed and squeezed, pressed and squeezed. I felt something being drawn from my head. I felt it surface through the skin as he squeezed and pinched some more with the bare fingers of his empty hand. Then he showed me what was removed. The sight repulsed me. He pressed and pinched and squeezed and pinched again. More came out. Piece by piece, he removed several small, ugly objects from my forehead. As he did, the pain dissipated. "What is it?" I grimaced, peering at the contents in his hand.

He looked at me in the eyes, and he answered. The Ojibway words were low and raspy and sharp and direct.

Ana interpreted. "He says someone used bad medicine on you. Someone wanted to kill you with this, and you would've died, but now you'll be okay."

He began doing to the back of my head what he'd done to the front, and again the pain became less and less. Each piece he removed he would show me, and I'd cringe and I would become

254

more puzzled and confused. Through my own bitterness, though, I felt myself growing stronger. When he was done, the pain was gone, and I sat there on the edge of the couch, staring again at the ugly pieces and slivers of what appeared to be rotten bone in his hands. They looked like decayed splinters and charred chips of brown and black bone.

"The old man says that someone hired someone who knows *geebik* to strike you like this, and that he's gonna send it back to both of them. He says it's wrong to use geebik this way, and the one who shot this into you should know better. Medicine always comes back. Good or bad. He says he will send the medicine back to both of them. . . . It will strike them in four days."

When Ana was finished translating, a hazy form shimmered alongside the old man. The dry air, heated by the gas stove, suddenly chilled. Ana and Elaine also saw the image forming near him. And the old man, relating to both realities, spoke to me again through Ana.

"He says that the ghost of my father is with us now, and he wants you to have this Indian name. He says that the name is Autumn."

The old man looked sharply at me once again. Tiny lights, like the ones that come from rattles and summon spirits, glistened in his old eyes like stars on a hazy night.

And while he sat looking into my eyes, he told me a great deal about myself and my purpose in this life. He also told me things I must avoid and things that I must do to protect myself. He explained how geebik was used on me and where I more than likely received it. Ana carefully interpreted.

He asked Ana for something to put the medicine in. Ironically, she discovered an empty prescription bottle in her bag. I watched him observe the ugly chips and slivers as he dropped them in, piece by piece, and tightened the cap. He put the bottle in his shirt pocket.

Before he left me that night, this man, over a hundred years in this life, told me one more thing. He told me about a specific color that I should wear whenever I do something for the People. He said such a color evokes the power of the earth and would help protect me and give me strength to do what needed to be done.

After they were gone, I laid on my bed luxuriating in life without pain. I fell asleep and never heard the drumming and singing that my neighbors would ask me about the next morning.

▲ ▲ ▲

Four days later, a woman serving on an Indian education board fell down a flight of stairs in her home and was seriously injured. She suffered a concussion and a broken leg from the fall. Word had it that on the same day an Indian deacon serving at one of the area churches suffered a stroke and was partially paralyzed.

CHAPTER 29

ASSASSINS
OF CHARACTER

W E WOULDN'T ALLOW the children to play near the front
window of the old rickety and haunted-looking house
where we lived on Dupont Avenue in Minneapolis. We were
afraid that a bomb thrown from an assassin's hand or that a bullet
shot from a killer's gun would end the precious lives of our children and possibly our own. It had come to that.

My encounter with medicine used in a bad way back when
I was a teacher at Heart of the Earth had made me aware of new
dangers that existed for a man like me, dangers of another real and
sinister nature. And although I had learned to protect myself, how
could I protect my wife and children?

It was 1981. I had been the cultural arts director of the Minneapolis American Indian Center for a little over a year. We left
our pretty home in Florida and our life near Uncle Nip so I could
return to Minnesota and take the job there at the Center and possibly do some of the things for the community in Minneapolis that
I felt so strongly needed to be done. What better way of instill-
ing a sense of pride in one's culture and one's self and people
than through art? If we can use the energy of our pain and anger

to create, if we can take what is beautiful in our lives and return that blessing by creating, then we can help restore the balance in the world.

I spent a wonderful and busy time as the Center's cultural arts director. And though I started with a staff of six young Indian artists, there were some twenty-eight Native Americans on some type of salary from my department within a year. We held popular exhibits of the people's art. We had established a museum where the younger Indians, between nineteen and twenty-five years old, learned the crafts and the ways of the people from Ojibway elders such as Old Man Bill, John Moose, and Larry Parent. And we had other elders who would volunteer their time and expertise and spirituality, elders like Bob Shaw, who was a Mohawk artist, and Amos Owens, who was a Dakota pipe keeper, and Carolyn Strong, an Ojibway grandmother and respected elder. We had ceremonies together and smoked the pipe together, and we prayed together in tipis painted by the young artists.

We gave tours where we would take people from all walks of life through our Indian gallery, and we had presentations where we would travel to schools and teach the unlearning of Indian stereotypes. Even the vice-premier of China and his entourage of Chinese educators had heard about us and asked to stop by the Indian Center on their way to meet with President Reagan. We had a great time with them, exchanging ideas, philosophies, and gifts. We also got to see the secret service mentality in action — one of the men in suits representing the United States was asked by an Indian man as the Chinese delegation entered the Center, "Which one is the vice-premier?"

And the blond, blue-eyed government man responded by saying, just as the delegation passed him, "The short one in the pajamas and slippers." When I heard this, I glanced at some of the members of the Chinese delegation and knew that they didn't need to know English to feel the sounds of those words.

258

That year we also had a photography exhibit called "The Longest Walk." It was mainly a black-and-white picture story documenting the American Indian Movement's walk across the United States from the San Francisco Bay to the steps of the nation's capital. The walk was a demonstration of support for native people's sovereignty and cultural identity. It was a protest against genocide.

Because of all we were doing — and because we were doing it as traditional Indians — we became a threat, not only to the government, but to specific and established Indian organizations like the state and local Indian education offices and the Intertribal Affairs Board. The offices were mainly occupied by federally recognized Indian administrators with large salaries. The function of these offices, as well as their administrators, depended on government funding. I never could figure out what was done with the hundreds of thousands of dollars allocated for Indian education. It sure wasn't having any great impact on the education of Indian children living in Minneapolis. In the Seventies and early Eighties, I can recall that the drop-out rate for Indian high-school students hovered somewhere around seventy to eighty percent. Sometimes it went as high as ninety percent.

But rather than become involved in a fight over that money and how it was being used, I directed the cultural arts department at the Indian Center to simply fill a few of those great gaps that existed in Indian education. And with the talent, knowledge, and devotion of young Indian artists and tribal elders, the cultural arts department became a valuable regional resource for elementary and secondary education. We also had a great impact on the arts. White owners of art galleries, which occasionally showed Indian art, were turning their eyes and attention toward our Minneapolis American Indian Art Gallery, a gallery built by Indians. And we were receiving local and national recognition for what we had achieved within two years.

This recognition became a great light of hope for many Indian people, but as I learned a great light can cast an even greater shadow. And the war with the shadow people continued.

It was an old war that had intensified during the founding of the AIM survival schools, when Indian students first began leaving the bigotry of the public schools and enrolling in the AIM schools. These were the students the offices of Indian education had failed to reach. There were many of them leaving — too many to justify.

Since I was a certified public school teacher, my Minnesota teaching certificate helped the AIM schools gain state accreditation. This, in turn, threatened the flow and amount of money allocated for Indian education in those public schools and Indian education offices, because that money depended on the number of enrolled Indian students in public schools. It was the money, not the welfare of the native children, that I and others in the community saw as the great motivator of state and local Indian education offices. A threat to the flow of that money created the hostility that resulted in an ominous and dark sense of war. And it was an old war fueled with old hatreds and a bitterness that began festering when I returned to Minnesota and took the position as cultural arts director of the Minneapolis American Indian Center.

The young and old and male and female staff of long-hairs and traditionalists who made up our cultural arts department were also reinforcing the knowledge that the Indian people in this urban community, one of the largest concentrations of Indians in the country, didn't need to sacrifice their identities in order to live and prosper in their own country. Our gallery and where we worked was right there on Franklin Avenue, right down from Addison's and Art's and all the other Indian bars where so many dreams died. We were proving that to be an Indian was something we really could be proud of. We were like a small tribe of artists and teachers and were even affectionately referred to in that way by many of the elders and other Indians in the community. We were showing the people by example what could be done when you're smart and talented and of good heart and not afraid of being Indian. We were creating beauty in an Indian world that had known too much violence and poverty. But we soon discovered that money does strange things to people who are weak and without identity and who have become too dependent on the very government that was responsible for destroying so much of the beauty of our culture and so much of the knowledge of what it meant to be an Indian.

If my involvement as cultural arts director wasn't enough to threaten one of the monster's heads of government, then my continued efforts to help the Indian prisoners at Stillwater to gain their religious freedom no doubt disturbed yet another head. And when I discovered that many of the young adult Indians employed in my department, and almost all of their children, were not registered on tribal rolls, I began writing strongly worded editorials in the Indian newspaper which I had named *The Circle* when it first began publishing years earlier. The editorials described situations, like the one in my own wife's family, where some of Simone's brothers and sisters, born of the same Indian parents, were not federally recognized as Indians because the tribal council on one reservation changed tribal enrollment rules. I wrote challenging words that questioned the white-bureaucratic way of defining Indians by percentage of blood in the first place. I wrote how paper genocide was being inflicted on our People by a few tribally enrolled and federally recognized Indians who had vested monetary interests in Indian lands and resources and were threatened by the idea of having to open up tribal roles for a whole new generation to share. I wrote that if this new type of genocide continued, the Native Americans could disappear on paper in the not-too-distant future, and then the government would feel justified in taking whatever lands and rights that the Indians have that remain. Such genocide has already been inflicted on the Indians of Central and South American countries like Brazil. My words about paper genocide disturbed another head of the great monster. This one belonged to the Intertribal Affairs Board.

Besides writing editorials about paper genocide, I also questioned the validity of such events as the annual Minneapolis "Song of Hiawatha" pageant. I questioned how the city of Minneapolis could spend thousands to endorse such an event each year with the support of the state and local Indian education offices, while the contributions of the real Hyonwatha — the co-founder of the Law of Great Peace of the Iroquois Confederacy — went unrecognized. I suggested that instead of selling beadwork from Taiwan in the city's gift shop at Minnehaha Falls, where the pageant took place, the city utilize the gifted Indian craftspeople in the area, and that only Native American art should be sold there instead of shoddy factory imitations. I knew too many Indian men who were artists and needed money to support themselves, their families, and their craft. I knew too many Indian women who were great beaders and had babies to feed and clothe.

And when I discovered that my wife and most of the young Indian women who worked in the Indian Center's cultural arts department back in 1980 were issued a coil-type contraceptive device at the Indian Health Board, a device which was reported as having already been banned by the government, I wrote about it. Wasn't it just a decade earlier that AIM had uncovered a government sterilization program on Indian women? Yet other heads of the monster that kept our people oppressed turned, showed their teeth, and growled.

When I suggested to the Indian Center's board of directors that we wanted to establish economic independence for the cultural arts department and become an independent and self-sufficient entity within the Center, we were denied by a close vote. Some of the board members stated their concern that the Indian Center's

262 board would lose control over the cultural arts department and the
gallery and thereby lose control over any money we might bring in.
My appeals to them about sovereignty and self-determination could
not change the outcome.

When we listened to the Indian Center's director and threw
all caution to the wind and applied for one of the largest educational
grants that the federal government provided, I think that's when the
monster decided to act. My reasons for applying for a grant that was
supposed to help Indian artists and help educate people were basically simple. The grant would give the government an opportunity
to fulfill one of its obligations to the People. That's what such a
grant, in writing, is supposed to do. So, why not apply for it? Well,
I found out why not. We were too close to the "big bucks." We were
too close to really changing things around. You see, I wasn't going
to profit from such a grant. The center was already paying me a
yearly salary to do my job. I think it was about $13,000 a year, near
poverty level. But I believed in what we were doing. We weren't
going to sell out to anyone nor were we about to languish as we saw
other programs in Indian education doing. We wanted to do it for
the People. I had no heart nor did I have the time to wage war
against our own people. We were too busy doing and creating.
According to Indian tradition, we wanted to "break away" and
really do something good for the People: elders, adults, parents, and
children. Our track record in the cultural arts department had proven
that we had the talent and the smarts to do it.

It was probably then that the assassins began planning to get
rid of me, or perhaps it was when we got the Minneapolis Public
School Superintendent, Dr. Richard Green, to monetarily support a
Native American-oriented Thanksgiving. Since the public schools
always do their "Thanksgiving thing" no matter what Indians have
to say, and since that is basically the only time Native Americans
are studied and discussed to any degree, then why not do it right?

We asked Dr. Green if he would help pay for Princess Red Wing to come to Minneapolis. That got the monster moving. The plan was that Red Wing would visit the schools where there were significant numbers of Native Americans, and that she, a descendant of the people who greeted the Pilgrims, would tell the true story of her ancestors and that first Thanksgiving. We had already gained the support for such a program from the Indian Center and small local colleges and even a TV station.

Dr. Green had leaned in favor of supporting the program even as the staff of the Indian education department protested, stating to him that we were reinforcing stereotypes at the Indian Center. "After all," an Indian education representative said, pointing her finger across the table at me, "look at him!"

She was referring to my braided hair, my beaded belt buckle that Simone had made for me, my beaded bracelet that one of the Red School House students had made for me, and my jacket that a Seminole grandmother had created and that I wore proudly. I think Dr. Green, a black man not unaware of the horrors that result when a people fight among themselves, saw through it all and agreed to lend public school support for the Thanksgiving program that we had proposed. This gave further cause for the assassins to prepare.

And when I recall years earlier how the local director of Indian education once accused me of teaching hate from books such as *Bury My Heart at Wounded Knee* and *Black Elk Speaks*, and literally pushed them off her desk and onto the floor, I guess that was a good indication where I stood — right in the monster's many faces.

I soon started receiving strange scribbled notes on clippings of newspaper articles that were about the cultural arts department's work in the community or about one of the artists we were exhibiting. Some of the writings made no sense. One forbade the marriages of Indians and whites in order to keep the races pure. Another called me a Cuban refugee who was going to get what I deserved.

I discovered one on my desk the day after my picture appeared in the *Minneapolis Star* with the vice-premier of China. It said that "All reds are better dead." I was careful at night when I left the Center to go home. I didn't want to be "done in" or have my "red ass kicked," as one of the scribbled notes had threatened.

Though I grew concerned, I don't think I became paranoid. I was, however, true to my wary deer nature, and I was cautious. I carried or wore small medicine bundles, and I used the medicine of heart that was given to me by the old man who had saved my life and by other elders and allies of the People who cared about me enough to help me as they could. And I was able to protect myself, my family, and the pipe in these ways.

But I could not protect the gallery or the art of the People late one winter's night when the Center was closed. That's when night-stalkers broke in and destroyed and stole much of the precious art that the young and old people had created.

Then we had our village wasted. It was located just outside the Indian Center, and it was totally destroyed. It was a village where we held celebrations. It was a village that the young Indians and the elders had re-created. I remember walking with the Indian artists among the torn and broken lodges. It was like a scene from another life. It was hard to keep our hearts strong after that, but we were some strong-hearted Indians and were determined not to give in.

I also felt the stress of worry for Simone and my children, for not only was I a political target, but Elaine Stately, Simone's mother, had also disturbed the control of the monster. Back then, Elaine too was a target of an assassin's nature. She had had her bouts with Indian education, and now she was on the board of directors of the Indian Center, which meant her political clout was getting stronger.

We had all heard what happened to AIM leader John Trudell's wife and children and mother-in-law, how they were murdered when his house was fire bombed. I hoped I would never know such pain. But I knew what such a spirit was capable of doing once it had bodies from which it could act, and I knew that the enemy would seize the opportunity to hurt me through my children or my wife if that opportunity was there. So Simone and I would keep our children away from windows in our home, and my dog E and I would often lose sleep listening for the approach of the shadow people. We also talked about returning to Florida and living near Uncle Nip again. After all, we reasoned, Uncle Nip wasn't getting any younger, and we wanted his influence on the children while he was alive, so that they would always remember him.

But then I felt the jolt of the assassin's first bullet. Though the threat was always there, I just didn't imagine it would come to this. I had protected myself and my family and the pipe the best ways that I could, but I couldn't protect any of us from what was about to happen. . . .

The winters in Minnesota are usually bitterly cold; at least, this was true for this "Florida man" during the winters that I lived there. It was a typical crispy day in January. The snow was piled alongside the slippery sidewalks, and the streets were black and grey from exhaust fumes, soot, and old snow. We had just finished the major photo exhibit of The Longest Walk. I was sitting at a table where I had been invited to participate in the monthly meeting of the Minneapolis Urban Indian Directors.

I sat scanning the pile of papers on the table in front of me that represented the business of the People. That's when I saw my name about halfway down one of the many pages of the letters I was flipping through. My eyes focused on the source: Minnesota State Department of Education. It was addressed to Dr. Richard Green, Superintendent, Minneapolis Public Schools. It was signed by the Assistant Manager of Indian Education. I began reading the contents:

"While most non-Indians are supportive of Indian professionals' efforts in the field of education, there are some who have taken it upon themselves to initiate activities that tend to be self-serving at best. I am referring specifically to the activities of Gabe Horn. . . ."

The letter went on to say that I was a non-Indian. It said that I lay claim to being an expert in American Indian culture. It said that I was "a self-appointed spiritual leader who performed religious ceremonies of the most sacred nature." It said that if "the preposterous claims of this individual received no visible recognition, then it would be a trivial matter," but I could "possibly gain funding simply by claiming to be Indian . . . that merits serious consideration."

The letter stated that "any assertion by me that an Indian is of royal hereditary blood (no doubt referring to my letter to Dr. Green about Princess Red Wing) is too absurd to discuss." In short, this assistant manager of Indian education debunked the hereditary claim of Princess Red Wing.

The letter ridiculed and disclaimed my statements about the power of Indian women as well.

It went on for the good part of nearly two whole single-spaced pages about how some Indian women had power, but others served in a less-than-equal status among the tribes, and that a number of tribes were patrilineal, and the rights of women in a number of tribes were severely limited.

I think I was getting the picture as my stomach began its descent back where it belonged.

In closing, the assistant manager of the Indian education section of the state office of education offered comfort to Dr. Green because "he was not the only one who was taken in by me."

I felt like I had been shot. I felt angry. It felt like something in me died then.

I could only turn to my people, so as soon as I could I brought the letter to the attention of the Indian directors around me. They too flipped through their numerous letters and typed forms until they came to the one that I'd been reading. It was like an ominous and invisible force had manifested in the crowded room and filled any space that was once air. One by one the men and women directors put the set of papers down on the table before them and sat, gaping and silent.

One of the men present, one of the founders of AIM, broke the silence. He said I shouldn't worry, that this was done to others, and it had once been done to him.

Others nodded and murmured their agreement. My own mother-in-law was there and said that it had also happened to her, that it would run its course and would eventually go away. But as she spoke I could see a veil of pain cover her face. It was a pain remembered from her own experience and a pain she felt because she loved me, the husband of her daughter.

The director of the Indian Center, a strong and powerful woman in the old tradition, stated that we should not just allow this to happen, and that she wanted a face-to-face confrontation with the individual who wrote this letter. The other directors agreed, and a date was set.

Within a few weeks another letter was circulated from the same source. This letter steered entirely away from accusing me of not being an Indian. The letter attacked, however, my right to pray among Indian people. It stated that "the practice of traditional Indian religious ceremonies, by someone not in any manner trained or authorized to perform such sacred teachings, must be questioned" and that there were "a number of individuals who were quite interested in asking me questions." The letter said that "the quintessential aspect of this knowledge is of such arcane and esoteric nature that it can only be authenticated by legitimate practitioners," and that I was "teaching Indian youth how to make a poor carbon copy at best."

This particular letter referred once again "to the monetary needs of recognized Indian programs" and "to the massive rip-offs in Indian education money that has created a serious depletion of monetary resources that legitimate communities and tribes need." It almost sounded like I wasn't living in a rickety old house bordering a city junk yard. It almost sounded like I could afford to keep my family warm in the bitter Minnesota winter. It almost sounded like I was making enough money to take my wife or children to the doctor if they were sick or a dentist if their teeth needed work. The letter could make someone who didn't know me believe that my family lived in a big house in the suburbs and that I drove a fancy car. It seemed to me that the letter was partially intended to make me a scapegoat for the kind of rip-off that the murdered Red School House teacher may have uncovered before he was run down on a lonely highway and left to die. I truly realized then what greed does to people who cannot control it. I truly realized then the value that people can put on money. Its appeal must stir something in the human DNA that distorts the way some people think and how they see life.

After the immediate effects of what I had just read subsided, I listened to the support I was hearing around the crowded table. The director of the Indian Center was right. I decided not to take this sitting down. I decided to stand up and say that this type of character assassination must stop.

I went to a lawyer from one of the most well-known law firms in the state of Minnesota and asked for help. I told him all about my life, including my participation in and organization of protests, and my teaching experiences and work with AIM over the years. I said that I did not have a federally recognized tribal enrollment number but that I had always been an Indian. "If I need proof in writing that I am an Indian," I said, "then my name is on the birch-bark scroll kept by Princess Red Wing."

The attorney had been sitting back in his leather chair on the other side of a long mahogany desk, listening. He shook his head slowly, raised his eyebrows, and pressed his lips together. Then he picked up the letters I had given him, read them over, and placed them back on his desk.

"Have you ever seen your F.B.I. file under the Freedom of Information Act?" I shook my head. I'd never considered that. "Does anyone know about the one who wrote these letters?" He gazed at the letterhead. "What do you know about the death of that Indian teacher you had mentioned, the one who was killed by a hit and run?"

"I only know what the rumors are — that he was murdered — that he knew something about people. . . ."

"Now, I can offer you our services," he said looking up at me, "but it's rather expensive and, since you haven't lost your job or income as a result of this action, we can't sue for a monetary award."

"What's this all mean?"

"It means that it will cost you a lot of money to take this to trial. Except for court costs, you won't get any of it back."

"How much?"

"My fee, that is if you want me to take the case, is a hundred dollars an hour."

I shook my head one last time and started to get up from the leather chair I was sitting in. I considered that maybe the Indian Center would back a suit on my behalf. But it wasn't likely. They didn't have that kind of money either. What Indian does? Besides, I had one or two enemies on the board anyway. They'd never vote to help me. But I wondered if they wouldn't see it as a way to help themselves. I wondered if by saying we don't support character assassinations, they'd be protecting themselves and even their children, who could face a similar fate someday.

The attorney must have seen my anguish. "Look," he said, "I'll write a letter demanding evidence for all the accusations this

270

individual made against you. I'll send you a copy. If he doesn't supply that information, and we know he can't, then at least you'll have that. That will help discredit his accusations and any credibility he might have through his title."

I accepted his offer, shook his hand, and thanked him, and he wished me good luck. He also reminded me that the Freedom of Information Act may not exist in the near future, so if I wanted to see some of what the F.B.I. might have on me, then I should do it soon.

My next action was to request help from the Minnesota Civil Liberties Union. After all, what right had a state office manager to attack my religious practices and to insist that I had no right to pray with other people in whatever way I chose to pray? Since a state letterhead was used to lend authority and credibility to the accusations about my spiritual practices among the People, I thought for sure this would be something Civil Liberties would pursue. I was wrong. They wrote me, saying that they didn't feel that a civil liberties issue was present in my situation.

I was down. I could find little help from the white man's world.

Support came from my beloved People as the confrontation with the assassins approached. There were the young artists who remained loyal and supportive. There were the elders who worked with me over the years: Old Man Bill, John Moose, and Larry Parent. Larry wrote a letter to *The Circle* describing the work that the young artists and I had done for the Center and the People. He described how we helped him out of his own depression and how comfortable we had always made him feel. John Moose handed me a pipe bowl he had made from pipestone that he had quarried. Old Man Bill helped interpret my dreams and was there at the front of the confrontation. And the elder Mohawk, Bob Shaw, visited me at the Center and lent his spiritual support as well as his insights.

The other elders at the Center, especially the women, also offered words of support and encouragement. I could tell that it hurt them because they saw how much these accusations had hurt me and how such an action had hurt the good spirit of the People, how it had hurt their sons and daughters and their grandchildren who worked with me.

All the while Simone remained strong and by my side.

I will never forget this show of love.

It was only the beginning. . . .

When I first saw my character assassin I thought about how much he looked like pictures I'd seen of Buffalo Bill. His hair was dark grey and, pushed back behind his ears, it wasn't quite long enough to reach the collar of his grey suit jacket. His face was pocked or scarred in some way. And though it was dark, it was not like that of other Indians I'd known. He wore sideburns and a long, thick mustache. Beneath his dark, heavy eyebrows, he had slits for eyes and I could not see their color. He was a large man and he strutted before the Indian Board of Directors who sat behind tables at the front of the Indian Center's auditorium. He appeared as if he were trying to make a show of his government-appointed power and authority. Little did he know that such behavior among the People was always suspect.

On one side of the crowded room were the Indian educators from the offices of Indian education. I recalled some of them sitting in the meeting we had with Dr. Green. There were people there from the Indian studies program at the university; I hadn't seen them in years, but could remember some of their faces and an occasional confrontation or two, especially when I said that Indian studies had to do with history and literature and not simply what they called language and culture.

There were a couple of white men in suits sitting in the back alongside someone from the state museum. The white men looked like feds of some kind, and glancing at the man from the state museum office, I remembered that confrontation when I had insisted that the state and local museums separate the bowls and stems of the pipes they kept for exhibition and that they return the remains of the people they kept in vaults in their basements. I remembered that we had created the Living Traditions Museum at the Indian Center.

I chose to sit toward the back of the auditorium, on the other side. I remember that my hair was braided that day but that I let it hang loose in the back. I remember how strong I felt when the Indian artists and the elders and I smoked the pipe in our tipi downstairs just moments before. They were there, including Old Man Bill, on the side where I sat, watching this abomination strutting and nervously jabbering in front of the People. And when the Indian men who were former prisoners at Stillwater entered the room and sat next to me, I felt my heart growing stronger.

The meeting was called to order and my assassin was told to sit down, that this was a Center board meeting and that he should do what he was told. On that board was an AIM leader who knew me as a teacher and another former AIMer who knew me as a friend. Both had smoked the pipe with me. And there was my beautiful mother-in-law who had been named on the pipe that I had been attacked for using. There were others on the board who had, at one time or another, found themselves in a circle with me. Most of them, though, like most people, had parts of their past that they weren't necessarily proud of and would be afraid to recall openly before a bureaucratic committee. Most had had their bouts with alcohol and had done things they were sorry for afterwards. All seemed to get very quiet as the assassin stood and handed out a sheet of paper. At the top of the paper it read: "Fact Sheet." It was about me. It reeked of a conspiracy — or some other *machi-manido* — in this world that stifles and shatters human identity.

Everything on it was either lies or a distortion of truths. One of the "facts" said that I conducted a "traditional pipe ceremony for a young Chippewa at Cass Lake." It was referring to the Red School House teacher who would never call himself a Chippewa. When his sister read this, she stood and demanded to know what involvement Indian education had with his death. It was a tense moment.

One of the language teachers at the university stood. She seemed very old. Her hair was white and thin. She slouched but not directly toward the floor like some old people do when age has caused them to bend like old stalks of corn. She appeared bent and sort of twisted. She called me a modern day trickster. She said I was a great danger to young people. She said I was a great evil.

Old Man Bill interrupted, reminding her that Manabosho, the Ojibway Trickster, had given the People many gifts.

Then the assassin tried to take control and pointed to the fact sheet, where it stated that I had "conducted pipe ceremonies at Still-water State Prison." One of the warriors then confronted him and demanded to know what was wrong with my bringing the pipe to them so they could pray. Another warrior stood and pointed his finger at the assassin. The warrior demanded to know where he was when they were fighting for their spiritual rights. "Where were you when the warden was denying us the right to pray with a pipe?"

The assassin replied by saying that he was working on a grant that would provide legitimate legislation for Indian prisoners. The audience around me laughed.

When I noticed Ana enter the auditorium, I felt my heart leap. I had not seen much of Ana since my days at Heart of the Earth. I was glad to see her. She knew the truth about me. She would say how we struggled together to educate Indian children. She would remember the ceremony of the old man when medicine had been used against me. She was there and interpreted what he said to me. She would remember the nights I stayed and prayed over the pipe with her and her relatives when her little daughter was so sick that she was not expected to live. She must remember how I and the other teachers at Heart of the Earth came together and decided that if Ana was fired for her drinking, we would all resign. I could remember when she told me one time long ago how she believed that I would help save their nation.

"Ana," I called out quietly. I waved and thought how grateful I was that she was there.

But, you know, I had forgotten how my dog E reacted every time he saw Ana, how he growled and often barked at her, how he never took his eyes from her. I had forgotten that maybe Ana had become jealous of me for some reason, that maybe she resented that I had gone on and that she kept falling.

Ana spoke loudly about how I came to the AIM school all broken up and how I told her that I wanted a pipe real bad. She seemed to dwell on this point even though I did have a pipe when I started teaching there. It was a beautifully crafted deer-antler pipe that was especially made for me by my Creek friend from Florida. One of the AIM people on the Center's board smoked on that pipe. When I received the one that is called the Great Mystery pipe a year or so later, I presented the other to one of the AIM singers at the Red School House. I never said I wanted a pipe, Ana. Why are you saying that?

Ana said that I disgraced her father's name, that I'd been going around telling people that her father had taught me about medicine.

But I never said such a thing, Ana, I thought, sitting there in my straight-back metal chair in horror. You know I would never say such a thing! Don't you remember you presented me an eagle feather that came from his medicine drum?

Then she turned, and as abruptly as she entered the room, she left, her fat, evil-looking sister trailing behind her. When Simone ran out after her and demanded to know why Ana had betrayed me, her sister threatened to beat Simone up.

"Ana, how could you do this to him?" Simone cried. The two women turned their backs to her and rushed down the stairs.

Then, just when I thought it was over, one of Ana's younger daughters stood up. She was one of the students who I taught at Heart of the Earth. She used to come over to my apartment in the projects and take E for long walks. She was a sweet kid then with a tendency to be a little spoiled. "If you ever say anything about my grandpa," she growled, "I'll kick your ass!" Then she too stormed away.

There was an embarrassed silence that fell on the room like a heavy blanket. Most everyone there must have felt soiled in some way. We used to be a great people, but it has come to this. The board sat quietly, fearful that maybe they too would be attacked the way I was. And what would be their defense? How would they defend themselves?

I could no longer be quiet. I stood and denied the accusations that Ana had made against me. I said that she was probably told a lot of things that weren't true by certain people representing the government who were probably in the room. I wondered aloud what horrible things they had told Ana. I wondered what they promised her for coming. Though I blamed them for manipulating Indian people that way, I knew in my hurting heart that I would never forgive Ana for her betrayal, and I would never forget it.

I paused and looked around at what I was seeing. I said that you could draw a knife down the middle of this room, that is how divided we are. I raised the "fact sheet" high in the air. I called it lies . . . lies and twisted truths. And I could hear the vision I was given on that cold winter's night years ago. I said that I never claimed to be a member of an extinct Florida tribe, and where was the evidence, since it was claimed that I wrote it down on a job application?

"And I'm not a Cuban refugee from Florida! I am Indian," I declared, still holding the fact sheet high. "I've always been an Indian.

I cannot provide you with a piece of government paper or a government number on a plastic card that shows me to be an Indian. Besides, I would not do such a thing! I would not allow myself to be defined in such a way. I would not be told who I am by people who represent a government out to exterminate what I am.

"I am an Indian . . . I am a Native American because that is what I am. My relationship to the Great Holy Mystery and Mother Earth make me what I am. My beliefs make me what I am. My acceptance among my traditional family members make me what I am. I have always been an Indian. If not on a government piece of paper, certainly in my heart and in the way I've lived my life. And isn't that what it's really all about — what's in the heart and the way we live?

"How can you say that Princess Red Wing is a fraud? She is a respected clan mother and grandmother of the Narraganset Tribe and Wampanoag Nation. She is one of the great teachers of our time. Your attempt to discredit her only serves to discredit yourself, and reveals the sort of man that you truly are."

I looked into the eyes of the board of directors. "You met Princess Red Wing. You know what good she did while she was here. Some of you danced and sang with her. How can you tolerate the words of this abomination, this liar before you? Her ancestors are the grandfathers and grandmothers of the Ojibway people."

I turned and faced my assassin. My eyes were like an owl's, and I wanted them to penetrate his black heart. "How dare you demean her!" I said. "How dare you tell me that I cannot pray with the pipe that I keep and protect with my life."

I tore and crumpled the fact sheet and tossed it to the floor; I said that I would no longer address the accusations of a liar, nor would I allow my ears to hear any more of his lies. "I have too much respect for the word and the Great Mystery!"

With that statement I walked out of the auditorium. Many of the young artists and former Indian prisoners followed.

As time passed, many people came up to me and congratulated me for standing up. But later, those in the Indian education office would ban my uncle's book, *Literature of the American Indian*, from being used by Indians in the school system. I was also told that in St. Paul, the Intertribal Affairs Board, which consisted of government-defined Indians, had banned me from speaking about Indians anywhere in the state, and that anyone who allowed me to speak or teach young Indians in Minnesota would be in danger of losing their federal and state funding. They referred to me as a dangerous radical. They said that I was an imposter.

Though our work in the cultural arts department and our brief Indian renaissance of a kind was still alive, you could tell that it was yet too vulnerable; maybe in time we will see that such challenges to our identity only strengthen us and help make us less vulnerable. The shadow people had, indeed, made their presence known. But, then, so had we.

After that confrontation, the threats kept coming, and my concern for the safety of my family eventually made us decide to go back to the Gulf shore and to our last days with Uncle Nip.

Those of us who were of good heart still manage to hang on together, in spite of the distance that separates our people, and still manage to display our people's art and make presentations whenever and wherever we can on behalf of what is still beautiful and good about being Indian. That will never change.

CHAPTER 30

KEEPERS OF THE CODE,
KEEPERS OF THE FAITH

I HAD A DREAM the other night, and I stood on the beach contemplating it in the same way I stood on a similar shore thirty-
six years ago, contemplating an island that became much more
than the imaginings of a small boy.

I walked barefoot to where the tide would reach as far as it
could. That hint of winter chill yet lingered in the wet sand and
in the salty air of this early spring morning. It stimulated winter
seeds among the dunes and carried with it the season's promise of
new life.

It had been a cold winter for Florida, but it helped bring
back some semblance of a balance on the land, for the insect
world had diminished considerably and many of the imported and
exotic plants had been killed off. The pelicans had it pretty bad,
though, because their food staple had already been seriously
depleted by netters and tourists. With the cold waters lapping up
towards the shore that winter, the fish that were left headed out
to the deeps. Calusa and Simone and some of the other local people, who care about such things, tried to help the pelicans out.
About twice a week they'd take buckets of donated fish out to Bird

Key and toss them to the birds. They'd come back with stories about how one pelican was hooked in the wing, another had a lure hanging from his bill. One had a plastic six-pack wrapper caught around his legs. Sometimes Calusa and Simone would swim or wade out into the cold water and try a rescue. Occasionally, they were lucky and brought a pelican in and were able to remove the hooks or plastic wrappers and set the bird free. Most of the time, though, they'd stand helpless, waist deep in the water, just out of reach of the starving and dying birds. But though the cold was hard on this threatened species, it did help to clean the algae from the water they fish in. And on this early spring day, the water of Mother Earth appeared so lovely and cool and clear.

I stood on its shore and breathed deeply the tangy air. My lungs filled with it. My brown chest swelled. My dark silvery-streaked and loosely braided hair lifted as a swift offshore breeze swept in. Goose bumps formed on my coppery skin, but soon melted away as the wind shifted, and the air became still and warm again in the transition of the day.

It was spring once more, I thought, and though it held a strong sense of familiarity in it, the air still carried a scent of newness too. The bright and pale yellow sun was rising behind me. The turquoise blue water was ahead. Above me and all around me was the Sky. Big and bright, it was the color of a blue jay's down. The world was a circle without end.

I couldn't get the dream out of my mind, and I kept scanning the shimmering Gulf searching for the sudden and soft emergence of the dolphins, but they did not come. And, oh, how I wanted to see them. How I ached to see them.

The other night I had a dream. It was about them.

The image of the dolphin's eyes who spoke to me penetrates me even now and is as vivid in the darkness of my mind as it was in the darkness of the dream. I had known dolphins ever since I was a boy, yet I had never had such a puzzling, almost frightening, dream about them.

How afraid I was as Simone and the children and I descended in the dream into the water. How strange it was to be in the spirit-home of these beautiful and magical beings who circled us. It was a feeling like Columbus and the Spaniards must have had when they first came to these shores and the native people emerged from the forests and gathered around them. How vulnerable the invaders must have felt and how vulnerable they were as these proud and gentle copper-colored and handsome people surrounded them. How easily Columbus and his crew could have been annihilated then. How they must have paused even in their greed-driven exploration just long enough to record in their own journals the splendor of what they were seeing. How even their suits of armor and crosses must have jingled faint and unfamiliar in the tropical breezes as they stood and swayed and stared in perfect silence as the original people stepped out from the treeline and onto the shell-white sand.

"Indios . . ." Columbus would call them, People in God . . . Indios. There is beauty in their smile, he wrote to the Spanish king and queen. There is sweetness and softness in their discourse. They all appear so youthful. The men are straight and tall. The women are shapely, their children are healthy. All are naked or nearly so, except for the white shell beads that hang from their necks and over their brown breasts and down from their ears. Their skin is smooth, and their black hair is combed straight and shiny and long and decorated with bright, colorful plumes and feathers the likes of which I have never seen. They seem to give freely of themselves to make us comfortable. . . .

Even the land around them, continued Columbus, is wonderful and welcoming. It is green with trees such as the world has never known, growing wild with fruits of many kinds . . . and the sea is clear to the white sandy bottom. There are fish of great varieties everywhere in it, and birds as tall as men wade along the island's shore. . . .

What wonder it must have been for Columbus and Cortés, for De Soto and Narvaez, to enter into a world that was not theirs, a world they had no reason to believe existed, but did. They were in a new world and didn't know it. They just knew that where they were was like no place they had ever been. Perhaps their awe and fear of the unknown are one of the common threads that bind all things in the Great Mystery. But for Columbus and the Conquistadors who followed, the awe must have been spectacular, the fear even greater. To the Indian, anything is possible and can exist in the Mystery. But the European arrivals, on the other hand, were not believers in a Great Mystery that bound all things into an incomprehensible totality. They believed in a God who created them in his image. They believed in a book that instructed them to dominate and rule over anything that was not like them, a book that made no mention of a people such as they encountered in this new world. As a result of their ignorance and their narrow perceptions and their arrogance, they couldn't understand and they couldn't become one with the world they had encountered.

I, however, am a believer in a Great Mystery in which all things exist, things far beyond my present awareness.

But like the Spaniards, my fear in the dream state the other night was of the unknown too. I was entering an environment of the dolphins. The sea was their world on this earth. In the dream I knew, though, that Simone and I and the children had to enter that world if we were to gain a better understanding of our world. With the dolphins in the sea, we would be with the great spirit of their kind and share their collective thought. This is the way we are to learn from the animals, I thought as I stood still scanning the Gulf, hoping to catch sight of those I loved, those beings I felt so much a part of. The white man captures the dolphins and studies them in a prison he has created for them because he has come to believe that his technology will help provide him with answers when he does not even know the questions. In short, the white man since his arrival has lost touch with the magical. He has lost touch with himself, and so, he is too afraid. I am not.

That night in my dream, if there was anything to balance my fear of the unknown, it was in my intention. The Spaniards' fear of the world of the Indios may have stemmed from their ignorance of it and their desire to dominate all of it, because their intentions were to rape the women and enslave the men and children and to steal from all of them. They had to destroy what they feared. They had to destroy what belonged to someone else. They had to destroy what was beautiful. Simone and I and the children entered the world of the dolphin in peace. I was also aware that I was in the great Mother's womb where the dolphins had chosen countless generations ago to remain. If there was to be communication with each other's species, it would best be done in dreams like this and in her womb where all things originated in this world.

This is what I thought as I gazed still at the sea.

The dolphins in my dream made us feel comfortable as friendly hosts do with visitors, as the Arawaks did for Columbus before he enslaved them and watched his men shoot them. Before they raped them. The wonder and joys felt by the children and Simone in the dream were tempered by their respect for the dolphins, whose home they had entered, whose species they called elder brother and elder sister. They would share an experience with the dolphins unique to each of them.

My dream focused on one elderly dolphin who singled me out and approached me. When he stopped before me, I reached out with my hand and rubbed his nose all the way up to the area between the dolphin's eyes. I did this out of love and the desire to communicate my friendship. I hoped that I hadn't acted too aggressively, that I hadn't allowed my desire to be friendly overcome my sense of respect, and that my own fear did not show the dolphin that I was not of good heart. I can remember the slick, smooth and rubbery texture of the dolphin's skin and the power of goodness that I had to use in order for the dolphin to feel my intent. My strong desire to let the dolphin know that I cared for him and his kind traveled through my hand. Through my hand, I let the dolphin know that I respected him, that I could be trusted, that I was a man of peace.

Maybe dolphins come into our dreams the way star-beings do, I thought, reaching for a pretty purple shell that was uncovered by the shifting tide, recalling times that I had seen these beings in other dreams and in my vision, and that I had traveled with them into the stars. I held the purple shell in the palm of my hand and studied it. I wondered if it was wampum. How appropriate, I thought, recollecting that a purple shell was the symbol of sincerity.

I looked up and searched the surface of the sea again, but the dolphins were not out there, at least not where I could see them and feel that rush of joy that comes from seeing them.

In my dream, the elder dolphin looked into me and studied me. He told me in the great silent language that he spoke, the kind that I had experienced in my vision, that he was searching for some understanding about the human species.

"Why do some humans kill us and care nothing about us and destroy our world, yet there are humans like you and your family who respect and love us and love this world as we do?" The questions caused me to sit back and regard my response. Was the dolphin asking me these questions in order to get me to deal with the answers, answers that he already knew and understood? Uncle Nip would do this to me sometimes. Nip would ask me a question that he would know the answer to, but by asking the question he got me to consider the response. Or was the dolphin asking because he really was trying to learn about humans and why we are so

different? One thing was certain: At that moment I understood the
extremes that the elder dolphin was speaking about. I too had wondered about this.

"It's what we believe," I replied. "It's in the power of our belief. . . . It all comes down to what we believe."

▲ ▲ ▲

That's what I said the day I addressed the Catholic bishop's
bicentennial hearings in Minneapolis back in '76. I'd only gone to
the huge auditorium in St. Stephens hoping to hear the director of
the Red School House speak. This was before I was to work there.
The speaker who was to appear at the hearings that night and
address his concerns about the welfare of Native Americans was
advertised as an Ojibway medicine man, an AIM activist, and an
AIM survival school director. I had heard his name around AIM circles, and I was anxious to listen to what the medicine man was
going to say to all these Catholics at these hearings, for the Catholics and I went back a ways. . . .

When I arrived at the church auditorium, the place was
packed. I had to stand out by the opened doors in the lobby if I
wanted to hear. There seemed to be a delay in the hearings and I had
the peculiar feeling that things weren't working out for the Catholics as they had planned and that somehow I would be involved in
something that I could never have foreseen.

While I leaned against a post in the crowded hallway, contemplating the situation and the feelings that accompanied it, a
young priest came up to me and started talking. It appeared we were
equally interested in hearing the medicine man and spoke anxiously
about his arrival. I decided that I liked the young priest. He was one
of the only priests that I ever remember liking. I figured that it had
something to do with mutual respect, sort of like that one Episcopal
priest who I recalled back in Wind River. Too bad he was killed, I
thought to myself.

This friendly young priest and I seemed to have mutual respect for each other, and that probably comes only to those people who are secure in their own beliefs and have no need to impose themselves on anyone else. Perhaps being spiritual leads a human on many paths, but those who don't try to impose themselves on others seem to be closer to the understandings than the ones who insist that they have found the way and that everyone else must follow them. Neither I nor this young priest conveyed that imposition, and each seemed secure in what he believed.

We couldn't help but be aware of the quiet rumbling in the restless crowd and all the eyes that followed the entourage of black-robed men who headed toward the young priest and me, standing back by the doors. Their walk through the crowd reminded me of some biblical story where Moses parted the sea so his people could escape their pursuers. Such was the way the crowd parted as the priests passed through.

The priests didn't stop until they reached their young colleague and me. They were stern and deliberate.

"Is he the substitute speaker?" one asked the young priest, while his eyes glanced at me. "We had a call from our special guest that though he couldn't make it, ill health, I believe, there would be someone here to take his place."

Now, the young priest who had befriended me knew through our conversation that we had both come to hear the medicine man. And it didn't take him long to figure out my regard for what the Catholic Church had done to me and to my people. He looked at me, looking at him. I nodded once. "Yes," the young priest responded, turning to the one who asked, "this is. . . ." He glanced at me again.

"Gabriel," I replied. "Gabriel Horn."

"Yes, this is Gabriel Horn, and Mr. Horn's here to substitute for the medicine man."

"Is this true?" asked one of the other priests, perhaps sensing that something was not right.

286

"Sure," I responded before he could contemplate further. "I'm a substitute."

"Well, then, let's go. You're on next. Come. Quickly. The bishops are waiting."

Indeed, I thought, the bishops are waiting.

They escorted me through that auditorium, parting the standing-room crowd again, just like Moses had parted the water. Next thing I knew, I was on stage with about fifty Catholic bishops from all over the world sitting in their bishop finery in bleachers on the stage. The priestly escorts sat me down at a table, just off to the right of where the bishops were seated, and positioned a microphone near my mouth. They pointed to a clock on the table and quietly raced an explanation past me about how the alarm would go off when my seven minutes were up. I took that to be some kind of foreshadowing, but smiled politely.

The head bishop, the one who was the master of ceremonies, was about to introduce me from a piece of paper one of the escorts handed him. As he stared at the name on the paper, he slowly lifted his gaze to me. The bishop tried to smile but remained rather rigid and appeared somewhat puzzled. There was something about my name perhaps . . . something about the way I looked that the head bishop seemed to me to find deeply disturbing. I didn't know why. But as he turned before the multitude of silent, anxious people to study me further, my eyes locked onto the large, gold cross lying flat against his chest and over his red and white regalia. It was not like any of the other crosses adorning the chests of the esteemed gathering. It appeared that he was wearing a gold cross exactly like the one that I had uncovered on the island when I was a boy — the island with the Spaniards that they wanted me to believe were just the imaginings of a little boy. Well, perhaps my imagination had finally allowed me to come face to face with an old enemy.

He reached one hand to the cross that hung from his neck. He held it as if meditating for a moment. "Our next speaker,

representing the American Indian Movement Survival Schools," he
began, "is a substitute for the ailing Eddie Benton Benai."

When the buzzer sounded marking my start, I began rather
slowly, like a large stone heading down a mountain. I first mentioned that the best thing that the Catholic Church could do for
the American Indians, both in this country and in Central and
South America, was to give back the lands they've confiscated from
Native Americans and the gold and the silver that they and the Conquistadors stole to fatten the Vatican vaults. I progressed rapidly into
suggesting that they stop supporting missionaries in this country
and elsewhere. That they should make the effort to elevate their
own spirituality rather than those of other people who are spiritual
in their own way. I said that the Native American has a religion
rooted in this land and not in the Middle East. That if they wanted
to make better use of missionary money then they should help
Indians who were jailed for defending Indian sovereignty and
human rights at Wounded Knee. These Indians needed bail money
and money to hire good lawyers to help regain their freedom.

The auditorium was silent. Several hundred people, perhaps
over a thousand, sat stunned and mute as my amplified words
echoed through the great hall. "Any Indians out there," I continued,
"who converted to Catholicism are no longer Indians, not in the
traditional sense. And any Indians out there who are working as
missionaries to undermine the religion of their own people are
betraying their own heritage.

"If you believe you have the right to dominate the animals
and all earth's creatures, and that you were put here to subdue, I
repeat, subdue, your Mother Earth, then you can no longer be an
Indian. You're a Catholic with Indian blood is all. . . . You're not an
Indian."

Just before they yanked the microphone from the table, I told
the audience that the Great Mystery is called Gitchie Manitou if
they were Ojibway, and Wakan-Tanka if they were Sioux. "We

believed in the Great Holy Mystery before the white man came to this land, your honorable bishops, not a God of the Jews."

288

They removed everything from the table as I politely protested that I still had three minutes left and that the alarm had not yet sounded. The head bishop, with the gold cross gleaming on his chest under the hot stage lights, tried to make a joke saying that he didn't know God was Jewish. No one laughed.

When I stood to leave, a dead silence filled the place once again. As I walked through the crowd toward the door unassisted by any priests, my eyes met the eyes of a very old Indian man, sitting way back in the crowd. I recall that they were strangely similar to the eyes of the dolphin who spoke to me in my dream just the other night. But back then I had never seen such eyes, such gentle, knowing eyes. Had we met before? For that instant, when the eyes of the old Indian locked with mine, I was totally reassured. Again I wonder if it was not the silent language that I was learning to hear. Abruptly, someone came between us, then many people.

As the hearing drew to a quick conclusion, and I reached the doors leading out of the auditorium, two Indian education teachers, holding little children in their arms, decided to confront me.

"You can't say we're not Ojibways because we're Catholics!" the fair-haired and fair-skinned father exclaimed.

I gazed at the little ones in their parents' arms. And they examined me as little ones often did. "Geez," I said, "they're adorable children." Then I switched my focus to the man and his short and heavy, dark-skinned wife. Her hair was as black as coal, but wiry-looking and cropped short above the shoulders. It reminded me of that look you see on Indians once they've surrendered themselves to the spirit-killers of their people. "You know," I said to her, "I was taught by my uncle that when you have Indian babies in such places you should be whispering 'false god, false god' in their ears. It has something to do with protecting their Indian spirit from those who might want to steal it."

Her eyes squinted and glared at me.

As I moved toward the exit of the building, this woman, this **289** same woman who was holding her baby, blocked my path. A crowd gathered around us and pressed in. "You don't even speak the language," she mocked.

I shook my head. "You just don't want to get it," I said. "Ojibway is a way of life. It is a religion. Don't you see? You can't expect a Jew to say he's Catholic, can you? What makes him a Jew is his religion. Should he get baptized and become a Catholic, he'd be a Catholic with Jewish ancestry."

The crowd around us swelled and pressed closer. Many blue eyes stared, many dark ones. Still before me stood these angry and confused Ojibway language and culture teachers, shifting their babies from one hip to the other.

"Are you saying that we're not raising our children to be Ojibways?"

I nodded my agreement to them both.

"They'll speak their language and know their culture!" the man said.

"That's not changing the fact that you're raising them Catholic, so they'll be Ojibway-speaking Catholics, not Ojibways, when they grow up."

Still holding his child, he edged closer to me; the crowd squeezed even tighter. "Look," I said. "Culture is what you believe. In the Bible it states that man was made in the image of God. How can that compare to a man being created in the image of Gitchie Manitou, the sum total of all things that always was and always will be? In the Bible it says for man to have dominion over the animals and subdue the earth! Aren't the animals our brothers and sisters? Aren't we equal and related to all things because the earth is the great mother we all share? The Bible says that your wife is supposed to obey you. Find a traditional Indian woman still breathing who will buy that one!

"And in those first pages of the white man's Bible, it says your kids, these innocent little babies, are born with sin.

"You can't get further away from being Ojibway than being Catholics or Mormons or Baptists or whoever else comes around proselytizing to native people. Why, I'd rather see you drunk on Franklin Avenue than in church with those kids on Sunday! What you do to yourselves is one thing. What you're doing to them is another."

The frozen crowd gradually shifted apart as several priests pushed through. Leading the way was the young one I'd met standing in the back when I first came in. "Come on," the young priest urged, "I'll help you get out of here."

As I turned to walk away, the woman tugged at her husband's arm, the kids dangling now near their waists. "He can't even speak the language," she sneered.

▲ ▲ ▲

The sun was above me, and the Gulf was calm. So was I. For a long time I had felt bad about that encounter with these people at the Catholic bishop's bicentennial hearings, for I never had the heart to fight my own people, but until now I never understood more how true the words I spoke back then were. The transition from morning to afternoon was occurring. The transition from knowledge to wisdom was also happening. Soon the winds would shift to onshore breezes, and the tide, like my own doubts about myself, would recede.

I tossed the wampum shell into the water, and caught sight of Simone coming up the beach.

"I was wondering where you were," she said, reaching for my hand and up to kiss me.

"I guess I was out here a lot longer than I figured," I smiled. "I guess it was sorta like when I start writin' . . . I just lose all track of time."

"You know," she said, "I kept thinking about your dream the other night and recalled that I had one too. And it was about dolphins! I don't know if I was asleep or awake, come to think of it, but I do remember what the dolphin told me."

I stood anticipating what she was about to say. My eyes urged her to continue.

"He said that they were keepers of the code, and what I believe he meant had to do with that silent language that they use when speaking to us. It's that silent language that you said happened in your vision. It may be how the star people talk to us. It may also have something to do with genetics. 'We are keepers of the code,'" she repeated. "That's what he said."

I took her hands in mine and brought them to my lips and kissed them. "And we are keepers of the faith, my beloved. We are keepers of the faith."

NOTES

Chapter Six: The book that is quoted on pp. 47–49 is *The Native American Book of Knowledge: Part I — We Have Always Been Here* by White Deer of Autumn (Beyond Words, 1992).

Chapter Seven: The quote from D.H. Lawrence on pp. 54–55 is from *Literature of the American Indian*, edited by Sanders and Peek (Glencoe Press, Macmillan, 1973).

This book was set in 11-point Schneidler type
by TBH Typecast, Inc., Cotati, California.

Schneidler was designed in 1937
by Ernst F. H. Schneidler (1882–1956),
who studied art as an architect
and worked as an illustrator and book designer.
The curiously unfinished quality of this admirable design
is a result of Schneidler's aversion
for anything polished and rounded-off.

Cover design by Kathy Warinner, Larkspur, California.
Editing by Marc Allen and Katherine Dieter.
Proofreading by K.D. Sullivan.

Printed by Malloy Lithographing, Inc.
Ann Arbor, Michigan,
on 55-pound cream-white Glatfelter stock.

New World Library is dedicated to publishing books and cassettes that help improve the quality of our lives. If you enjoyed *Native Heart*, we highly recommend the following books from New World Library's Classic Wisdom Collection:

> *Native American Wisdom* edited by Kent Nerburn and Louise Mengelkoch. Taken from speeches and writings of peoples from all tribes, this book presents the best of Native American wisdom on topics such as the land, the ways of living, and the ways of the heart.

> *The Soul of an Indian and Other Writings from Ohiyesa (Charles Alexander Eastman)* edited by Kent Nerburn. Ohiyesa has been described as "the Native American Thoreau." This sensitively edited new edition presents the profound and beautiful reflections of this important writer on nature, the education of children, and a life of honor.

For a complete catalog of our fine books and cassettes, contact:

New World Library
58 Paul Drive
San Rafael, CA 94903

Phone: (415) 472-2100
FAX: (415) 472-6131

Or call toll free:
(800) 227-3900
In California: (800) 632-2122